Time, History, and Belief in Aztec and Colonial Mexico

Time
History
and
Belief
in
Aztec
and
Colonial
Mexico

Ross Hassig

University of Texas Press, Austin

Copyright © 2001 by the University of Texas Press
All rights reserved
Printed in the United States of America
First edition, 2001

Requests for permission to reproduce material from this
work should be sent to Permissions, University of Texas
Press, P.O. Box 7819, Austin, TX 78713-7819.

∞ The paper used in this book meets the minimum
requirements of ANSI/NISO Z39.48-1992 (R1997) (Permanence of Paper).

Library of Congress Cataloging-in-Publication Data

Hassig, Ross, 1945–
Time, history, and belief in Aztec and Colonial
Mexico / Ross Hassig.
    p.   cm.
Includes bibliographical references and index.
ISBN 0-292-73139-6 (cloth : alk. paper)—
ISBN 0-292-73140-x (pbk. : alk. paper)
   1. Aztec calendar. 2. Aztecs—History. 3. Aztec
cosmology. 4. Manuscripts, Nahuatl. 5. Time—
Social aspects—Mexico. 6. Mexico—History—
Spanish colony, 1540–1810. I. Title.
F1219.76.C35 H37 2001
529'.32978452—dc21   00-041783

To Professor G. William Skinner
an exacting mentor who has made it a rewarding journey

Contents

Illustrations

Figures

Tables

Maps

Preface

The Aztecs had a strange culture with bizarre practices and beliefs, or so many conventional discussions would have it concerning one of anthropology's favorite whipping boys. They have been at the center of my research for some twenty-five years, yet I have never seen them this way. To me, the challenge is not only to understand them in their own terms but also to understand them as a group seeking the same things that all groups seek: to make sense of their world and to inhabit it as best they could in rational ways, albeit from a different cultural perspective.

Studying the Aztecs blends anthropology and history, though not always harmoniously. To oversimplify: history tends to emphasize the specific facts of the events of concern whereas anthropology tends to emphasize theoretical explanations. In both cases, the tendency is the result not only of the orientations of the respective disciplines, but also of their structural organizations. For academic purposes, history tends to be specialized by time and place, with a heavy emphasis on specifics as a way of knowing that time and place, whereas anthropology tends to be divided on the basis of theoretical issues.

Anthropological studies have traditionally focused either on complex non-Western societies with long and complicated histories or on simpler societies for which there is little historical record. The former are often walled off as belonging to area specialists who possess a mastery of exotic languages, complex historical backgrounds, and archaeological data. As a result, these areas are often ignored by those who study simpler societies—traditionally the majority of anthropologists. These traditional societies, however, are of little interest in and of themselves to most people, anthropologists included; their interest lies in being exemplars of some theoretical consideration that can then help enlighten us about other, similar, groups.

Anthropology has a long-standing concern with its epistemological underpinnings, in part owing to an emphasis on the theoretical sinews that hold the disparate field together. But the struggle to create a satisfying intellectual structure has become self-consuming, leaving too little concern for explaining the world, even if this must be done conditionally. Much of the current divisiveness in anthropology can be traced to the struggle over the proper relationship between theory and data. Today, the focus on *how* we know something has become greater than the focus on *what* we know; our inability to frame a completely satisfactory explanation has led to a paralysis that is belied by our own ability to negotiate the world around us; and whatever theoretical orientation is adopted tends to be applied to the world as a leitmotif more than as a way to engage the data, even provisionally. In short, theory dominates anthropology in a way that it does not in history precisely because theory is what is shared in anthropology—what holds it together as a discipline and makes a Melanesianist interested in a culture in South Africa or lowland South America.

This disciplinary predisposition to emphasize theoretical over descriptive orientations merges in Mesoamerica with a second trend—that toward explaining matters through ideology and symbolism. This is not the only predisposition, of course, but more practical orientations tend to be found in such areas as politics and economics,[1] whereas ideological approaches tend to dominate such intellectual issues as calendars,[2] notions of time,[3] and the nature of history.[4] If there is one topic that is calculated to make most Mesoamericanists run screaming into the night, it is the calendar. Enormously complex and still incompletely understood, the calendar is almost mandatorily studied, even though it is of little practical concern to those of us who do not focus primarily on the ritual or symbolic.

But the calendar is significant because the Aztecs and other Mesoamerican societies are generally considered to have a cyclical concept of time and, consequently, a cyclical notion of history that was largely displaced after the Conquest by the Western perspective of linear time and history, with the indigenous calendrical beliefs and practices surviving only at the village or folk level. But the issue of time, which forms a major part of this book, has been only spottily examined in pre- and post-Columbian Mesoamerica. Whether it has been studied, and to what extent, varies by academic discipline and time period. The pre-

Columbian era is especially rich in calendrical studies, but in the post-Columbian era, little attention has been paid to time except to note the fragmentation and demise of the indigenous calendars (and, in passing, to clocks in architectural studies where they appear as part of the fabric of colonial buildings).

This study seeks to make the Aztec calendar, and Aztec notions of time and history, more immediately useful and interesting by confronting the traditional interpretation. I assert that the traditional emphasis on time in Aztec culture as a cyclical phenomenon that patterns behavior is the result of a theoretical predisposition that short-circuits empirical research rather than being solidly grounded in the data, and that it is fundamentally miscast.

My basic argument is that the Aztecs did not have a primarily cyclical notion of time or history; rather, they manipulated time by way of their calendar, for political purposes. And, while I do not discard the ideological approach wholesale, I nevertheless offer a different view of Aztec society. I argue that focusing primarily on Aztec ideology as a way of making sense of their behavior and society has produced an inadequate and seriously distorted assessment. Instead, I argue that the Aztec elite deliberately knit together their political ambitions and ideological beliefs into a coherent, self-referential justification for domination that simultaneously crafted the mechanism of imperial control. If my argument holds, it alters the prevailing notions of Aztec time and history; it also has implications for how we interpret the broader Aztec society, as well as affecting our approach to both pre-Aztec Mexican cultures and the colonial era, and, perhaps, casting doubt on some of the ways we view contemporary Mesoamerican communities.

In the first chapter of this book, I present the traditional explanation of Aztec time and history. This interpretation is then examined to show how it can satisfactorily explain three different types of evidence of Aztec perspectives, the *Codex Borbonicus*, the Great Temple (Templo Mayor) of Tenochtitlan, and a stone monument called the Teocalli de la Guerra Sagrada (Temple of the Sacred Warfare). In the second and third chapters of the book, I go beyond the issues examined from this perspective, raising others suggesting that the prevailing interpretation may not be wholly satisfactory and that other factors may need to be considered. In the fourth and fifth chapters of this book, I consider evidence suggesting that the Aztecs, in fact, did not have a cyclical notion of time, but a linear one and that their temporal concepts as embodied in the calendar were manipulated for political purposes. Then, as an elaboration on this political orientation toward time, I examine the implications for Aztec and other Mesoamerican societies. And in the sixth and seventh chapters of this book, I extend the analysis into the colonial era, where the shift to European notions of time has generally been passed over in silence, presumably because adopting these concepts has been seen as normal or as a logical part of general patterns of assimilation and Christianization by the Spaniards. In fact, the imported temporal notions did not totally displace the indigenous ones, nor were they the entire suite of European temporal concepts, nor was their imposition of equal concern to all segments of Spanish society— suggesting a further political element in the Mexican adoption of European time.

Acknowledgments

Many people have contributed to the writing of this book, through explicit suggestions, critiques, references, and even casual comments that sparked a relevant thought. First among these is J. Richard Andrews, who in addition to being a sounding board for, as well as a valuable initiator of, ideas, has been tireless in lending his Nahuatl expertise to clarify concepts and translate passages. I am also greatly indebted to Professor Richard Henry of the Department of Astronomy and Physics at the University of Oklahoma, who offered considerable advice, information, and guidance throughout the astronomical sections of the book. I also owe thanks to Chris Kyle for having read the complete manuscript, and especially to Tim Pauketat for semi-voluntarily spending every evening of a week-long research trip to Mexico reading the manuscript. The tenor of his criticisms and the colossal size of the recommended revisions reflect the eagerness with which he embraced the task.

I would also like to express my thanks to the John Simon Guggenheim Memorial Foundation for a fellowship in 1997–98, to the School of American Research for a residential grant that year, to the Graduate College of the University of Oklahoma for a series of small grants that allowed me to pursue this topic, and to the Sainsbury Research Unit of the University of East Anglia for a research fellowship in 1999 during which I finished the manuscript. Without the support of these institutions and the encouragement and critique of both those in Santa Fe and in Norwich, this book would not have been completed.

This book is dedicated to Professor G. William Skinner, an outstanding cultural anthropologist and an inspiring mentor and role model. Of all my academic mentors, I owe him the most. He showed me what was possible in anthropology and gave me his considerable support; whatever I have accomplished I owe in overwhelming measure to him.

Time, History, and Belief in Aztec and Colonial Mexico

Chapter 1

Time and the Interpretation
of Other Cultures

When Hernán Cortés stepped ashore in what is now Veracruz, he not only began the conquest of Mexico, he became the pivotal illustration of two conflicting interpretations of the nature of time and historical understanding. As widely understood, albeit debated, from one largely European perspective, Cortés's arrival was a unique occurrence, a watershed event in the history of Mexico that forever altered the subsequent history. But another, indigenous, perspective, takes Cortés's arrival as a predictable, even expected, event within a larger cyclical pattern, and as such it did not divide time as much as fulfill it. And had he not landed, someone else would have. So which perspective is correct?

The debate thus framed is not so much about facts as about fundamental theoretical orientations. It is over our view of history, explanation, and how we see the relationship of conceptual constructs—beliefs—to actions. Facts may be adduced and brought to bear on the issues under debate, but what the facts are and how they are weighed depends in large part on the struggle over the interpretive strategies. That Cortés's arrival is generally considered to have been a course-altering event rests not just on the merits of the man and his actions, but on a Western linear perspective of time and the broader cosmological view to which it is inextricably linked.

Originating in a religious concept of a beginning and an end,[1] and later harnessed to the Enlightenment notion of progress,[2] change for

1

the West is ongoing, continuous, and cumulative but not repetitive. In linear (or secular) time, change is directional and continuous, with the past differing from the present, which, in turn, differs from the future,[3] but it is without inherent direction. It merely passes.[4] To be recognized as linear, time must change in relation to something else. Sometimes this passage is phrased in religious terms: for instance, Christianity sees the significant beginning as dating from the birth of Jesus and continuing until His return, in a straightforward linear progression.[5] Basically, linear systems are tied to a beginning point from which time can be calculated endlessly, and they do not pose questions about the nature of the future because, while it is an outgrowth of the past, it is not deterministically embedded in it.

But suppose time and history are not linear. There are two major competing perspectives that affect how people act in many of the world's cultures. Those who see Cortés's conquest of Mexico—or economic depressions, wars, and the myriad other historical occurrences—simply as an unimportant incident in an otherwise essentially unchanging world embrace a steady state view of time, which yields a history embodying no significant change.[6] For them, time has neither a direction nor a presence: everything just is. Of course, few deny the reality of aging, or other such changes to the individual, but these are regarded as ephemeral, whereas what is real and significant is enduring and unchanging, with no significant difference between past, present, and future.[7]

As a variation on steady state, time is sometimes seen as partially stationary, with only a distant future, which is a position espoused by millenarian movements.[8] And there is evidence of the truth of this proposition, especially in earlier times and in relatively unsophisticated communities where things changed so slowly that it was largely imperceptible to the individual, or it was at least not seen as change. In an environment in which there is little seasonal variation, there is little temporal change to demarcate events clearly in the mind, with the result that, where they occurred becomes more important because this is the major element that changes and with which other events can be readily associated. As an example, Karl Barth[9] reports a highland New Guinea group with a poorly developed conceptualization of time whose members remembered events spatially, by what happened in terms of location rather than by time.[10]

And still others, who see Cortés's arrival, economic depressions, wars, and so forth as part of a larger, periodic pattern, have effectively adopted a cyclical notion of time (and as one variant, spiral time combines linear and cyclical time). In cyclical perspectives, time is seen as changing in real but endlessly repetitive ways.[11] I can see myself age, my children grow up, and my parents die, so things do indeed change, but these are subsumed under a larger, endlessly repetitive temporality in which fundamental conditions are unchanging in the long run. The past, present, and future may differ from each other somewhat, but they nevertheless repeat the same essential patterns found at other times. There can be purpose to life, as actions have meaningful immediate consequences, though not in the sense that what one does will make a difference ultimately.[12] Time changes on a small scale, but is essentially unchanging on a large one. Such notions of time are often tied to a cosmological scheme and assume that the future is inscribed in the present and is readable. Important events and their causes do not occur ex nihilo; rather, their causes lie in earlier patterns that the present examples replicate. Thus, their significance is already established and one's perspective is affected not merely by these events, but by one's position in the cycle.

There is evidence for this conceptualization of time as well. After all, life is comprised of many different cycles, among which are the work week and the annual cycle, embodying, as they do, seasonal agricultural, and ritual cycles which have proven to be powerful analytical devices.[13] But the domestic cycle is also an important aspect of our notion of the repetitive nature of life.[14] Thus while adherents of this perspective do see variations, so many examples can be placed in a cyclical conceptualization that it seems logical that all change can be seen in this way as well. Vedic India is often used to illustrate a cyclical time culture in which it was believed that the world went through a series of ages, with minor variations occurring within an overall repetitive pattern.[15] The same historical events can be viewed in very different ways under these three contrasting perspectives on time, so it is not merely the events and the importance one places on them that make history, but the temporal context we employ.

Every culture grapples with the notion of time and conceives of it in its own way. Yet even in the West, where the commonsense, historical, philosophical, religious, and physical notions of time have been extensively considered and repeatedly reformulated, and a linear sense of time dominates, there still remains considerable diversity of opinion.

But even if the actual nature of time were, or could be, known, how various people conceive and use it can still differ. And how time is conceived in a society is embodied in its calendar.

Calendars tend to emphasize the cyclical nature of time,[16] perhaps as a guiding cultural concept, but certainly because calendars inherently chronicle cycles, whether weeks, months, years, centuries, and so forth. Calendrical time is generally thought to be based on ecological cycles—typically the solar year with its seasons—and on days,[17] which are intuitively obvious units of time and are widely recognized as such, though when they begin and end differs among cultures. Likewise, everywhere seasonality is at all pronounced, so too is the solar year. But beyond days and years, the way time is divided is remarkably varied. Some calendars use lunations but, otherwise, subdivisions of the year tend to be generated culturally without much regard for natural periodicities.[18] For example, other than the inexact quartering of lunations, there is little basis in nature for a 7-day week.[19] More complex time calculations tend to follow sedentism because these often depend on astronomical phenomena which cannot be easily recognized without long-term observations from fixed locations.[20]

Larger cycles begin to be employed when societies achieve the complexity of states. Often these lack an ecological basis and arise from numerological and other social considerations. Moreover, time becomes rationalized as smaller cycles, including the solar year, are made to conform to the logic of larger cycles, and vice versa. Time becomes a synthetic, rational, intellectual system that is far more elaborate than the ecological or annual cycle. But once that happens, the calendar is forced out of sync with nature because days and years do not always easily fit with the larger system, which tends to place greater emphasis on cycles than on the inconveniently uneven seasons.[21] Among these calendrically significant astronomical events are equinoxes, solstices, and, even more complex, the rising and setting of the various planets and stars against fixed horizon markers.[22] Elaboration of a commonsense ecologically based calendrical system to one that recognized temporal patterns based on more complex astronomical phenomena (and numerological calculations from their mathematical system) must nevertheless have been an intellectual revelation on a par with the overthrow of the pre-Copernican world in the West.[23]

Time is a difficult notion to define,[24] though it apparently moves in one direction only, as there are no known systems—biological or physical—that operate in a temporally contrary fashion.[25] But that is little comfort to the people and cultures that must deal with time, as it can be divided in many different ways and conceived in a multitude of fashions,[26] each with its own consequences for how those people or cultures see their world. And while all state-level societies have some form of calendar, these are not conceived similarly and do not have the same social consequences.

The Problem of Aztec Time and History

Mesoamerican cultures are generally considered to be characterized by cyclical time. Of these, cyclical time is best documented among the Aztecs (Mexica) of central Mexico, who are most widely known from their fatal encounter with the Spaniards in 1519–21, their many human sacrifices, and their exotic gods and rituals. Decapitated though their culture was, the Aztecs have bequeathed a legacy of art, history, religion, myths, and cosmology that enormously enlivens the pantheon of great civilizations, adds an interesting and unusual perspective on the world, and continues to fascinate us centuries later.

In the Aztec view of cosmology, this was not the first world.[27] Rather, the world had been created and destroyed four times previously over a span of 2,028 years. The first world, or Sun, was 4 Ocelotl (4 Jaguar), over which the god Tezcatlipoca presided. Giants roamed the earth, but jaguars devoured them, ending that age. The next Sun was 4 Ehecatl (4 Wind), over which Quetzalcoatl presided, but this world was destroyed by hurricanes and all the people were turned into monkeys. The third Sun was 4 Quiahuitl (4 Rain), presided over by Tlaloc, and when it was destroyed by fiery rain, the people were turned into turkeys. The fourth Sun was 4 Atl (4 Water), presided over by Chalchihuitl-Icue, and was destroyed by a great flood. After the destruction of the fourth Sun, the gods assembled and built a bonfire into which one was to throw himself as a sacrifice to begin the next world. When none of the great gods did so, the lowly Nanahuatl (Pustulous-one) jumped in, the fire purified him, and he emerged as Tonatiuh, the sun. But before he would begin his journey across the sky, all of the other gods had to perform sacrifices and give their own blood, whereupon he rose in the east as he has ever since. This world is 4 Olin (4 Quake) and will eventually be destroyed by great earthquakes, and the earth on which we live is but one level of the cosmological world. There are 13 levels of Topan (Above-us), the region above the earth, and 9 levels of Mictlan

(Place of the Dead), the region below the earth (counting the earth as level 1 in both cases).

As with all historically known societies, the Aztecs are inextricably in the past: what we know of them depends on our interpretation of what they and others left—histories, descriptions, monuments, temples, and the archaeologically recoverable detritus of everyday life. After all, it is not only social relations that are infused with cultural values, perspectives, and beliefs, but everything. Moreover, we do not view objects and events and then interpret them in terms of our beliefs, as that suggests some are knowable separate from our perspectives; rather, our beliefs are an inherent part of the object or event as we experience it. So how can we penetrate our own perspectives to yield a clearer view of the Aztecs?

A standard way of interpreting cultures in Mesoamerica is the eminently reasonable strategy of doing so in light of their beliefs. Indeed, how important ideology is in the operations of any society is a much debated topic,[28] and one that is by no means limited to Mesoamerica. A prominent recent example of this approach is Marshall Sahlins's interpretation of the Hawaiians' reaction to the landing of Captain James Cook in 1779.[29]

Adopting the position that history is the reenactment of cultural structure, Sahlins holds that the Hawaiians, or at least the decision makers, interpreted Captain Cook as Lono, their year god. Because he appeared at the appropriate time and performed a series of acts that could be interpreted consistently with those expected of Lono, Cook was thought to be that god and was killed in accordance with Hawaiian rites for his return. Such an approach assumes that natives, or anyone, interpret objects and events in ways that are consistent with extant beliefs. This is entirely reasonable, for how else are people to interpret their world other than in terms of the known? And in the Aztec case, it is their cosmological views, myths, and notion of time that are taken as patterning their behavior.

Given the multiple interrelated periodicities of their calendar and the inherently cyclical nature of calendrical systems, the idea that the world was expressed in, and patterned by, temporal cycles is generally considered to have been very much a part of the fabric of Aztec life.[30] Moreover, this notion of time necessarily had a direct impact on the Aztecs having conceived of history as cyclical as well, since notions of time and concepts of history are strongly congruent, so that in a cyclical system, past events structured the present and patterned the future.[31] And Aztec views of their own past are seen as inextricably woven into their cyclical notion of time.

Aztec Calendar

Focusing on time and its meaning for the Aztecs is problematic since they inherited a far older Mesoamerican calendar and tradition that traces back almost 2,000 years.[32] The Aztecs themselves were doubtless ignorant of whatever purposes and motivations initially gave rise to the calendar—after all, they thought their major cultural traditions had been invented by the Toltecs, rather than earlier groups whose histories, traditions, and even presence had long been forgotten.[33] Thus, Aztec meaning is not a historical bequest but a contemporary reconceptualization that arose based on the calendar's structure and patterns, leaving unaddressed such issues as why it was so structured originally or why it functioned as it did.

Nevertheless, their calendar was comprised of multiple interrelated periodicities and the resultant notion of time is taken to have had a direct impact on how the Aztecs conceived of history, which is generally considered to have been cyclical as well, with past events structuring the present and patterning the future.[34] The Aztec calendar was based on multiple interlocking sets of escalating cycles far beyond those of calendars elsewhere, so some brief consideration of their system is in order.

Among the Aztecs, timekeeping was primarily a priestly responsibility, but it does not appear to have been esoteric knowledge that was jealously guarded by specialists to the exclusion of everyone else. The calendar system was taught in the elite schools, the calmecac, whose attendees included the sons of the upper nobility, some sons of lower nobles, and those who regardless of social class were destined for the priesthood.[35] Thus, many of the nobles had a potentially comprehensive understanding of timekeeping, and everyone—commoners and nobles alike—must have had a basic grasp of the calendar, at least as good as that of today's populace of our own calendar system. As a result, most of the people could calculate market days, birthdays, specific gods' days, and so forth. The priests, however, kept both the sacred and the secular calendars and, as scholars and scribes, were responsible for the written copies that survive today.

The Aztec calendar, which shares the basic structure of virtually all

Table 1–1. The 13 day numbers and the associated 13 Lords of the Day.

1. Xiuhteuctli	Turquoise-lord
2. Tlalteuctli	Lord-of-the-land
3. Chalchihuitl-Icue	Her-skirt Is Jade
4. Tonatiuh	He-goes-becoming-warm
5. Tlazolteotl	Filth-goddess
6. Mictlan-Teuctli	Lord-in-Mictlan
7. Centeotl	Ear-of-maize-god
8. Tlaloc	Land-lier
9. Quetzalcoatl	Plumed-serpent
10. Tezcatlipoca	Smoking Mirror
11. Chalmecateuctli	Lord-who-is-a-resident-in Chalman
12. Tlahuizcalpan-Teuctli	Lord-at-the-Dawn
13. Citlalli-Icue	Her-skirt Is Stars

Mesoamerican calendars, is typically described as a series of interlinking cycles that generate increasingly larger cycles, culminating in the 52-year Calendar Round (Xiuhmolpilli, the Mesoamerican "century") or the 104-year double Calendar Round (Huehuetiliztli) that structures their history.[36] This 52-year cycle is built up by the intersection of two separate but interlocking cycles, one of 260 days, the tonalpohualli (the count of the days)[37] and the other of 365 days, the xihuitl (the year).[38]

Each of these cycles—260 days and 365 days—is the result of the combination of still smaller cycles. One of these smaller cycles is based on a series of numbers, from 1 through 13.[39] A sequence rather than a count, these numbers do not function in a mathematical fashion, but only as a set of serial demarcators, although each day number is also associated with one of the 13 Lords of the Day.[40] The numbers are indicated by a series of 1 to 13 dots, totaling the amount designated.[41]

The second basic cycle consists of 20 symbols of apparently arbitrary origin. Unlike the 13 day numbers, the 20 day symbols have no directly associated supernaturals. (Even though the glyphic depictions for the day symbols are sometimes the god of the element indicated as the referent symbol, they are meant to indicate the element and not the deity. Thus, for instance, wind is usually depicted by the sign for Ehecatl, god of wind. These two cycles of 13 and 20 run in tandem to produce day names, which are a combination of a day number and a day symbol.)[42]

Table 1–2. **The 20 day signs.**
[These day signs are also repeated by Serna [1953:120 –122], and Castillo
[1991:209] also says that the first day of the sequence is 1 Cipactli.]

1. cipactli	alligator
2. ehecatl	wind
3. calli	house
4. cuetzalin	lizard
5. coatl	snake
6. miquiztli	death
7. mazatl	deer
8. tochtli	rabbit
9. atl	water
10. itzcuintli	dog
11. ozomatli	monkey
12. malinalli	grass
13. acatl	reed
14. ocelotl	jaguar
15. cuauhtli	eagle
16. cozcacuauhtli	vulture
17. olin	(earth)quake
18. tecpatl	flint
19. quiahuitl	rain
20. xochitl	flower

To illustrate, if the system began with the day number 1 and the day symbol cipactli, each cycle would continue running and, in our example, generate paired numbers and symbols until it reached 13 Acatl. At that point, while the day symbol sequence would continue, the day number sequence would begin again, with 1, generating the fourteenth day—1 Ocelotl. Both day and number cycles would then continue through 7 Xochitl, exhausting the day symbol series, which would then begin again with cipactli, while the day number sequence would continue uninterrupted with 8, producing the twenty-first day, 8 Cipactli, and so on. This compound cycle continues through 260 days before both 13-day-number and 20-day-symbol cycles reach simultaneous completion, having generated 260 uniquely named days (13 × 20 = 260) before the entire sequence begins anew.

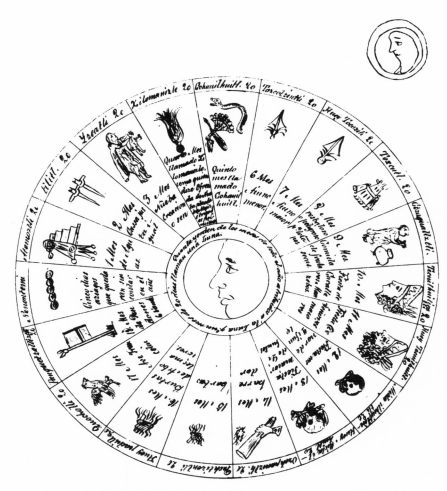

1-1. Late colonial indigenous calendar wheel depicting the xihuitl months. AGN-Historia, vol. 1, exp. 19, fol. 249; 1790 (Courtesy of the Archivo General de la Nación, Mexico City)

Table 1–3. **The 9 Lords of the Night.**
[This sequence is also provided textually by Serna [1953:163–164].]

1. Xiuhteuctli	Turquoise-lord
2. Itztli *or* Tecpatl	Obsidian *or* Flint
3. Piltzinteuctli	Child-lord
4. Centeotl	Ear-of-maize-god
5. Mictlan-Teuctli	Lord-in-Mictlan
6. Chalchihuitl-Icue	Her-skirt Is Jade
7. Tlazolteotl	Filth-goddess
8. Tepeyollotli	Heart-of-the-mountain(s)
9. Tlaloc	Land-lier

Although these are the basic calendrical cycles, there is a complicating third one, also tied to the tonalpohualli, the 9 Lords of the Night.[43] The 9 Lords of the Night cycle continuously with the other two tonalpohualli sequences and have an important astrological role in determining good, bad, and neutral days on which to celebrate auspicious occasions or begin significant undertakings.[44] Their calendrical role, however, is poorly understood and they seem superfluous as it is the day number and day symbol cycles that combine to produce the 260-day tonalpohualli cycle.

Although the tonalpohualli cycle is produced from both the 13- and the 20-day series, contrary to Seler's emphasis on the 20-day cycle,[45] it is the 13-day-number series that structures it. It is the primacy of that cycle that organizes the tonalpohualli into periods of 13 days[46] (conventionally called "trecenas" in Spanish), with each such period being dominated by a god or gods.[47] This means that each day in the tonalpohualli cycle is under the influence minimally of one Lord of the Day, one Lord of the Night, and at least one god for the entire trecena period, plus the associated voladores (fliers) tied to each of the 13 days.[48] The voladores are not identified by name in colonial text sources, so their individual identities are debated (I am following Seler[49] and Caso[50]). In one manuscript, the *Tonalamatl Aubin*, the voladores also have associated gods protruding from their beaks so there may be yet another god for each day.[51]

The other major calendrical cycle is based on the solar year, or xihuitl, and is comprised of 18 months of 20 days each.[52] The 20 days

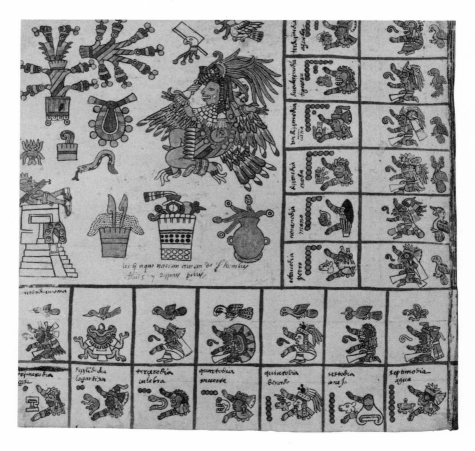

I-2. Fifteenth in the trecena cycle. Bottom horizontal and left vertical rows depict the 9 Lords of the Night (duplicating 4) plus 13 day names; the top horizontal and right vertical rows depict the 13 Lords of the Night plus the 13 voladores, and the Trecena god is Itzpapalotl. Folio 14, *Codex Borbonicus* (Courtesy of the Bibliothéque de l'Assemblée nationale Française, Paris)

Table 1–4. Voladores (and associated gods) in the Tonalamatl Aubin.
(Seler 1900 – 01:34; 1990 – 96, 1:191)

1. Blue hummingbird	Tlahuizcalpan-Teuctli
2. Green hummingbird	Ixtlilton
3. Hawk	Xochipilli
4. Quail	Xipe Totec
5. Eagle	Yaotl
6. Screech owl	Huahuantli
7. Butterfly	Xiuhteuctli
8. Striped Eagle	Tlaloc
9. Turkey	Tlaloc
10. Horned owl	Yayauhqui Tezcatlipoca
11. Macaw (Red Guacamayo)	Xochipilli
12. Quetzal	Centeotl
13. Green Parrot	Xochiquetzal

are not directly tied to lunations, which are 29.53 days long, but lunar cycles were recognized, though they played no major role in the Aztec calendar. Instead, the 20-day month is probably numerologically derived, owing its origin to the Mesoamerican vigesimal (base-20) counting system rather than our decimal (base-10) system.[53]

In contrast to the tonalpohualli, whose basic unit comes from the 13-day cycle, the xihuitl takes as its fundamental unit the 20-day cycle. To be complete, however, the days of the month must have an associated day number and are thus generated from the number/symbol configuration of the tonalpohualli. And because there are 20 day symbols and 20 days in a month, the same sequence of names occurs in every month in a given year, so each month in that year will begin with the same day symbol (though not the same day number), in contrast to the trecenas, which begin with the same day number but not the same day symbol.

Since the months of the xihuitl take the 20 day symbols as their basic structure, which have no direct supernatural associations, this is the more secular cycle, as the ecologically oriented names of many of the months suggest. Each month has a feast dedicated to a specific god, though whether this occurs on the first day of the month or the last is

Table 1–5. The 18 months of the Xihuitl.
(variant month names italicized in brackets).

[Serna [1953:127–133] uses the same sequence, beginning and ending on the same month, but he records Tlaxochimaco for month 9, Xocotlhuetzi for 10, Teotleco for 12, and Tepeilhuitl for 13. Castillo [1991:211–213] also follows this sequence, but with Xilomanaliztli as month 1, Xochihuitl as month 18, and he conflates two months, Tititl and Izcalli, as Izcalli Tititl for month 17.]

1. Atl Cahualo	Water is abandoned
[Cuahuitl Ehua	*Tree/Pole Rises]*
[Xilomanaliztli	*Spreading (i.e., Offering) of Green Maize]*
2. Tlacaxipehualiztli	Flaying of men
3. Tozoztontli	Short vigil
4. Huei Tozoztli	Long vigil
5. Toxcatl	Drought
6. Etzalcualiztli	Eating of bean porridge
7. Tecuilhuitontli	Small festival of the Lords
8. Huei Tecuilhuitl	Great festival of the Lords
9. Miccailhuitontli	Small festival of the dead
[Tlaxochimaco	*All Give Flowers to Things]*
10. Huei Miccailhuitl	Great festival of the dead
[Xocotl Huetzi	*Fruit Falls]*
11. Ochpaniztli	Sweeping of the road
12. Pachtontli	Small Spanish moss
[Teotl Eco	*Gods Arrive]*
13. Huei Pachtli	Great Spanish moss
[Tepeilhuitl	*Festival of the Mountains]*
14. Quecholli	Macaw
15. Panquetzaliztli	Raising of the flags
16. Atemoztli	Descent in the form of water
17. Tititl	Shrunk *or* Wrinkled thing
18. Izcalli	Sprout

debated.[54] Owing to the logical demands of the vigesimal counting system, 18 months of 20 days each is as close to numerological perfection as the solar year will permit. This count generates only 360 days, however, so 5 days are added following the eighteenth month to bring the xihuitl into line with the solar year.[55]

These 5 added days, called nemontemi or nen ontemi (waste; lit., It becomes full in vain) days, neither comprised a separate, shortened month nor fell within any of the 18 conventional months, and thus bore no unit name in the xihuitl. However, since the tonalpohualli cycle continued to run independently of the operation of the xihuitl, each nemontemi day did possess a day name derived from the former. Adding these 5 days brought the xihuitl count into approximate accord with the solar cycle, but the year was no longer evenly divisible by the 20-day-symbol count, as it would have in a 360-day year. Instead, the added days meant that the start of each new xihuitl advanced 5 days from the previous year in both the day-number and day-symbol counts.

The year names were based on the day symbol of the first (or last; it is debated) day of the month. Thus, for instance, if the first year began with tochtli, that year would be 1 Tochtli, and the next year would be 2 Acatl, which is the day symbol of the first day of the second year, the day symbol sequence having moved forward by five because of the insertion of the nemontemi days. The 2 Acatl year is second not only because acatl is the second day symbol in the sequence, but also because the 13-day-number cycle only runs through 28 full cycles (or 364 days) in a solar year, which means that the cycle has already begun again before the beginning of the next year. Thus, the following year starts not with 1, which fell in the ending year, but with the number 2, naming both the day and the year as a consequence. As the years continue, the next one begins on 3 Tecpatl, 4 Calli, 5 Tochtli, and so on, through 13 Tochtli, when the 13-day-number cycle begins again with 1 (Acatl). The 13-day-number cycle is repeated four times, generating 52 uniquely named years in a 52-year cycle ($4 \times 13 = 52$) that can be divided into four 13-year quarters.[56] Since the xihuitl is only 365 days long, rather than the actual 365.2422 days of a full solar cycle, some leap year correction needed to be made in order to keep in line with solar reality. How this was done is uncertain and colonial writers differed on this subject, perhaps because the native calendar was tied to the Christian one as of 1548 and no longer made its own leap year adjustments.[57] Among the suggested mechanisms for dealing with the difference between the calendrical year and the solar year are no leap year correction at all,[58] the addition of a day every 4 years,[59] or the addition of 13 days every 52 years.[60]

The two cycles of 260 and 365 days, respectively, ran continuously, with their conjunctions of day names, months, and years producing a still larger cycle of 52 solar years (260 × 365 = 94,900, which is 52 xihuitl cycles or 73 tonalpohualli cycles), known as the Calendar Round, before beginning anew.[61] At that point, just like the day-symbol and day-number cycles of the tonalpohualli, both xihuitl and tonalpohualli cycles reached completion together. With the entire 52-year cycle thus completed, time ended, and the beginning of the next Calendar Round cycle was marked by the celebration of the New Fire ceremony.[62]

Drawing on fray Bernardino de Sahagún's[63] description of this event, when the four 13-year cycles had made a circle and the 52-year cycle had ended, the fires were extinguished throughout the land, all the household statues of the gods were thrown into the water, the pestles and hearthstones were thrown away, and everything was swept from the houses. When night fell on that last day of the 52-year cycle, demons (tzitzimime) descended to devour people. The houses were deserted, everyone went up on the terraces, children wore masks of maguey leaves, women were placed in granaries, and no one slept.

As night fell, the priests in Tenochtitlan began their procession, wearing the garb of the gods. They marched along the causeway to Itztapalapan, where they reached and climbed the hill of Huixachtecatl (lit., Person-from-Huixachtlan[64]). And at midnight, when the Pleiades reached their zenith, they knew the next cycle would begin. The fire priest of Copolco then laid a fire drill (a stick spun in the hands to create heat and ignite a fire) upon the chest of the person to be sacrificed and worked it until a flame erupted. He then quickly cut open the captive's chest, wrenched out his heart, and cast it into the fire, which rapidly consumed the body of the captive as well.[65]

When this fire became visible to everyone in the towns below, the people cut their ears in autosacrifice and splattered the blood in the direction of the new fire. The fire priests lit the first torch from the fire in the sacrificial captive's chest, took it to the Great Temple in Tenochtitlan, and placed it in the brazier in the Temple of Huitzilopochtli. Runners carried the flame from Huixachtlan (lit., Place beside the thorny trees [i.e., acacias]), the temple atop the hill of Huixachtecatl, to all of the other towns of the land, where it was first taken to the temple and the priests' houses, and then to the wards (calpollis), where it was spread to every neighborhood and house. Incense was offered and amaranth-seed cakes were eaten before sunrise, and then everyone fasted from first light until midday, when more captives were sacrificed. In this way, all the household fires for the next 52-year cycle came ultimately from the new fire kindled on the sacrifice's chest. This ceremony, also called the Binding of the Years, marked the completion of the 52-year cycle. Every second Calendar Round also coincided with the 8-year Venus cycle and was a Double Calendar Round, though these seem to have borne no additional calendrical significance than the usual Calendar Round and are not pictorially distinguished in the codices.

Because the Aztec calendar was comprised of cycles combining and building on each other—13-day cycles, 20-day cycles, 260-day cycles, 365-day cycles—and culminating in endlessly repeating 52-year cycles, each Calendar Round possessed its own starting point at the first day. But without still larger cycles, there could be no longer term starting point, or zero date, and the Aztec calendar was left numerically adrift, with an endless series of repeating cycles.

No single early historical source documents all of the features of the Aztec calendar. But the *Codex Borbonicus*, a very early colonial manuscript,[66] is the most comprehensive and is of indigenous authorship. The first and last two pages are missing, but following Glass and Robertson[67] and reading left to right, part 1 (fols. 3–20 plus the missing fols. 1–2) is a tonalpohualli depicting 18 of the 20 trecenas. Part 2 (fols. 21–22) shows the associated Lords of the Night with the year bearer days of the 52 xihuitl years of the Calendar Round. Part 3 (fols. 23–36) is an 18-month calendar year, with folio 34 showing the New Fire ceremony[68] in the month Panquetzaliztli. Part 4 (fols. 37–38 plus the missing fols. 39–40) repeats one of the month ceremonies and continues with year dates through 1507. Thus, the general Aztec notions of time and the calendar are most completely embodied in this manuscript.

This calendar, in which temporal cycles form an integral part well beyond years, possessed no zero starting date. As a result, this calendar, based on an endless repetition of cycles, provided the framework for what is perhaps the best known example of a cyclical culture.

I-3. Festival for the month of Panquetzaliztli nominally depicting the New Fire ceremony. Folio 34, *Codex Borbonicus* (Courtesy of the Bibliothéque de l'Assemblée nationale Française, Paris)

Ideology and Evidence

There are sound reasons to think that ideological constructs do pattern social practices, and the fundamental understanding of time—its nature, the way a society divides and counts it, and how it influences perspectives on past, present, and future—is perhaps the best example of this. Aztec myths of the cyclical creation and destruction of the world and their cosmological location within multiple otherworldly layers find major reflection in their notions of time. But the question is whether these myths provide otherwise unavailable insights into Mexican events, objects, and perspectives, rather than merely suggest an aesthetic appreciation of them. This has already been observed in the *Codex Borbonicus*, but another, less explicit, reflection of underlying beliefs that may nevertheless be understood in that way is seen in the remains of the Great Temple (Templo Mayor) of Tenochtitlan (whose modern excavation began only after 1978)[69] in light of Aztec cosmology.

Upon reaching Tenochtitlan, one of the Spanish conquistadors[70] described the Great Temple as square and approximately 150 paces long and 115 or 120 paces wide. At the height of two men, the building was set back 2 paces on all sides, with stairs on one side. It continued to be built up in this fashion until it reached the top, with a total of 120 or 130 stairs; on top were built towers, and the pyramid was dedicated to Huitzilopochtli.

Today, all that survives from the Spanish onslaught are truncated remains. But because Mexican pyramids were typically expanded by building over existing ones and incorporating their bulk into the rubble fill of the interior, walking toward the center of the pyramid takes one from the remains of the most recent structure back through time to earlier and earlier examples. The first temple was begun by the Aztecs the year after they founded their capital of Tenochtitlan; subsequent Aztec rulers sought to expand it.[71]

The principal investigator of the site, archaeologist Eduardo Matos Moctezuma, has identified seven stages in the construction of the pyramid.[72] The earliest temple (Stage I) is historically recorded as having been constructed of earth, but it could not be excavated because of the high water table. The remaining structures were all excavated and assigned to the reigns of their respective kings. These have been interpreted as reflecting the Aztec cosmological view, in which the celestial

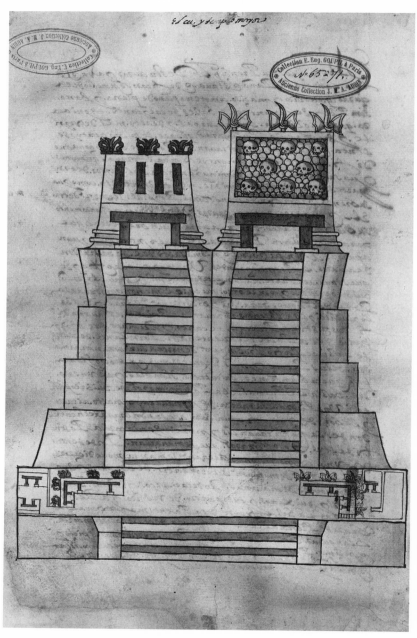

I-4. Great Temple. Folio II2v, *Codex Ixtlilxóchitl* **(BNP 65-7I)** (Courtesy of the Bibliothéque nationale de France, Paris)

Table 1–6. Aztec kings and years of reign.
[See Hassig [1988] for full references to these dates.]

1372–1391	Acamapichtli (Reed-fist)
1391–1417	Huitzilihuitl (Hummingbird-feather)
1417–1427	Chimalpopoca (He-smokes-like-a-shield)
1427–1440	Itzcoatl (Obsidian-serpent)
1440–1468	Moteuczoma Ilhuicamina (He-frowned-like-a-lord He-pierces-the-sky-with-an-arrow)
1468–1481	Axayacatl (Water-mask)
1481–1486	Tizoc (Chalk-pulque)
1486–1502	Ahuitzotl (Otter, lit. Water-porcupine)
1502–1520	Moteuczoma Xocoyotl (He-frowned-like-a-lord The-younger)
1520	Cuitlahua (Excrement-owner)
1520–1525	Cuauhtemoc (He-descends-like-an-eagle)

Table 1–7. Construction stages of the Great Temple.
[From Matos Moctezuma [1988:70, 176].]

Stage I	1325
Stage II	1375–1426 glyph date 2 Tochtli (1390)
Stage III	1427–1440 glyph date 4 Acatl (1421)
Stage IV	1440–1468 glyph date 1 Tochtli (1454)
Stage IVb	1468–1481 glyph date 3 Calli (1469)
Stage V	1481–1486
Stage VI	1486–1502
Stage VII	1502–1520

plane of the world (that on which we live) intersects with the 13 levels of the heavens (Topan) and the 9 levels of the underworld (Mictlan).[73] Thus, the Great Temple represents a blending of the Aztec view of the symbolic universe[74] and their own history as embodied in their migration legend.

The Great Temple has dual stairways and is considered to be divided into halves, represented by the two temples of Tlaloc on the left (north) and Huitzilopochtli on the right (south);[75] the southern temple represents Coatepetl.[76] The historical world, as the Aztecs present it, involves their departure from their mythical ancestral home of Aztlan in the year 1 Tecpatl (A.D. 1143), followed by a long period of wandering, sometimes from Aztlan to Chicomoztoc (Seven-Caves-Place), the caves from which the major central Mexican groups legendarily emerged, before moving into the Valley of Mexico. In one account, at Coatepetl, the goddess Coatl-Icue was impregnated by a ball of feathers but, on learning of this, her daughter, Coyolxauhqui, summoned her brothers, the Centzon Huitznahua (400 Southerners),[77] and they decided to kill their mother for thus disgracing them. But Coatl-Icue was pregnant with the god Huitzilopochtli, who spoke to his mother from the womb, telling her not to fear, and when his brothers arrived, he sprang from the womb fully grown and fully armed, and slew them and his sister. It is this place that is thought to be represented on the southern half of the Great Temple, while the northern temple represents Tonacatepetl, the mountain where Tlaloc is the patron deity.[78] There is additional support for this interpretation in the Coyolxauhqui stone, which depicts the goddess's dead body at the base of the pyramid, as at the mythical Coatepetl.[79] Thus, the Great Temple is a symbolic depiction of the earthly, underworldly, and heavenly planes, the legendary Aztec origin story, and the symbolic contrast between Tonacatepetl and Coatepetl, Tlaloc and Huitzilopochtli, water and blood, agriculture and

I-5. Teocalli de la Guerra Sagrada, front (Drawing by Doni Fox)

war (the sun is northerly during the summer or agricultural season and southerly during the winter or war season[80]).

There are also historical elements in this construction of the Aztec migration. The Aztecs record that after they reached the Valley of Mexico, they tried to establish themselves in a series of places, and finally settled on an island in western Lake Texcoco. The accounts of why they ended up there differ, ranging from being forced to flee into the marshes by the king of Colhuacan, to searching for a snake-eating eagle on a rock, as foretold by their gods. But however they reached that spot, they founded their capital of Tenochtitlan in 1325 (2 Calli).

This symbolic approach offers a compelling interpretation of the Great Temple, tying its physical form into Aztec cosmological, mythical, historical, and calendrical notions. But this example is by no means an isolated case without parallel in the rest of the Aztec world, as can be seen by examining Alfonso Caso's classic analysis of the Teocalli de la Guerra Sagrada.[81] Built into part of the National Palace in Mexico City, this stone monument, discovered in 1926, is carved in the shape of a temple (teocalli).[82]

The lower front of the monument has two carved dates flanking the stairway, 1 Tochtli (Rabbit) on the left and 2 Acatl (Reed) on the right, which represent year dates. A cord around the acatl glyph marks the Binding of the Years.[83] Above the dates are depictions of two bowls, known as eagle vessels (cuauhxicalli), which were used as receptacles for the hearts and blood of human sacrifices. The lower portion of the eagle vessels are decorated with two undulating lines and two discs, which probably represent jade and together symbolize blood. The center portion of the right eagle vessel has feathers that reflect the name of the vessel, whereas the left one has jaguar skin reliefs. Above these are

I-6. Cartouche containing the 2 Acatl glyph with the binding to denote the celebration of the New Fire ceremony, lower right front, Teocalli de la Guerra Sagrada (Drawing by Doni Fox)

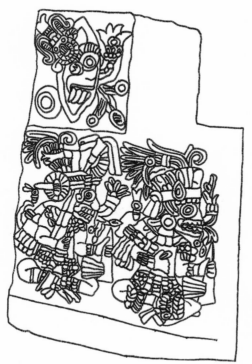

1-7. Figures depicted on the left side, Teocalli de la Guerra Sagrada [Drawing by Doni Fox]

inverted hearts, and from the center of the right vessel comes an eagle feather; the analogous portion of the left vessel has been defaced. The vessels reflect the eagle warriors and the jaguar warriors who were dedicated to the cult of the sun, indicating that the fundamental idea of this monument was the ritual war through which sacrificial captives were taken in combat.

There are two figures on each side of the monument, each holding copal bags in their rearmost (foreground) hands and a maguey spine with other spines inserted in it for ritual autosacrifice in their foremost (background) hands. The figures on the left side of the monument are Tlaloc, god of water, though the rear depiction has elements of Mictlan-Teuctli, Lord of the Underworld (and thus the dead) and the front one has elements of Tlahuizcalpan-Teuctli, the god who is the planet Venus. The figures on the right side of the monument are Xiuhteuctli, god of fire and of the year, in front, and the rear figure, though difficult to interpret, is probably Xochipilli, god of flowers.

I-8. Figures depicted on the right side, Teo-calli de la Guerra Sa-grada (Drawing by Doni Fox)

All four deities show their exposed teeth and each of the four gods has a symbol in front of his mouth, where word or song glyphs are customarily located. The dual symbols here represent a flow of water and an object that appears on the fire serpent (xiuhcoatl). Taken together, and following the analysis of Eduard Seler,[84] these depict the atl-tlachinolli sign (atl = water, dart-thrower, and tlachinolli = burned thing), and signify ritual war for the purpose of taking hearts and blood for the sun so that it will continue on its course.

The upper body of the monument has date glyphs on both right and left sides. On the right side is 1 Tecpatl (Flint) and on the left is 1 Miquiztli (Death). Both dates begin trecenas (the twenty 13-day divisions of the tonalpohualli) and correspond with the north. Both glyphs bear a smoking mirror symbolic of the god Tezcatlipoca and from the mouth of each emerges the atl-tlachinolli glyph.[85] Between these two dates are 52 years in the tonalpohualli, which symbolize the 52 years of the century and the Binding of the Years. Moreover, the trecena, 1 Tecpatl, was dedicated to Huitzilopochtli, Camaxtli, and a deity from Huexotzinco, all gods of war. The trecena I Miquiztli was dedicated to Tezcatlipoca and also apparently to Mictlan-Teuctli and Tonatiuh, sun gods, and to Tonatiuh and Tezcatlipoca in his manifestation as Tecuciztecatl. Thus, I Tecpatl and I Miquiztli represent the sixth and tenth trecenas, which are presided over by the sun.

The front of the upper body contains a solar disc flanked by two figures. In the center of the disc is the glyph 4 Olin (Quake), which is the day the sun began moving in the legend of the creation of the fifth Sun, indicating that the primary dedication of this monument was to the sun. The figure on the right is Tezcatlipoca and that on the left is Huitzilopochtli, both gods of war. Both have atl-tlachinolli glyphs in front of their mouths and both carry maguey spines in their foremost hands. There is also a glyph in front and above Tezcatlipoca, which remains uninterpreted in Caso's account.[86]

The platform base between the lower and upper bodies of the monument has a carving of Tlalteuctli, the earth monster. Flanking this figure are two shields. Behind the shield on the left are four darts and a flag, and eight feathers; the shield is also decorated with eight feathers.

I-9. Solar disk flanked by two figures, upper front, Teocalli de la Guerra Sagrada (Drawing by Doni Fox)

Behind the shield on the right are four arrows and a flag; the shield bears no decoration but may originally have been painted.

The platform on top of the upper body of the monument has a date (2 Calli [House]) in a square cartouche and is probably a year date. Around and enclosing this glyph is a woven ball of zacate fiber (zacata-payolli) into which were placed maguey spines for autosacrifice. From the middle of this ball comes the smoking mirror symbol also seen on the 1 Miquiztli and 1 Tecpatl glyphs on the sides, and two rods that are probably maguey spines. Flanking the ball are two rolls of paper bound with four ties, which symbolize sacrifice, and from each of which comes the head of a fire serpent.

The back of the monument has a relief of a figure in the earth, from whose mouth comes a nopal cactus, upon which is an eagle. The figure, surrounded by water, is the goddess of water, Chalchihuitl-Icue. The fruits of the cactus are transformed into human hearts like those depicted on the eagle vessels, and an atl-tlachinolli glyph emerges from the eagle's mouth. The entire scene represents Tenochtitlan, which was founded in the year 2 Calli (2 House; 1325).[87]

Caso interprets the Teocalli as a monument to the sacred war (xochi-yaoyotl), dedicated to the cult of the sun, and flanked by four deities representing death. The stone also commemorates the founding of the Aztec capital of Tenochtitlan, so the overall effect is to commemorate mythical and historical events, sacrificial actions, and gods related to Tenochtitlan on an undated monument of major ideological significance.

But as pervasive as these perceptions of time and history were among the Aztecs, did they extend beyond this one city of Tenochtitlan, or were they largely confined to the Aztecs and their capital? No Aztec-era monuments quite like the Teocalli have been recovered outside Tenochtitlan, but there were other dual temple pyramids, though all extant examples are in or near the Valley of Mexico. Given the systematic destruction of Aztec religious monuments by the Spaniards following the Conquest, this dearth of monumental evidence is perhaps not surprising. But evidence of a widely shared ideology is available in the calendar.

Though the calendars in Mexico differed in month names and gods commemorated, they all shared basic organizational similarities,[88] which strongly argues that they formed part of the general cultural substratum of Mesoamerica. With rare exception, they were based on two

cycles of 260 and 365 days, respectively, generating a basic 52-year cycle, and they all possessed divisions into units of 20 days and 13 days,
though some had further divisions as well, such as the 65-day divisions
of the Zapotec calendar[89] and the 2–14 number sequence in the Azoyu
manuscripts from Guerrero rather than the usual 1–13.[90]

Indeed, Alfonso Caso argues that the calendars of central Mexico
were all coordinated and exhibited a basic uniformity that cross-cut
different geographical, political, and linguistic areas. Thus, the ideology of cyclical time and mythical history through which actions can be
understood is fundamental to Mesoamerica and can be readily seen in
the codex, monument, and temple examined. The working out of the
Aztec calendar, and the references to Aztec history, myths, and cosmology, can be seen in these objects and offer an excellent key to deci-
phering their meanings, tying creations to beliefs. These shared notions are often taken as strongly patterning Aztec behavior and thus
provide a template by which these people can be understood. This ideological approach to the interpretation of other cultures is thus clearly
productive. The codex, pyramid, and monument can be explained in
terms of Aztec history, calendar, and cosmology, but if we broaden the
focus to approach the examples from a different theoretical perspective,
this explanation seems less satisfactory.

Chapter 2

Outside the Focus

The primary challenge to this standard interpretation of these Aztec relics comes not from internal inconsistencies but from competing theoretical orientations that place the objects in a different light.
Gananath Obeyesekere's recent critique of Sahlins's interpretation of
Hawaiian history illustrates the problem. Though sympathetic to Sahlins's general approach to history,[1] Obeyesekere challenges his specific
interpretation of Captain Cook as a god. He argues that, while Sahlins
has explained Cook's death in terms of Hawaiian myth and ideology,
the events and circumstances surrounding his killing do not adequately
fit the ritual model of Lono's return. Rather, he argues that these same
events can be better understood as political acts by the chief designed
to affect local alliances.[2] He emphasizes political concerns, sees Hawaiians acting in ways that are meaningful to them in their current
circumstances, and does not see them forcing events into their precon-
ceived conceptual frameworks. While not explicitly framed in these
terms, the fundamental argument is over how strongly ideology patterns interpretations of the world.[3]

Given how well such ideological interpretations seem to account for
the evidence, how can one meaningfully challenge them? Since basic
thematic positions are essentially first principles, they are articles of
faith that admit of little challenge in terms of their internal logic, re-
ducing the debate to how precise the fit must be to sustain an analogy,

such as between the actions of Lono and Cook. After all, differences will always emerge in such analogical reasoning and the argument is over how much is acceptable before one considers the parallel to be no longer sustainable. So the adequacy of the analogy alone must not be the crux of the criticism. The critique must instead be mounted on the relation of the interpretive stance to the data it purports to explain,[4] so the struggle is over the facts of the case. But a reinterpretation can rarely succeed by using the data presented by the original interpreters, since they will present only those that support their case, not disingenuously but because their theoretical orientation defines what is and is not pertinent to their thesis. A data critique requires reexamining the primary sources, both to glean facts that do not fit or were omitted as irrelevant to the original interpretation, and to broaden the field to allow alternative interpretations. My concern is not, of course, with the adequacy of either Sahlins's or Obeyesekere's interpretations, but with how well the Aztecs have been assessed. The interpretation of Aztec notions of time, history, and the calendar presented above have been broadly accepted and appear to explain actions and records in the form of codices and monuments in a convincing way. So the question is whether an effective challenge can in fact be mounted against this conventional interpretation.

Omissions, Misunderstandings, and Inconsistencies

If the Aztec analysis focuses on time, history, and the calendar, each as a thing-in-itself, the conventional interpretations are satisfactory. But focusing on these phenomena as dictating Aztec behavior makes them the center of the interpretation and offers little scope for considering other information not crucial to their internal workings. While the conventional description presents few problems on its face, several considerations raise the specter of a calendar that does not operate as a simple reflection of Aztec religious ideology. Even matters not explicitly addressed in the *Codex Borbonicus* inevitably raise issues by logical extension.

There is no need to create an alternative interpretation if the conventional one is satisfactory. But at least four problems with the calendar reflect on the general notion of time for the Aztecs and yet do not yield to ready resolution under the prevailing interpretation. One is the point at which the day begins. Alfonso Caso[5] argues that there are only four times when the day is likely to have begun: sunrise, midday, sunset, and midnight. He dismisses both sunrise and sunset as starting points because, although easily observed, they change throughout the year as the days shorten in the winter and lengthen in the summer, and he argues that they are therefore unsuitable. Midnight is a fixed point that does not vary, but without clocks or a notable nightly astronomical phenomenon to mark it, it is not very useful. Noon, then, was the starting point of the day, he concludes, because it did not vary and was easily identifiable by the sun reaching its zenith.[6] Despite Caso's argument from utility for the Aztecs, his reasoning did not deter many other civilizations from basing their days on movable starting points. For instance, day began at dawn for the ancient Egyptians, at sunset for the Babylonians, Jews, and Muslims, at sunset and later midnight for the Romans, at dawn in western Europe before clocks,[7] at half an hour after sunset in fourteenth-century Italy,[8] and at sunset for the traditional Maya today.[9]

Despite the ease with which noon can be determined, as a starting time for the day it is awkward, forcing attendees to begin walking to market the day before the present day has begun, for example. Besides, as a practical matter, the functional day would likely have started at quite different times for different members of society. Farmers would logically begin the day at sunrise, as would the military, whereas priests might well begin it at another point for ritual purposes. The same may have been true of the calendar, which may have begun at one point for calendrical considerations, but at others for various social activities, with the result that the fundamental question of what single time the day starts may be entirely specious.

Lest it seem unlikely that a society would have different beginning times for the day for different groups, consider that the day begins at midnight in the West for the vast majority of matters, yet since a division would be very awkward for astronomers concerned with recording celestial events from sunset to sunrise, from Ptolemy's time until 1925, the astronomical day began at noon.[10] So Caso's dismissal of day markers that vary seasonally is a cultural assumption that is not at all borne out comparatively or historically. Besides, the notion of sunrise, sunset, or the zenith does not convey the sort of specificity to which Caso alludes. After all, is sunset when the sun first touches the horizon, is last visible above it, is centered on the horizon, or after the light fades following setting?

A second problem with our understanding of the calendar concerns the notion of Aztec "hours," which does not emerge directly from the historical documentation, but as an extrapolation from the logic of the system. It has been suggested that each Aztec day is divided into 13 hours and each night into 9 hours,[11] which, if true, reflects a greater emphasis on the day than the night, dividing the former into more numerous, and more useful, units than the latter. This does not reflect a greater length for the day over the night, even if the dawn and gloaming are included in the day, since these vary seasonally. As the day is conveniently marked by the position of the sun, at least for such gross periods as antemeridian, midday, and postmeridian, there was little need for additional public time indicators. At least for some rituals, the Aztecs noted (1) dawn, (2) when it was time to eat, (3) noon, and (4) sunset during the day; and at night, they marked (5) dark, (6) bedtime, (7) the sounding of the trumpet (i.e., midnight), and (8) near daybreak.[12] At night, the priestly novices signaled temporal durations by regularly replenishing the temple fires,[13] so some notion of standard (but variable) durations was employed, though fixed hours are a relatively recent idea anywhere in the world,[14] except in latitudes near the equator, where days and nights were naturally of relatively equal length, as in ancient Babylonia.[15] In battles during the Conquest, however, the Aztecs reportedly relieved their troops every quarter hour,[16] which, if true, would suggest some still-unknown means of calculating time with roughly that precision. In any case, the divisions of day and night, if they were calculated, were unequal in nature, and varied in duration throughout the year, though they may well have been symbolically equal. But this idea has been criticized[17] and is not essential to understand how the calendar functioned.

A third problem involves when the year bearer days fall within the xihuitl month and year. Every month in that year began (or ended) on only 1 of 4 day signs—calli, tochtli, acatl, or tecpatl—which were accordingly known as the year bearers, but where that day fell in the month is still debated.[18] Resolving this issue does not affect our overall understanding of the logic of the calendar system, but since many calculations of dates begin with Aztec day dates—notably based on the date of the fall of Tenochtitlan, which was August 13, 1521, or the day 1 Coatl in the month Huei Miccailhuitl—when that year bearer fell during the indigenous month significantly affects the correlation by days if not months.[19]

A fourth problem, and one that is much debated, is which month began the year. One reason for the various opinions about the year-starting month is that these apparently differed by locale; different places had slightly different calendrical traditions, which suggests that perhaps the idea that all the Mexican calendars were synchronized is wrong. After all, Caso's position is not based on direct evidence of dates, but on a reasoned consideration of the available data.

In the absence of pre-Columbian monuments bearing dates in different calendrical systems for the same event, it is difficult to test whether Caso is correct. The ideal evidence of Caso's claim would be indigenous dates in the various calendars, each tied to a Christian date early in the colonial period before the calendar was altered by contact,[20] which would lay the foundation for an accurate comparison of indigenous systems by way of the Christian calendar. Since these links do not exist, however, the primary evidence connecting Mexican calendars is their striking similarities.

They all share the eighteen 20-day months, each with its own ceremony and patron deities. And where the same god was celebrated, or where the meanings of their names were similar, Caso claimed these were not only the same month, but agreed day for day.[21] Thus, for example, he equates the Tarascan goddess Cuerauaperi with the Aztec goddess Toci (also called Teteo Innan), which he then uses to link the Tarascan month during which Cuerauaperi's festival is held with the Aztec month during which Toci is worshiped.[22] In essence, Caso's logic is that we know the sequence of the months in the Aztec calendar and we know when the year began; if we know any of the months or commemorated gods in another Mexican calendar, we can correlate the months of the various calendars and know when the other Mexican calendar systems should begin, too. So everything falls into place as long as a correlation can be established between any month in the Aztec system and its analog in the other systems.

Caso's perspective on the calendar arose less from observing similarities in timing among the various calendars than from his belief that the ancient Mexicans shared a mentality about the sacred nature of the calendar. Thus his pairing of months was "justified" even when the data themselves were less than compelling.[23] But if the pairing of these months can be shown to be inaccurate, then the overall correlation and, consequently, the model that the various Mexican calendars operate in sync, can be demonstrated to be incorrect. There is no direct evidence to refute this correlation, but there is an indirect way to assess it—by looking at social practices that are dated among various groups and ty-ing them to regular and thus datable events that can then be compared. The classic case of this is war.

Although there could be minor conflicts at any time in the year, large-scale warfare in Mexico was patterned by environmental con-straints. The major factor affecting the timing of military campaigns was the rainy season, which usually began in late May/early June and continued through mid-September in central Mexico.[24] Thereafter, the dry season began, stretching from around late September through mid-May. This pattern meant not only that the men from whom the bulk of the army was drawn were in the fields working, but that during the rainy season it was difficult to move large forces over sodden dirt roads and across swollen streams.[25] Moving large forces was significantly easier during the dry season, and only then, after harvest, were large amounts of foodstuffs available to feed the army.[26]

Major military campaigns were typically mounted from late autumn through spring owing to climatological factors as well as the availabil-ity of men and supplies. Their initiation was marked by the festival of Panquetzaliztli.[27] This month began, according to Caso, on Novem-ber 21[28] (calculated for the year 1519), and the rainy season generally ran from Etzalcualiztli (May 25–June 13) into Ochpaniztli (Septem-ber 2–21). The emphasis on war during the dry seasons—a practical necessity rather than just a ritual—was widespread in Mesoamerica.[29] And it is this correlation between seasons and warfare that offers an al-ternative means of assessing the correlations among the various Mexi-can calendars.

The Tarascans record the beginning of their war season with the feast of Hanziuánsquaro,[30] whose exact date is uncertain. Caso suggests that the month of the same name—so the festival doubtless occurred within it, probably on the first day—ran from July 18 to August 6,[31] based on the similarities with the Aztec month of Miccailhuitontli. There may indeed be similarities between the festivals, but Caso's cor-relation would put the beginning of the Tarascan military campaigns right in the middle of the rainy season when conditions were worst and contrary to the evidence that they, in fact, did not carry out wars at that time.

While this correlation is not definitive proof that Caso is wrong on this point, his model depends more on predilection than on an analyti-cal demonstration of calendrical synchronization. As a result, the link-age between the dry season, warfare, and specific months is better evidence against Caso's general calendrical correlation than the evidence he has marshaled for it, and strongly suggests that he is wrong and that at least some of the central Mexican calendars were not all synchronized after all.

If Caso is wrong about the coordination of the various Mexican calendars, as he almost certainly is, what does that say about Mesoamerican calendars generally, and the Aztec one specifically? First, calendrically tied ritual behaviors cannot be coordinated throughout central Mexico or Mesoamerica generally. And second, the calendar does not seem to be a system that runs solely on its own internal logic. Where there *is* uniformity, something other than the calendar must account for it. In short, a strictly ideological approach to understanding Aztec behavior will not work because the calendar itself does not conform to the patterning observed. If we may reverse Caso's perspective, it is not the divergence of calendars that needs to be explained, but rather their convergence.

The Manipulation of Time

I do not advocate rejecting understanding Aztec behavior in terms of ideology simply because there are logical problems in our comprehension of Mesoamerican calendars as approached from this perspective. After all, many of the patterns revealed by this approach are compelling, and further data or more insightful analysis may reveal the problems to be chimeras. But what does throw the ideological interpretation into question are a couple of well-documented cases of the calendar being deliberately manipulated in apparent violation of that ideology. An inquiry into what was altered, how, and why should help lay the foundation for a reassessment of time in Aztec society.

In the reckoning of the 260-day tonalpohualli cycle, each day was good, bad, or indifferent, and actions taken on these days accordingly shared their qualities. For example, it was said that anyone born on the day 1 Ocelotl would die in war, be taken away, abandoned, or seized;[32] one born on 1 Mazatl would become a ruler and gain fame if he was of noble lineage; and if he was a commoner, he would also surpass others and become a valiant chieftain.[33] Major undertakings were also ostensibly begun on auspicious days or were deferred until a beneficial day arrived. Examples of major enterprises that might be shifted to more favorable days include the beginning of a major trading expedition (1 Coatl)[34] and the start of a military campaign (1 Itzcuintli).[35] The point at which these undertakings could be initiated was flexible and could be shifted a few days forward or back without significant hardship. But other events were fixed, such as the day of one's birth or the naming ceremony that followed four days later.

A strictly ideological interpretation of the calendar's effect on behavior would be warranted if the tonalpohualli cycle actually determined the divinatory quality of the days, as well as the likely outcome of enterprises begun then or the quality and prospects of people born then. But these seemingly fixed days could be, and were, manipulated; if your birthday is inauspicious, shift to your naming day, and, if both days are ill-omened, pick a completely different one even if it has no necessary relation to you. In short, there was a calendrically based set of auguries, but these were all avoidable, all manipulatable,[36] which suggests that, for the Aztecs, time was not the fatalistically determined aspect of life it is often portrayed to be. Ordinary individuals did not manipulate time itself, but they did alter their relations to it and its anticipated effects on them. In fact, this sort of temporal elasticity was more in keeping with how the Aztecs were likely to have regarded time than our own rather absolute notions of it.

In a society in which there were no markers of regular durations, whether mechanical clocks, hourglasses, or water clocks, time was task focused, inherently contextual, and thus necessarily elastic.[37] There was little notion of time as an absolute, abstract, and quantifiable commodity. At an everyday level, days and nights varied in length, as did seasons, and even the heavenly bodies wandered across the horizon. Is it any wonder that time would be viewed as flexible and even manipulable?

The manipulation of time was not limited to the idiosyncratic actions of individual Aztecs, however. It was also changed at the official level. For example, the conventional interpretation of the tonalpohualli suggests a complete 260-day cycle built up of complete lesser cycles, yet this is not entirely accurate. The basic unit of the tonalpohualli is the trecena, which is based on the 13-day-number and associated 13 Lords of the Night cycles combined with the 20 day symbols to generate the 260 days that comprise the tonalpohualli cycle. Each trecena is largely complete, since each repeats the same 13 day numbers, the same 13 Lords of the Day, and the same associated voladores; it also has a god or gods of the 13-day unit, though these differ among the surviving versions of the tonalamatl, perhaps reflecting different constellations of gods favored by the city where that particular tonalamatl originated.[38] The 20 day symbols, however, run continuously and overlap the trecenas, holding the collection of otherwise autonomous units together as a series until they run through their cycles 13 times. But there is less integration with the 9 Lords of the Night.

All 9 Lords of the Night are represented in each trecena, although not always in a single 1-through-9 sequence; 4 are duplicated, and the series inevitably overlaps one or both adjacent trecenas. This pattern may be glimpsed in the tonalpohualli section of the *Codex Borbonicus*, where the first day of that 260-day sequence begins with the day 1 Cipactli, the first Lord of the Day and the first Lord of the Night (by projection from the missing fol. 1). Yet in part 2, the 52-year Calendar Round, the Lord of the Night associated with the first year of the count, 1 Tochtli, is not Xiuhteuctli, the first one in the series, but Mictlan-Teuctli, who is the fifth. Though an integral part of the tonalpohualli, the 9 Lords of the Night cycle plays no direct role in the xihuitl and is secondary to the 13 day numbers and 13 Lords of the Day, which define the periodicity of the trecenas, as well as the 20-day-symbol cycle. In fact, unlike the other cycles, the 9 Lords of the Night cycle does not fit the 260-day tonalpohualli cycle evenly. Calculating strictly arithmetically, the completion of the 9 Lords of the Night cycle coincides with those of the 13- and 20-day cycles only every eleven trecena cycles, which means that, if the cycle were allowed to run independently and without alteration, the 9 Lords of the Night would not reach completion at the end of a tonalpohualli, a xihuitl, or even a 52-year cycle, as do the other calendrical cycles. The last day of the tonalpohualli, the 260th day, should be only the eighth Lord of the Night; thus allowing the cycle to run arithmetically introduces a randomness into the system that clashes with the orderliness of the rest of its other parts. But is there a solution?

The Zapotec calendar doubles the Lords of the Night on the first day of the tonalpohualli cycle,[39] counting two on that first day so that the 9-day cycle ends with the other two major cycles after 260 days. But while the Zapotec example offers a plausible explanation for how the Lords of the Night were treated in the Aztec case, it is neither a necessary solution nor one that finds any support in the historical accounts. There is no example of the doubling of the first day of the tonalpohualli in the Aztec case, though there is something similar in the *Tonalamatl Aubin*,[40] which probably comes from the Tlaxcallan confederacy.[41] In the last of the 20 trecenas of that tonalamatl, the final day has 2 Lords of the Night,[42] which suggests that the Aztecs might have double counted on the last day.[43] If they did, they subordinated the

9 Lords of the Night cycle to the 13- and 20-day cycles in the calendrical system.

Such a double count would seem to suggest that the Aztecs slightly altered their calendar. But would this argue against interpreting their behavior as cyclically structured, since they interfered with that cycle? Or would this argue for cyclically structured behavior, because they sought to force their calendar into a more cyclically dominated system than the strictly mathematical working out of the variables would allow? Whatever the resolution, it is apparent that the Aztecs considered the 9-day cycle to be essential, or the entire tonalamatl would not have been described. A simpler display showing the calendar system plus the 20 trecena gods would have sufficed, as a similar system did for the highly repetitive xihuitl months, in which only the 20 festivals are presented. The fact that the Aztecs explicitly depicted every permutation of the entire Tonalpohualli cycle, rather than a logical scheme from which the totality could be deduced, as they did with the xihuitl months, suggests that there is something about the one eccentric element—the 9 Lords of the Night cycle—that demands a full explication, and that we have an incomplete understanding of the working of the calendar, or at least of the 260-day calendar.

But a more significant—and official—alteration of the calendar was the shift of the New Fire ceremony, which is alluded to in a number of colonial sources but most explicitly discussed in the *Codex Telleriano-Remensis*.[44] The New Fire ceremony marked the end of the previous Calendar Round and the initiation of the succeeding one.[45] Thus, logically it had to occur on the evening and night of the last day of the nemontemi period of the last year of the 52-year cycle that was reaching completion, and it concluded on the night and early morning of the first day of the first year of the 52-year cycle that was beginning, which is confirmed by the early chroniclers.[46] But the Aztecs held their New Fire ceremony in the year 2 Acatl,[47] which was not, and could not be, the start of a logically functioning 52-year Calendar Round cycle.

In Aztec cosmology, the world had been created and destroyed four times before, and the current world was thought to be finite as well. So if the Aztecs believed that the world might end at the completion of a 52-year Calendar Round cycle, why—or, more importantly, *how*—would the New Fire ceremony have been moved from its logical position at the end of one Calendar Round/beginning of another, to a time a full solar year (1 xihuitl) into the succeeding Calendar Round and 105 days into the second tonalpohualli cycle?

Did the Aztecs, in fact, move the New Fire ceremony? Logically, they must have, since only a year that began with the number 1 (1 Tochtli, 1 Acatl, 1 Tecpatl, or 1 Calli) could begin a Calendar Round count. There is always the possibility, however, that our understanding of the Aztec calendar is seriously flawed—and it is certainly incomplete— such that a 2 Acatl initiation date for the Calendar Round is logical. But as I see no arithmetical resolution, the ultimate recourse must be to history.

Was there a different date for the New Fire ceremony before the Aztec era? The answer is a clear yes. At Xochicalco, a site in central Morelos occupied from A.D. 650 to 900,[48] a carved stone monument discovered at the base of the hill bearing a 1, a New Fire ceremony glyph, and the year date 1 Rabbit (1 Tochtli) is interpreted as commemorating the first New Fire ceremony.[49] Moreover, the Aztecs' predecessors, the Toltecs, also celebrated their New Fire ceremony in the year 1 Tochtli.[50] So in pre-Aztec times, the New Fire ceremony was celebrated on 1 Tochtli, as one would logically expect: between that time and the Spanish Conquest, there was a shift. The numerous date glyphs make it clear that they used some day symbols,[51] including year bearers, that were different from those later employed by the Aztecs,[52] so some change

2-1. Calendrical glyphs, left front, Pyramid of the Plumed Serpent, Xochicalco (A.D. 650 – 900) (Xochicalco, Morelos, Mexico) (Photo by Ross Hassig)

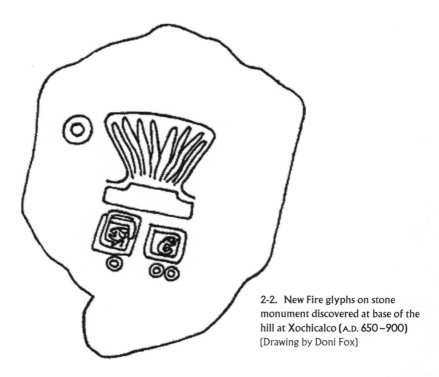

2-2. New Fire glyphs on stone monument discovered at base of the hill at Xochicalco (A.D. 650–900) (Drawing by Doni Fox)

occurred between that culture and the Aztecs, and the carvings on the front of the Pyramid of the Plumed Serpent at Xochicalco apparently commemorate a calendrical change.[53] But when did this calendrical shift happen, and why?

As with many calendrical matters, when the New Fire ceremony was shifted from 1 Tochtli to 2 Acatl is disputed. The dates that have been suggested are 1194–95, 1350–51, 1454–55, and 1506–07. The earliest is 1195,[54] or some similar date, when the first New Fire ceremony is considered to have been celebrated by the Aztecs. As reflected in most Aztec historical chronicles, this year was 2 Acatl and does have an accompanying New Fire glyph, which would mean that the change in New Fire date had already taken place and thus did not occur during Aztec times, but there is no direct statement of such a shift. The second date, 1351 (2 Acatl),[55] has been suggested because in the years during which the previous three New Fire ceremonies were presumably commemorated if it was still held in 1 Tochtli (1194, 1246, and 1298), the Aztecs had suffered military defeats. It is suggested that they decided to shift the ceremony to a more propitious year as a result, and moved it forward one year to 2 Acatl. These military defeats could well have provided a reason for the shift, but there is no direct evidence that it happened in that year. The third date, 1455 (2 Acatl), was changed from 1454 (1 Tochtli) because the latter was a famine year, which is historically documented.[56] But the fourth year, 1507 (2 Acatl), had seen the shift from 1506 (1 Tochtli), and it is a change at this time that has the strongest evidence in its support.[57] The *Codex Telleriano-Remensis* expressly states that King Moteuczoma Xocoyotl shifted the New Fire ceremony from 1506 (1 Tochtli), which was a famine year, to 1507 (2 Acatl).[58] But if the New Fire ceremony could be shifted so easily from one year to the next, what does this say about its role as a determinant of Aztec behavior? To answer this question, there must be some consideration of the purpose of the New Fire ceremony.

Perhaps, in accordance with traditional interpretations of the ceremony, the New Fire ceremony was in fact needed to inaugurate the beginning of the succeeding 52-year cycle, since time had come to an end with the previous series' completion. But how does this explain the first New Fire ceremony, as it would surely have been held when many people still living could remember the beginning of that 52-year period which had started without one? Perhaps the initial rationale was merely to commemorate the end/beginning of the Calendar Round, and the ceremony's role as essential to the perpetuation of time and the world was an accretion, sanctified by time, and fully embraced only by later groups.

In trying to understand the calendar generally, there are constant problems with contradictory sources.[59] Reconciling these is often difficult, if not impossible, forcing one to make a reasoned choice among the various firsthand accounts, as is frequently the way with historical research. But in the case of the New Fire ceremony, the earliest, most complete description is by Bernardino de Sahagún.[60] Many of the subsequent descriptions of the New Fire ceremony seem to derive from Sahagún, and I do not seek to compare his description with those of other early colonial sources,[61] as the conflicts are minimal. Yet Sahagún's account also has problems.

Three of Sahagún's major statements in the *Florentine Codex* that relate to the New Fire ceremony are problematic, not individually, but when taken together. First, the New Fire ceremony comes at the end of the last year of the Calendar Round.[62] Second, the year begins on February 1; this is contested and other dates are given, but they all fall

Año detrezecasas yd̄.
1505 vuo grande han
bre. Enla provincia d̄ me
xico. yvan por pan hazi
a la provincia d̄apango

Año d̄ vnco nejo yd̄. 1506
vuo tanto ffaton en la provin
cia d̄ mexico. que se comi an
 las senbradas. yansi sali
Andeno the. con lunbres a hat
Carlos senbrados. Es te año
A sae teomontecuma. Vn onbre
des tamanera dizen los viejos
que fue por a plicar a los di
oses por que Bian que avia
dozientos años. que sienprete
nian hanbre el año d̄ vnco
nejo
σ eneste año se solian a taz
los años segun su cuenta
ypor q̄ sienpre les hera año
trabajoso Lamando monteca
ma a dos canas

2-3 a,b. Historical events from the years 1504 through 1509. Note the famine in 1506 and
the New Fire glyph in 1507. Folios 41v–42r, *Codex Telleriano–Remensis* (BNP 385) (Courtesy of
the Bibliothéque nationale de France, Paris)

1507 1508 1509

mexpanilli

Año. de dos cañas. y de 1507 huo
neclipse de sol y tenblo la tierra
y se ahogaron pr 1800
onbres de guerra al el
rio de tuçac. que es adelante
de ytzuca camino de la mis teca
vendo que y van a sinjeptar
provincias Este Año se aca
bo la yglesia del fuego nuevo
por que siempre de cincuenta
en cincuenta y dos açendian
lunbre nueva Esta y glesia es
tava en el cerro visar thlqua
trolepes de mexico. cabecul hu
tlabac de aqui se lleva va lum
bre nueva para toda la tierra
por que dezian que el que tuvi
ere a quel dia lunbre Encasa
ueian de acaecer mil cosas

Año de quatro casas. y de 1509 vieron vna
claridad. de noche que duro mas de quarenta
dias Dizenlos que la vieron que fue desde la
nueva españa que Era muy gran de v muy
Res plan de ciente y que Estava a la parte
de oriente y que salia de la tierra y llegava al
cielo En este Año. se alço El pueblo de coço
la. que Es seis leguas de huaxaca. contra los
mexicanos los quales fueron sobre El y no de
xaron onbre A vida según dizen los viejos que
En ellos se hallaron esta fue vna de
las marabillas q ellos vieron an
tes q viniesen los xpianos y pe
savan q era que al coatle al
qual esperaban

consistently in the first quarter of the year (from late January through early March).[63] This means that the last day of the 5-day nemontemi period of the last year of the previous Calendar Round would be January 31, so that the start of the year would be on February 1, if we use that date. This is the case both as an historically recorded matter and as a logical one. The third fact that helps date the New Fire ceremony is that the sacrifice of the captive on whose chest the fire would be rekindled for the New Fire ceremony occurred when the Pleiades reached its zenith at midnight.[64]

These three facts, all recorded by Sahagún in the same source, pinpoint the date of the New Fire ceremony. The first two indicate that it was midnight before February 1 (February 12 Gregorian). While this date seems quite specific, in February or thereabouts, Sahagún's third statement relating to the zenith (within 5°, the range of variation for naked-eye astronomy) of the Pleiades at midnight at the Hill of Huixachtecatl would place the ceremony in 1507 on October 26 (November 6 Gregorian) as an equally certain mathematical fact.[65] Though both facts are firmly and simultaneously attested, both dates cannot be true.

Rafael Tena[66] accepts the astronomical argument as producing the more certain date and argues that the New Fire ceremony was not held at the end of the Calendar Round, but on November 6 (Gregorian) in the month of Quecholli. To reconcile this with the December 9 date for the New Fire ceremony in the *Crónica mexicana*,[67] however, he says it was then advanced 30 days to coincide with the feast of Panquetzaliztli, which was also the day of Huitzilopochtli's birth, during which festival the heads of the sacrificial victims were put on the skull rack.[68] Is this, then, when the New Fire ceremony was held?

Sahagún offered some support for this view in the *Primeros Memoriales*,[69] where he stated that the year began on 1 Tochtli but the New Fire ceremony was on 2 Acatl, which contradicts the aggregate of his *Florentine Codex* statements. Yet accepting this interpretation means directly contradicting the vast majority of sources that describe it as occurring at midnight on the last day of the ending Calendar Round, which was in February or March. These two equally specific and fixed times—the historical date and the astronomical occurrence—are absolutely irreconcilable. There must be a problem with the data as presented, and there are three major possible sources of this error.

First, perhaps the early Spanish priests—none of whom witnessed a New Fire ceremony—erred in stressing the Pleiades as the pivotal celestial marker simply because it was a common one elsewhere.[70] In early February, the star cluster Praesipe, which is similar to the Pleiades but somewhat fainter, reaches its zenith at midnight,[71] and the two clusters may have been confused in the accounts. This seems unlikely, however, since the Aztec priests watched the Pleiades regularly and sounded a trumpet when they reached their zenith.[72]

Second, when the Calendar Round ended (on February 1), the Pleiades would reach zenith at sunset, and perhaps that is the key marker rather than zenith at midnight. After all, without some means of keeping time other than by the sun—say, a mechanical clock—how could the Aztecs determine that it was, in fact, midnight? The Pleiades reaching its zenith at midnight cannot both be the definition of midnight and a means of establishing it. Indeed, it seems clear that what was called midnight was the Pleiades' zenith, whenever that occurred, and not the sun reaching a position 180° from zenith.

Third, Sahagún may simply have been in error. After all, he never witnessed what he described, and this aspect of his description contradicts others. It cannot all be true, but I will leave the issue for the moment. Nevertheless, there was one certain change in the New Fire ceremony—not a shift from February to November, but one from the year 1 Tochtli to the year 2 Acatl. The question is, why?

Any change can be made most easily if it is consistent with cultural traditions and disrupts the existing situation to the least extent possible. If any calendrical change is contemplated, the logical time would be at the end of the Calendar Round, when the lesser cycles also reached completion. But while the movement of the calendar at that point makes a lot of sense, why would the New Fire ceremony be shifted at all? Moreover, the New Fire ceremony shift was not merely temporal, but locational as well. Perhaps some answers can be found by examining the history of the New Fire ceremony.

Aztec chronicles record a total of eight New Fire ceremonies over the course of Aztec history, in 1143, 1195, 1247, 1299, 1351, 1403, 1455, and 1507.[73] Because the Aztecs founded their capital of Tenochtitlan in 1325 (2 Calli),[74] only the last four New Fire ceremonies could have been held there. When they founded their capital, they were a relatively unimportant group; they were tributaries of the Tepanec empire, which they and their allies overthrew in 1428.[75] But even by 1455, although the Aztecs had subdued or co-opted most of the Valley of Mexico, the Chalca city-states in the southeast corner of the valley remained independent and openly hostile until they were finally conquered in 1464.[76]

Thus, the hill of Huixachtecatl above Itztlapalapan, which is widely considered to be the site of the New Fire ceremony, was probably in Aztec control for the last two ceremonies, and incontestably so for only the last one.[77] No matter how important the ceremony may have been to the Aztecs, it seems highly unlikely that they could have conducted the New Fire ceremony in 1351 or 1403 at a site that was not under their control—and that in fact was the territory of a city-state (Colhuacan) which at the time had higher status and even provided the first Aztec king, Acamapichtli.[78] And, even though the cities of the central and western portions of the southern lakes had become Aztec allies and/or tributaries by the time of the 1454–55 New Fire ceremony, the Chalca city-states were in direct line of sight of Huixachtecatl, and were still independent and hostile, rendering the hill's use problematic for that year. Moreover, although Aztec hydraulic works were begun as early as the reign of King Itzcoatl,[79] the majority could not be completed until the full southern lakes were under Aztec control following

2-4. New Fire pyramid (Huixachtlan) atop Huixachtecatl (now the Hill of the Star), above Itztlapalapan (Ixtapalapa, Mexico, D.F.) (Photo by Ross Hassig)

the conquest of Chalco, so it is probable that there was no causeway stretching between Tenochtitlan and Itztlapalapan in 1454–55. Only by the 1507 New Fire ceremony had all the southern valley cities been subdued. So while it is possible that the New Fire ceremony might have been held on Huixachtecatl in 1455, the evidence is equivocal.[80] Moreover, Moteuczoma Xocoyotl ordered a temple built on top of Huixachtecatl for the 1507 New Fire ceremony[81] and, as the surviving ruins are quite modest, this appears to have been the first permanent temple and not the elaboration of an existing one. Thus, it is likely that 1507 was the first year the ceremony was celebrated on Huixachtecatl, and its locational shift likely corresponded with its temporal relocation from 1 Tochtli to 2 Acatl. The previous ceremony was held at the Templo Mayor in Tenochtitlan,[82] as suggested not only by the Aztecs' earlier geopolitical situation but also by the expansion of that structure dated in the New Fire year of 1454.[83]

The foregoing litany of questions and difficulties indicates considerably more uncertainty about time and the calendar than the conventional interpretation would suggest. Indeed, time seems to have been more flexibly used in the lives of individuals than an ideological interpretation would suggest, and was not uniform throughout Mexico. But if this is true, what does it say for our understanding of the Aztecs and about their own view of history?

Chapter 3

Reinterpreting Aztec Perspectives

It seems apparent that the standard view of Aztec time, history, and myth is not as satisfactory as it first seemed. The difficulty in interpreting the Aztec past lies not in contradictory or inconclusive data—that criticism can be marshaled against virtually any explanation given the grossly incomplete nature of the historical and archaeological record—but in the fundamental theoretical orientation from which the issue is approached. In the case presented thus far, much of the debate in this sort of ethnohistorical reconstruction centers on the adequacy of explaining objects and practices in terms of underlying beliefs. The idea that one can understand the actions of people from another culture in their own ideological terms arises from the undeniable fact that values infuse everything and, in that sense at least, we do not have an objective understanding of the world but a conceptually constructed one that is best explained from the vantage point of that culture.

Sahlins argues for an ideology-driven interpretation while Obeyesekere argues for a practical one; in either case, whether cultural perspectives pattern new interpretations is not a yes or no matter. Where cultural notions and practices do not match, ideological constructs do not appear to be dictating behavior. True, the bulk of the way the calendar functions is consistent with Aztec cultural notions. However, rather than taking these as *dictating* actions, perhaps a stronger case could be made for taking cultural notions as patterning or justifying actions as useful—as a template for action at best and as a rationalization for acts at worst. After all, there is no culturally monolithic ideology because, while ideology is handed down from generation to generation, beliefs are nevertheless constantly tested against the world we experience. So the question becomes, how strongly or how long do people adhere to their cultural precepts? At what point does the fit between such precepts and novel events become so poor that new or altered interpretations emerge? Rather than being either ideologically or practically driven, actions occupy a sliding scale ranging from strongly patterned to weakly patterned, or from ideology-as-action to ideology-as-idiom. If people behaved in the manner suggested by the extreme strong end of the continuum, there would be endless replication as beliefs are acted upon, whereas at the extreme weak end, cultural perspectives would have no significant influence on new situations because extant beliefs served as no more than the language in which they are discussed. Such extremes would embody conditions of no change at the strong end and so little continuity at the weak end that there would be no societal cohesion.

Most examinations of other cultures fall between these extremes, but any of them can quickly become interpretive stances rather than analytical approaches. This is especially true as one approaches the extremes: at the strong end the answers are already in hand in the established beliefs of the natives whereas, at the weak end, the answers lie exclusively in their relationship to the world.

Wolf[1] argues for the inherent integration of ideology with power and notes especially that the former cannot be understood without the latter. I agree that interpreting a culture in terms of its ideology alone is inadequate and would frame an approach in terms of how strongly an ideological approach is held. If the position is taken that cultural perspectives only weakly structure the nature and context of responses and that other factors weigh more heavily in which actions to take, the focus is placed on the society rather than on the calendar, and the outcome is an interpretation that stresses its social functions, not its internal workings, as is currently the case.

It might be suggested that this shift misses the point of a calendrical interpretation. But calendars are social creations and do not exist in and of themselves, so only this type of interpretation is likely to yield an assessment of their uses and roles in society. That is, at least in the case under consideration, if not in all instances, calendars are weak ideological constructs into which other social concerns intrude and alter their use. They are created neither sui generis nor for their own purposes, but for social ones, and a societal perspective is likely to lead to alternative assessments of the data and the calendar's uses. Moreover, a social perspective offers a means of critiquing the current view, which is unlikely to be altered by an internal perspective because the symbolic purposes of the calendar are, in this position, justifications of it. Furthermore, the internal focus invariably emphasizes the calendar's temporal functions to the almost total neglect of the social purposes to which they are intimately tied. This criticism does not seek to strip ideological interpretations of all value—they do, after all, point to real relations between actions and beliefs. They simply do not go far enough in terms of social usage, nor do they explain matters that fall outside the focus set by the ideology as understood. Having thus set the task does not mean that a perspective that takes formal ideological constructs as only weakly patterning behavior is therefore defined as superior to a strongly patterning perspective; rather, widening the possible interpretations offers the possibility of generating an alternative view that can be contrasted with the conventional one to see which might account for more of the available evidence and thus be more convincing.

As a theoretical statement, Wolf's approach is broadly satisfactory— ideology does not originate or stand on its own and thus cannot be used alone to interpret a culture. It is an inherent aspect of power. The difficulty with this position is that, while Wolf offers a compelling assessment of the relationship between ideology and power as theoretical constructs, his approach does not address the content of these categories. In other words, it is one thing to specify the relationship between ideology and power, and it is another thing altogether to say what these are: what constitutes power in Aztec society and what is the ideology to which it relates? Thus, the point of contention is not simply the epistemological one of whether people interpret the world from their own cultural perspectives, but the historiographical one of whether we are interpreting their culture adequately by adopting this approach.

If a given set of beliefs or, more accurately, a given set of perspectives on beliefs, is taken as true, the subsequent analysis becomes a matter of reconciling recorded data with those beliefs in an interpretation that necessarily cannot be in error. Assessing the relationship of beliefs to actions is thus not merely a matter of one's theoretical orientation, but is also a historiographical problem of what facts link to theory regardless of its nature. Instead of going from ideology to action, which selects what actions one will examine, can one instead begin with actions and then make them intelligible? Yes and no; identifying an action depends on some theoretical criteria of significance to select the facts, but it does not preordain their interpretation and force them into a conceptual framework. And, after all, it is consequences that frame the historical question.

How, though, is ideology accurately identified? One problem with interpreting encounters in terms of indigenous beliefs is that one must know these, yet all too often generic beliefs are taken as true for all people in that society. Even from those periods where it is readily apparent that accounts of the religious beliefs and practices of others should be accepted only with caution and critically assessed, recorded beliefs are taken at face value because the historiographical tradition has long done so and, perhaps more compellingly, because these views fit, or can be made to fit, with the general facts of contact history. In short, indigenous beliefs and ideology are often accepted uncritically as monoliths.

It is easy to assert what someone believes or even what that person is doing, but convincingly demonstrating the accuracy of that interpretation is hellishly difficult, especially in the case of early societies for which the historical record is weak, and particularly when cultural beliefs are being manipulated disingenuously. All symbols are polysemic, with no single meaning. Deriving an ideology from the historical record and archaeological remains, which are then tied to actions, is thus merely an assertion, a theoretical claim, not a stance based on known facts. And while it is tempting to argue that one can begin with actions rather than symbols because actions are at least known, what those actions mean is as arguable as the symbols, since actions meant to achieve one purpose are often cloaked in the rhetoric of another. For instance, during the sixteenth century, a debate raged among the Spaniards over whether the Indians should pay more or less tribute. This pitted secular priests (parish priests answerable to the bishop), who argued that the Indians could well afford to pay more, against regulars (members of monastic orders who fell outside the bishop's control), who argued that they could not. The ostensible argument was over the well-being of the Indians, but the issue actually in dispute was whether the seculars would be able to oust the regulars from the areas they had settled and Christianized.[2] Seculars required far larger supporting payments per capita than regulars, and the debate found the seculars arguing for a larger tribute because that would allow them to take over, whereas the regulars argued against it in an effort to prevent secular intrusion. Both debates—Indian tribute levels and priestly control— employ the same rhetoric and symbols, yet seek radically different ends. And what makes the task even more difficult is the disingenuousness of leaders who use symbols to generate public support for one goal while their actual purpose is different, but one that will also be accomplished if the publicly invoked action is carried out.

Thus historical interpretation from actions is, at best, only marginally more secure than that from symbols. Neither offers an unequivocal evidentiary base on which less certain analyses can be layered. But placing at least equal emphasis on actions does have the advantage of not only allowing symbols to be used to define what actions are relevant, but also of allowing actions that would be excluded under a symbolic focus to be incorporated and used to assess the adequacy of the ideological interpretation. In short, symbols and actions must both be used to assess the other in an ongoing interpretation. Standard descriptions of either ideological positions or actions cannot simply be accepted at face value, since that defines what is accepted as true and forces the other to be tailored to conform. Nor can either be assessed in isolation, as is often the case with ideology, which is frequently studied in and of itself, as though it were a monadic reality. As Wolf[3] argues, ideology is not just ideas, but the mental constructs that are publicly manifested and employed to underwrite power.

History and Interpretation

History is not merely the chronicling of events, but rather of meaningful events; thus how people see the world will affect what they perceive as significant, how they act and react, and therefore what they record. The complete and accurate reconstruction of a past culture is thus simply impossible, as data limitations alone should make clear. What one confronts in seeking to address eighteenth-century Hawaiian or sixteenth-century Aztec cultures is not the issue of what that culture *is*, but how we *know* it. In short, the interpretation of past cultures depends less on their nature, which can only be incompletely known, than on the historiographical process itself, with its own focus, potential, and limitations. Moreover, there is a difference between knowing a culture ethnographically and knowing one historically. Just as particle physics has the Heisenberg uncertainty principle, which states that a particle's mass and its velocity can each be determined but each to the exclusion of the other, and thus not at the same time—hence the uncertainty—so too does ethnohistory have an uncertainty principle.

Although many things come to light in historical records, the analyst is nevertheless dependent upon the vagaries of record keeping, document survival, and the good fortune of discovery to reveal them. In contrast, the ethnographer can actively inquire, although some things, such as wealth or ethnic background, may be more difficult to discover during someone's lifetime than posthumously. However, the importance of an event or circumstance depends not on the thing itself but on its consequences, so a significant occurrence can only be recognized historically. For instance, an ethnographer may focus on a murder in his/her village as the most significant event of the day, week, month, or year because he/she believes it is important, not of itself, but in terms of its longer range consequences, based on the impact such events have had elsewhere. But in that same village, an Abraham Lincoln, a Gandhi, or a Hitler might be born and the ethnographer will have missed this more significant event because it cannot be immediately recognized as important. Thus, while ethnography offers the best data, history offers the best questions, and the two can never be completely brought together.

Beyond the problems of data, however, lie those of causation. In historical analysis, a fact is not a physical condition or event, but a meaningful incident selected out of the innumerable events of the day because it is significant to the people involved. Because it is meaningful to other historical actors, they take it into consideration and it influences their subsequent actions. But since norms and actions all too often differ, the focus must be primarily on actions, rather than just on verbal claims or written statements; ideological claims are often made to justify actions taken for very different reasons.

The focus is not on actions per se, but on cause. Cause, however, is not an observable fact but a historical relationship, a link between two events that is seen as sequential and in which the prior is indispensable to the occurrence of the latter. But this link is an analytical assessment rather than an objective reality. A historical cause is the considered assessment of cause and consequences. A historically significant event is virtually never apparent from a given action, but rather from that action's consequences, many of which are known only far in the future. And it is this historical notion of causation, which is akin to motivation, rather than the mechanical interaction of events, that precipitates many of the problems.

Explanation seeks to account for effects, and causes are invoked only in relation to effects, to explain them. Causes are not always transparently significant when they occur and need only be explained in relation to their effects. But because causes are not always immediately perceived as important, they are less likely to be recorded when they occur (and if they are, it is typically in a sketchier version) than are effects, and the greater the separation between these in time, the less that will generally have been recorded and be known of the cause.

As odd as it may seem at first glance, it is not always easy to distinguish a cause from an effect. Every cause is, presumably, also an effect, yet we label them causes because of their relationship to the effect of interest. Effects are the events on which the historical analysis focuses and are thus defined *as* effects, and once this has taken place, the search is then on for their causes. In essence, then, they are effects because we seek their causes, which we do because we see them as having had a subsequent impact. Thus first and foremost, pivotal events are such because we consensually agree that they are. And we do so because we share basic epistemological notions about history and causation, and the perception of pivotal events is our common cultural currency.

Effects are what is important in history, yet our analyses focus on cause because we believe we already know the crucial historical link between the cause and its effects. But while we know the effect, or it would not have been the important focus of the inquiry, the same is not true of the cause. The cause is discovered only by reasoning back from the effect.

In feeling our way blindly through the historical record, the most impressive bumps—in records as well as in impact on the people— are the effects, and we then must tentatively feel our way back to the fainter, more poorly recorded, causes. We look for effects, which establish the major points in time, and then reason back to their causes. The route of research is thus from effect backward, though this is obscured by the normal manner of presentation, which is from the cause forward, because history, common understanding, and causal reasoning emphasize a progressive chronological presentation. History can thus be roughly divided into annals or chronicles, which are the records of effects, and formal history, which is the conceptual effort to link them to causes.

Seeing the subjects of the research as different, as "the Other" in that now threadbare term, results from presuming "different cultures therefore different logics." And whatever the epistemological status of that metaphysical claim, the methodological truth is that they must necessarily be understood in our terms as well. Just as unifying a calendar is an attempt to bring other groups and societies into a single time in which all acts and events can be related, so history is, or should be, an effort to embrace other groups and societies in a single intelligible past, albeit one of many different perspectives. That which is inexplicable in human society, past or present, is either thus far inadequately understood, too-hastily abandoned, leaving a heavy burden of proof on the shoulders of those who would flee the issue, or simply unknowable and incapable of being glossed over by projected meanings.

The causal links that are important in historical analysis, however, are ours, what we see as significant, and not necessarily those of the natives, at least not primarily. To take two examples from Western history, in the fourteenth century, the Black Death (bubonic plague) struck Europe and the general perception of its immediate cause was corruption of the air, but it was seen as the work of God as a final cause,[4] and explanations were tailored accordingly. But the modern understanding of the Black Death emphasizes the *Pasteurella pestis* bacteria spread by flea-bearing rats.[5] In seeking an explanation of the fourteenth-century Black Death epidemic today, knowing the natives' perception of its cause is essential to understanding their responses, but it is wholly inadequate to understand the causes and consequences of the plague itself. To render that pandemic explicable entails grasping the natives' view insofar as possible, but making it intelligible in terms of our own more comprehensive understanding of plagues. Thus, we note fourteenth-century records of visiting shrines, or of pledging to undertake pilgrimages or to donate property to the Church, but these play a secondary role to the more crucial incidental reports of poor sanitation, overcrowding, or other conditions we now know would facilitate the spread of the plague. As another example, the fifteenth-century *Malleus Maleficarum*, which enjoyed papal support, asserts that witches do exist and perform supernatural feats with the aid of the devil, and that they may be tortured to exact a confession, without which they cannot be condemned to death.[6] While these beliefs were firmly held and acted upon, no modern analysis of the various witchcraft trials of the past would be content to explain them in these terms, rather than importing social, psychological, political, or economic motivations. In short, it is the analyst's notion of cause that structures historical reconstructions, not just the natives'. The latter is assuredly part of the content, but the structure is the analyst's, so history is the interplay of our notions of events and those of the natives, never the natives' alone.

Dealing with other cultures thus requires coming to grips with alien perspectives, customs, and values, and this most often entails working through the records of a different culture—different in time if not in identity—to understand a third alien culture. The difficulty is therefore not merely understanding a different culture, but one from your own perspective, while reading through an intermediary recording culture (in the Hawaiian example, eighteenth-century British; in the Aztec example, sixteenth-century Spanish).

Such a reading is made doubly difficult because of the skewing of content by cultural interest. The people of each culture record what they see as important—or what those who make such decisions deem important, which adds a double screening to historical accounts. For example, given the radically divergent cultural traditions of Spaniards and Aztecs, a pivotal event in the causal chain as seen within one cultural framework will not necessarily be the essential cause from the other cultural perspective, even of such a seemingly fixed event as Cortés's landing on the Veracruz coast. And this will have a major impact on historical accounts, since each culture will record (or ignore) events according to their significance from their own perspective. The probable result will be two very different records, each of which is likely to skew the historical interpretation, though in different ways.

Even if the problems of significance and double cultural analysis can be overcome, can a strong interpretation of Aztec time, history, and the calendar be critiqued? The presentation of the orthodox view seems sound, but any argument has a theoretical structure that dictates the inclusion or exclusion of data, so critiquing a stance generally requires opening the context wider. Only by marshaling evidence more broadly is there any possibility of revealing data that conflict with orthodoxy, stimulating extramural questions, and prompting new interpretations.

Continuing this line of thought, if we see cultural notions as dictating actions, and yet we reconstruct that culture in terms of our own understanding of what is significant based on how we feel the key factors work (e.g., disease is biological, not moral), what does this do to their beliefs? If we take ideology as strongly causal and yet select events or actions as significant that differ from those the people of that culture would emphasize, then clearly their beliefs, even though held, did not directly cause what was significant in the explanation. The actions we chose were related to their beliefs, but these may not have been the most significant ones in their view. Our reconstruction of their history is thus also a revaluation of their beliefs that uses these but reconstructs a logical, consistent, yet necessarily skewed, interpretation of them. Even a strong approach to the past, therefore, does not really begin with the subject people's beliefs and then use them to explain what happened, but begins with *our* understanding of history, actions, and cultures, picks what is important, and then selects from among their beliefs and reorders their importance or reinterprets their significance to render intelligible the events we have chosen. Actions and beliefs are always related, but we already have basic background beliefs we cannot fully shed and, in any case, the goal of history is not to do so. Does this mean that history is a chimera? No. The goal is to render the past (whether of ourselves or others) intelligible in our terms. But does that merely produce a modern myth? I think not. We are just assessing significance and the beliefs associated with those actions or events, in relation to what we know to be causally patterning. We may consider other "explanations," such as the morality of the Black Death, but relegate these to the sidelines because, while such beliefs patterned behavior, they were ineffectual in altering the course of history. This amounts to a sort of evolutionary weeding out that would eventually have occurred in that society as causal relations became more clearly understood.

Beliefs must be critiqued and assessed in relation to something else, and, given the context here, I suggest it be against actions. This preserves the ideology-action nexus, but does not begin with beliefs and then force all actions into conformity. Rather, it opens a world of motivational possibilities to explain actions rather than assuming that the analyst knows the culture to which he/she ties the people's behavior. In fact, both culture *and* actions demand simultaneous interpretation, and assuming knowledge of the former offers only an illusorily secure anchor for the latter.

All culture is learned, by observation, practice, and trial and error, and selectively adopting the patterns and practices that are meaningful. As a result, we learn culture differentially, and nobody perfectly embodies that of their society. Complex societies increasingly rely on finer and finer social coordination—taxes must be paid, armies marshaled, and courts held, and all require synchronizing participants on particular days—which the increasingly specific use of time allows. And while religious groups may have elaborated on traditional notions and units of time to create the complex system and use it for their own internal purposes, it is politics that harnessed time and drove it to power.

Where does this leave the epistemological status of the historical analysis? There are two bases of at least partial stability for the interpretation. First, interpreting ideology and actions in relation to each other offers some corrective to speculative excess, as Wolf argues. And second, the most certain background for historical analysis is previous historical analysis, earlier theories and interpretations.

Aztecs and Noncyclical Time

Did the Aztecs actually believe that time was sacred and immutable to them and that its cyclicity strictly structured their lives and history? To question this notion of sacred cyclicity further, perhaps we should examine how it worked in their view of history.

The Aztec calendar was composed of an endless series of repetitive 52-year periods,[7] years of the same name but in different cycles that can easily be conflated and seen as influencing each other. Examples are not usually offered when the assertion is made that Aztec history was based on a cyclical notion of time that patterned the people's lives, though there are two classic examples of this—the return of Quetzalcoatl in the year 1 Acatl in the guise of Hernán Cortés and the famine of 1454 (1 Tochtli), which recurred in 1506 (1 Tochtli).

One of the common explanations for Cortés's success in conquering Mexico with so few Spaniards is based on the idea that the Aztecs thought he was the returning god, Quetzalcoatl, and therefore they did not resist effectively.[8] The logic of the argument is that Cortés reached Mexico in 1519, which was the year 1 Acatl in the Aztec calendar.[9] That year is associated with Quetzalcoatl, though largely through a conflation of the god with a historical Toltec ruler and priest of his cult, Ce Acatl Topiltzin Quetzalcoatl (1 Reed, Our Lord Quetzalcoatl),[10] who left Tollan in the tenth century.[11] The legends vary, but his departure is generally associated with his disgrace or his having lost a religious struggle to abolish human sacrifice. Whatever the cause, he left Tollan and, in most accounts, went to the Gulf coast, where he either immolated himself and became the planet (and god) Venus, or he sailed east on a raft, vowing to return.[12] Since his birth year was the same named year (in the 52-year cycle) as Cortés's arrival (1 Acatl), the Aztecs thought the latter was Quetzalcoatl and effectively surrendered to him.

Despite the neat fit between rapid conquest and indigenous beliefs, which supports a strong interpretative approach, those more inclined to a weak approach plausibly argue that this "explanation" does not fit with the actual events of the Conquest, such as the Aztecs' vigorous military resistance, and note that the thesis arose decades after the fact, most likely as an ex post facto indigenous rationalization of defeat rather than being an actual cause.[13] This is not to say that the Aztecs ignored the supernatural in explaining the Conquest—one would expect them to draw on their own background to interpret unprecedented events in a meaningful way, especially in light of all the seemingly godlike capabilities the Spaniards possessed—but there is little evidence that they continued this notion or acted on it.[14] But more to the point for a cyclical interpretation of history, even though Cortés reached Mexico in 1519 (1 Acatl), he was not the first Spaniard to do so. In 1517, which was the year 12 Tecpatl, Francisco Hernández de Córdoba landed in Mexico and sailed along the Yucatan coast to Chanpoton, but did not reach the Aztec area. Juan de Grijalva also landed in Yucatan, and then sailed north along the Veracruz coast in 1518, which was the year 13 Calli, where he met with Aztec nobles who then reported these events to King Moteuczoma Xocoyotl.[15] The arrival of the Spaniards thus did not occur in the auspicious year of 1 Acatl, and Cortés's "return" the next year was not matched to the date of Quetzalcoatl's departure from Mexico, upon which his return was premised, but merely to his birth year. As a result, Cortés's arrival, which led to the Cortés-as-Quetzalcoatl interpretation, did not match an earlier event that it was supposedly recapitulating; moreover, the Aztecs reacted to it in strictly human terms, by dispatching observers to the coast.[16]

The second and more compelling case of cyclical history, the reoccurrence of the famine of 1454, has a more direct relationship between events 52 years apart, since the earlier famine was not a quasi-mythical event set in a distant past, but the repetition of an earlier famine during the same named year in the following Calendar Round. In 1454 (1 Tochtli), the Valley of Mexico underwent the worst pre-Columbian famine on record, an event so devastating to the Aztecs that, when the next 1 Tochtli (1506) approached a full Calendar Round later, the people were anxious lest they should suffer another such famine.[17] And, indeed, a famine was recorded for 1506, albeit a significantly less devastating one. But is this evidence of a cyclical notion of history? If history is patterned by its temporal cyclicity, why was 1454 (1 Tochtli), which was a famine year,[18] not patterned by events of 1402 (1 Tochtli), which was not?[19] The famine of 1454 was itself novel, a new event that altered the nature of that year from what it had been in the previous 52-year cycle. It might be argued, as has Rafael Tena,[20] that previous 1 Tochtli years (at least the 1 Tochtli years of 1246 and 1298) witnessed military defeats, so that named year was simply generically ill-fated, and famine was merely another evil of that type. Yet why would 1506 be anticipated as a famine year specifically, rather than some other evil, such as a military disaster? Even if that can be explained away, the natures of 1454 and 1506 were significantly different.

The Valley of Mexico might suffer insect or rodent infestations or early and late frosts in any year.[21] But private and state stores and the importation of food from elsewhere make single-year calamities inconvenient but far less than disastrous. The famine of 1454, though the worst on record for the Aztecs, was not the result of a single year's catastrophe, but of an unusual series of locust plagues, floods, frosts, and droughts over several years.[22] Although the year 1506 had experienced major crop losses that might lead to another famine of the magnitude of the famine of 1454, the situation was quite different. The Aztecs had greatly increased the agricultural productivity of the Valley of Mexico by expanding the system of artificial islands (chinampas) for agricultural purposes,[23] which yielded an estimated 40 million kilograms of maize[24] per year over that available to Tenochtitlan in 1454, their storage facilities were not depleted, and they had vastly increased their empire, so many of their tributaries could be called upon to funnel needed supplies into the capital.[25]

So was there a famine in 1506? No—at least not anything close to the magnitude of the one in 1454. Pictorial sources show a rodent infestation that adversely affected the harvest in the autumn,[26] and textual sources also mention drought,[27] but that would have been unlikely to affect the chinampa crops during the rest of the year, and of course the existing stores would have been largely unaffected. So why was 1506 recorded as a famine year? Insofar as it was considered a bad year, the cause, I argue, lies elsewhere than in a single crop failure.

What may well have made 1506 an anxious year for the Aztecs was the lack of a New Fire ceremony. The ceremony that should have been held on the last night of the ending 52-year cycle in 13 Calli (1505) and thus inaugurated the year 1 Tochtli (1506) was deferred, and to the extent that the people believed that the world would end at the completion of one of the Calendar Rounds and that the New Fire ceremony was essential to the perpetuation of the world, not celebrating it would undoubtedly generate considerable anxiety. But because the historical chronicles were official accounts, it was easier (and more politic) to credit the year's bad character to a repetition of the previous cycle's famine than blame it on the shift of the New Fire ceremony and, especially, on the elite, which had initiated it.

Part of the difficulty in trying to assess whether the Aztecs had a predominantly cyclical or a linear notion of time lies in our persistence in looking at time as an abstraction rather than in stepping back from that approach to time and dealing with it as it was lived. Most analyses of time in Aztec society, especially those that emphasize cyclical perspectives, take a God's-eye view rather than an ego perspective. Time can be analyzed in an abstract fashion to yield a view that is not often experienced by people in the lived world and, given the multiplicity of people and offices, various notions of time may have been held by a variety of people or officeholders at different times for diverse purposes.

Virtually everyone in complex societies has both linear and cyclical notions of time, and this was doubtless true of the Aztecs. Everyone could see the cyclical aspects of their lives as one season gave way to the next, as crops were planted, ripened, and were harvested, as the annual cycle of labor for the state took its toll, and as religious festivals came and went in a predictable pattern. But at the same time, many aspects of Aztec daily life were assuredly linear. While households may experience a cycle, this is more an analytical perspective that can be taken when looking at a demographic household. For the individual, one is born, grows through childhood, reaches adulthood, marries, raises a family, grows old, and dies. And this was, of course, recognized by the Aztecs, both as to the various stages of life,[28] and most definitively as to retirement (i.e., at 52, the age at which one no longer had military or tribute obligations to the state).[29] Thus, for the individual, while their yearly existence had cyclical aspects, there was also a straightforward linear progression through life, and both were explicitly recognized.

The recognition that the same person or group operates on both cyclical and linear time does not preclude emphasizing a cyclical view, of course, and this is best exemplified by religious practitioners. The essence of religious ritual, particularly in Aztec society, was the endless cycle of sacred rites, a constant repetition of what Mircea Eliade calls "Cosmic time,"[30] which repeats the original sacred event in its ritual reenactment. Thus, for religious purposes, time is inherently cyclical, each commemoration being reenacted on the anniversary of its original (or mythical) occurrence, according to whatever calendrical cycle is employed (that is, it need not be tied to a solar cycle, as is the case in the West). A place can become sacred through actions or rituals and remain so over long time spans, which accounts for the rebuilding and expansion of the Great Temple just as surely as it does for cathedrals in Europe. But a time can only be sacralized through ritual repetition, with each reenactment symbolically recreating the original event. To the religious, then, cyclicity takes on a dominating importance that is only partially shared by others in that society whose lives are also structured by more linear concerns.

It is this emphasis on cyclicity and the sacredness of dates and time that make ritual practitioners the perfect keepers of the calendars, especially after religions have become bureaucratized and dogmatized. Since the calendar is typically maintained by clerics, religious ideology often becomes the common currency for all events because it is inherently tied to the temporal cycle, which makes a strong ideological perspective on events easy—indeed almost too easy—as the interpretation of choice. Moreover, Aztec religious and political ideology were interlocking and mutually supporting—the supernatural justified (or served as a rationalization for) political actions and state expansion directly funded priests and temples.[31] Once developed, this inherently ritual temporal structure can be shifted to more mundane uses, so just because ritual is employed to structure time and just because religious practitioners are the originators and elaborators of the calendars in many societies does not mean that these calendars do not have secular purposes as well. Such is clearly the case in Western society.

Religious ritual can be tied directly to temporal repetition, but political authorities are likely to emphasize linear time over cyclical because political events are more random and temporally chaotic: this military campaign succeeds but that one fails, this year sees a famine but the past decade did not, this king enjoys a very long reign and that one dies prematurely. Political life is fraught with the unpredictable, and while it can piggyback some of its significant events onto ritual time, political occurrences cannot be strictly tied to the ritual cycle. Many things may give political life a cyclical pattern, such as the Aztec campaign season, which was dictated by weather and the agricultural cycle, but regular or regularized events need be overseen only by bureaucrats or managers: political leaders are needed precisely because life is punctuated by major events at unpredictable times that then demand decisions and actions, and for this a linear perspective dominates.

This linear perspective can be clearly seen in Aztec architecture. Ritually timed constructions occurred in the ancient Near East[32] but, despite claims that the Aztecs built structures to coincide with such ritual temporal cycles as the 52-year Calendar Round,[33] notably in the case of the dual pyramid at Tenayuca,[34] this is demonstrably untrue of the Great Temple.[35] Building phases did not coincide with ritual cycles, but with kingly reigns, and calendars are commonly based on the latter worldwide.[36] Thus, while the kings may have used religious explanations and justifications for actions and events, they nevertheless built structures—even temples—that were primarily keyed to political events, not religious ones. Such temporally eccentric building campaigns reflect the linear notions of time that dominated Aztec political events and actors.

Aztecs and Ideology

The Aztecs did not merely inherit their official cosmology; they altered it as well.[37] All of their changes may never be known, given the dearth of information. After all, the Spanish chroniclers arrived among the ruins of Aztec society and, in seeking to record native beliefs, left descriptions of what they encountered at that time, but they were not always aware that there had been earlier changes. Thus, changes must be teased from information not always intended to reveal it. And if Aztec accounts alone are used, little would be discovered. But by comparing Aztec accounts with those from elsewhere in Mexico, and by interpreting recovered Aztec monuments in light of these discernible differences, some changes can be gleaned and the time of their occurrence estimated.

The major changes in Aztec cosmology, which are not generally found outside the Valley of Mexico, are a shift from a 4-Sun to a 5-Sun world, and a change from a 9-level Topan (heaven)[38] to a 13-level one.[39] These alterations seem to have occurred relatively recently, as they had not yet been thoroughly or consistently integrated into fundamental Mesoamerican cosmological conventions elsewhere. For instance, the two major sources recording the duration of the previous four worlds both list these as 2,028 years.[40] Breaking this down into the durations of the four respective worlds, the *Leyenda de los soles*[41] lists them as lasting 676, 364, 312, and 676 years, in contrast to the 676-, 676-, 364-, and 312-year durations recorded in the *Historia de los Mexicanos por sus pinturas*.[42] Although the two sources agree on the total duration and on the lengths of the four time periods, they differ on the order in which they occurred, which suggests that thought on the time periods had not yet become thoroughly orthodox. In both cases, however, the years are evenly divisible by 52-year periods, yielding Sun durations of 13, 7, 6, and 13, or of 13, 13, 7, and 6 Calendar Rounds, respectively—same lengths but in different sequences.

The 13 Calendar Round periods are logical and expectable, given Aztec ritual numerology, but not the 6 or the 7 Calendar Round periods. However, the 6 and 7 Calendar Rounds add up to 13, strongly suggesting that, in the 4-Sun version of the creation of the world, the previous three worlds had each lasted for a total of 676 years, or 13 Calendar Rounds. So when the Aztecs added a fifth sun, rather than insert an additional Sun of 676 years duration and create a 2,704-year earlier Suns' history to compete with the orthodox 2,028 one, they merely divided one of the previous Sun's durations roughly in half and left the total duration intact. That created 364 and 312 years, respectively, because the division was not made by dividing the number of years in half (2 Suns of 6½ Calendar Rounds, or 338 years each), but rather by dividing the total number of 52-year Calendar Rounds but treating each Calendar Round as an indivisible whole. As there were 13, the rough bisection of this duration left two unequal periods, though these were the closest equal full Calendar Round equivalents, which are 6 and 7. This change meant that the 4-Sun version of Mesoamerican cosmology and the 5-Sun Aztec version both left the previous worlds with a total of 2,028 years, albeit allocated in different ways, and further suggests that each of the previous worlds was originally considered to have had 13 Calendar Rounds and thus, so too, presumably, should the current world for a ritually and numerologically satisfying total of 52 Calendar Rounds in all. But because the completion of such a duration may well have heralded the end of that world, based on the Aztec numerological pattern of overlapping and communally completing cycles, this provided a likely reason why the Aztecs merely divided an existing duration rather than inserting an additional one of 13 Calendar Rounds.

Such political manipulations of time and religious predictions are not unprecedented. In ancient Iran, Emperor Ardashir was faced with the end of his dynasty in less than two centuries, based on Zarathushtran's prophecy that the empire and his religion would be destroyed in 1,000 years. So he merely asserted that his own ascension was some 250 years earlier than it had actually been in order to permit greater dynastic longevity within the prophecy.[43]

If the Aztecs were to add a fifth Sun by inserting a fourth Sun into the past, also giving it a duration of 13 Calendar Rounds would have had ritually dire implications for the Aztec world, since an entire cycle of 52 Calendar Rounds would have been completed. And while it is demonstrably true that the world was continuing, any such notion would likely entail a severing of the present world from that of the past, undermining the Aztecs' legitimacy as inheritors of the Mesoamerican tradition. Thus, in this suggested reconstruction, the Aztecs avoided that problem and kept the duration of the previous worlds at the same total length by dividing one Sun's original duration into 6 and 7 Calendar Rounds, and allocating them between two of the previous Suns. This upset no cosmological traditions regarding the previous total duration of the worlds, or the lesser cycles of 13, 20, and 260, all of which continue in the same number and in full completions for any of the newly established Suns' durations, while allowing the existing Sun to continue for its allotted time. Thus, the Aztec cosmological change was inserted without disturbing either the world in which they lived or the aggregate durations of the previous worlds, and it could be absorbed with minimum disruption of either the Aztec worldview or that of others still retaining the older 4-Sun version. Yet by proposing Suns that endured for less than a full 13 Calendar Rounds each, the Aztecs also introduced still more uncertainty into their cosmological world. Now, there was no guarantee that the current Sun would continue for a full 13 Calendar Rounds since, now, two previous ones had not, making each impending New Fire ceremony an even more anxious and important time, and boosting the role of the priesthood.

In a similar cosmological shift, while most of central Mexico believed in a 9-level Topan (heaven), the Aztecs added four more to produce one of 13 levels.[44] The 4 additional levels were apparently inserted between the old levels 8 and 9, keeping the first 8 levels undisturbed and converting the old 9 into the new level 13.[45] But the newly inserted levels are only sketchily described in the *Codex Vaticanus*, the only extant pictorial representation of the Aztec Topan/Mictlan. Why did they shift from 9 to 13? That is unclear, though 13 is the next ritually significant calendrical number above 9, and moving to 13 would allow the levels of Topan to be evenly paired with the 13 Lords of the Day. Moreover, it would further emphasize the 13-day cycle, which reaches even completion each tonalpohualli and each Calendar Round, in contrast to the 9-day cycle, which does neither.

In both cases—the shift from 4 Suns to 5 and the change from 9 levels of Topan to 13—the alterations are noticeable, not merely because

Table 3-1. Topan / Mictlan and associated gods.
(Codex Vaticanus 1979: fols. 1v–2r; Garibay [1973:103; Histoyre du Mechique 1905:22–23].)

13	Omeyocan	Ometeuctli
	(It is In the Place of Omeyotl [i.e., Duality])	
12	Teotl Tlatlauhcan	Tlahuizcalpan-Teuctli
	(It is In the Place of Teotl-tlatlauhqui [i.e., the Red God])	
11	Teotl Cozauhcan	Yohualteuctli
	(It is In the Place of Teotl-cozauhqui [i.e., the Yellow God])	
10	Teotl Iztacan	Tezcatlipoca
	(It is In the Place of Teotl-iztac [i.e., the White God])	
9	Itztapal Nanatzcayan	Quetzalcoatl
	(It is In the Place where Things Make a Grating Sound like Flagstones [i.e., grinding against one another])	
8	Ilhuicatl Xoxouhcan	Tlalocan-Teuctli
	(It is In the Heaven of Ilhuicatl-xoxouhqui [i.e., the Green Heaven])	
7	Ilhuicatl Yayauhcan	Tonacateuctl and Tonacacihuatl
	(It is In the Heaven of Ilhuicatl-yayauhqui [i.e., the Swarthy Heaven])	
6	Ilhuicatl Mamalhuayocan	Mictlan-Teuctli
	(It is In the Heaven of Mamalhuaztli [i.e., Castor and Pollux])	
5	Ilhuicatl Huixtotlan	Tonaloque
	(It is In the Heaven Beside the Brine)	
4	Ilhuicatl Tonatiuh	Tonatiuh
	(It is In the Heaven where Tonatiuh [the Sun] lives)	
3	Ilhuicatl Citlalicue	Chalchihuitl-Icue
	(It is In the Heaven where Citlalicue [Her-skirt Is Stars] lives)	

Table 3–1. (*Continued*)

2	Ilhuicatl Tlalocan Ipan Metztli Xiuhtli
	(It is In the Heaven which is the place of Tlaloc, which is Above the moon)
1	Tlalticpac Xiuhteuctli
	(It is On Top of the Land)
2	Apanohuayan
	(It is At the Place where Everyone Passes Beyond Water)
3	Tepetl Imonamiquiyan
	(It is In the Place of the Mountains' Defile)
4	Itztepetl
	(It is the Obsidian Mountain)
5	Itzehecayan
	(It is In the Place where the Wind Blows with Obsidian Fragments)
6	Pancuecuetlayan
	(It is In the Place where things Vigorously Wave like Banners)
7	Temiminaloyan
	(It is In the Place where People are Repeatedly Shot with Arrows)
8	Teyollocualoyan
	(It is In the Place where People Are Eaten at the Heart)
9	Iz Mictlan Opochcalocan
	(Here it is In the Place Beside Dead People which is In the Place where there are no Smokeholes)

variant traditions persisted beyond the Valley of Mexico, but because of the conceptual incompleteness of the fit, a difficulty that would perhaps have been smoothed over in time. Precisely when these changes were made is uncertain. Durán[46] records Nezahualpilli admonishing Moteuczoma Xocoyotl on his election as king to contemplate the 9 heavens, which suggests either that the shift had not yet taken place in 1502 or that it had occurred but was still contested. I know of no data that would resolve the matter definitively, but I assume the Topan change was roughly contemporaneous with the 5-Sun shift, which seems to have occurred early in the reign of King Moteuczoma Xocoyotl, or at least it was most publicly expressed then on the Calendar Stone.

3-1. Aztec Calendar Stone, depicting Aztecs' cosmological view of the universe (Drawing by Doni Fox)

The best known Aztec monumental sculpture, the Calendar Stone,[47] was probably a sacrificial stone that was placed flat in front of the Great Temple and that depicts the official state cosmological view. In the center is the face of either Tonatiuh, the sun god, or, more likely, Tlalteuctli, the earth monster (the matter is debated[48]), framed by the glyph 4 Olin. Within this glyph are the calendrical glyphs for the four previous Suns—4 Ocelotl, 4 Ehecatl, 4 Quiahuitl, and 4 Atl. Outside the olin glyph are four others—1 Quiahuitl, 7 Ozomatli, 1 Tecpatl, and a headdress. Around all of this is a ring containing the 20 day symbols, then another ring depicting chalchihuitl (jade), a stream of blood, chalchihuitl pendants, and sun rays. At the bottom are the facing heads of Xiuhteuctli, god of fire and time, on the left and Tonatiuh, the sun, on the right, emerging from the mouths of serpents, whose bodies form the outermost ring of the monument. At the top, between the two tails, is the glyph 13 Acatl in a cartouche. These various glyphs have been interpreted mythically, such that 13 Acatl refers to the birth of the Sun and the four glyphs flanking the olin are directions. But 13 Acatl probably refers to 1427, the beginning of the reign of King Itzcoatl, who founded the Aztec empire, the headdress is the name glyph of Moteuczoma Xocoyotl, and 1 Tecpatl may refer to the date of the Aztecs' departure from Aztlan, but it more likely refers to 1428, when the Aztecs began their empire, though 1 Tecpatl is also the birth date of Huitzilopochtli. The day glyphs probably refer to ceremonies.

Although the Calendar Stone does not bear the date of its creation, the name glyph places it during the reign of Moteuczoma Xocoyotl (1502–1520). Moreover, another monument that bears a scaled-down version of the Calendar Stone solar disc and 4 Olin glyph does have a date, the Teocalli de la Guerra Sagrada, indicating that this cosmological shift had taken place in or by 1507.[49] These changes were most likely designed to create ideological perspectives that supported the polity and legitimated the new political hierarchy.[50]

There may well be further implications from these changes, including the possibility that the Aztecs previously had only 9 hours of day, as there may only have been 9 Lords of the Day. After all, the Codex Tudela[51] depicts a partial tonalamatl with the 9 Lords of the Night and the 13 voladores, but no Lords of the Day.[52] Such possible shifts are not of direct concern here, however. What is clear is that the Aztecs consciously manipulated official ideology.

Chapter 4

Why the Aztecs Manipulated Time

The variance between the standard view of Aztec time and the difficulties that are evident after a closer examination of the calendar suggest more than that the conventional view is inadequate or that it has neglected inconvenient aspects of the colonial descriptions, with the result that our understanding is incomplete. The discrepancies point to a faulty initial understanding of Aztec time, history, and the calendar. Instead of an Aztec cosmology in which the calendar inexorably structured life and behavior, the available evidence can perhaps be better understood as a deliberate Aztec practice of manipulating time, as happened elsewhere in the world.[1]

Because calendars are often assumed to be logical systems, or systems related to regular ecological and/or astronomical patterns, a standard explanation for the rise of complex calendrical systems around the time of the emergence of state-level societies is the need to regulate agricultural activity, especially when it is conducted on a large scale.[2] But many agrarian societies lack the complex calendars of states and yet function perfectly well.[3] So, if agrarian societies can function without complex calendars to coordinate productive behavior, then is the emergence of such calendars satisfactorily explained in these terms?

Where complex calendars are especially effective is not simply in coordinating social activities with ecological changes—the level of calendrical complexity generally found in states and empires is unnecessary, and there are too many other cues open to everyone, such as solstices, lunations, and seasonal changes in flora and fauna—but in coordinating various aspects of human behaviors. Complex calendars are a means of social coordination and control, but because they are based on more than ecological factors, they are not fully comprehensible to everyone and inherently lend themselves to hierarchical uses.

The calendrical anomalies already pointed out cannot be explained from a normative view of time in which the calendar is taken to be an independent system against whose dates other events can be arrayed. These anomalies are not merely apparent perturbations in a system too inadequately grasped, but can be better understood by recognizing that, while the calendar does have an internal logic and is partly based on ecological cycles, it is bent to political purposes and serves the state. As Pierre Bourdieu notes,[4] the calendar as written down is an abstraction and does not completely capture its socially interwoven and functional nature. That is so because everyday life, especially among farmers, does not depend on a calendar. Is there a farmer anywhere so ignorant as not to know when to plant or when to harvest? The formal calendar is, instead, a means of imposing social control, whether religious or political, and is devised for that purpose—to regulate the giving of tithes and tribute, and the providing of obligatory labor. Its maintainers are religious or statal, and it is they who are its primary beneficiaries.[5] Thus, any analysis that seeks to understand the calendar simply by examining its internal logic will always be inadequate because nonsystemic, historically specific political alterations disturb its logical functioning. In short, the calendar does not generate a temporal structure that patterns events, nor is it simply a temporal backdrop against which political events can be set; rather, political concerns create the calendar, manipulate it, and use it for practical purposes.[6]

The calendar has been one of the most effective instruments for exercising power in human society.[7] This is especially true of institutions, such as empires, that persist over long periods and need to coordinate broad-based behavior. Time can be structured many different ways as can easily be seen by the plethora of weeks and months of different durations around the world. Each such temporal division, whether rooted in religion, politics, economics, astronomy/astrology, or history, is, to a major extent arbitrary, and inherently political, if not because it arose as a conscious political choice, then certainly in how it is used.

However a specific calendar and its divisions arise, once in place the calendar structures other, especially public, behavior, becomes routinized, and takes on a reality all its own. Only when there is a change in the temporal system is the pattern of time resisted, as an alteration from what is "normal." An example of this close to home were the often acrimonious debates over the use of daylight savings time in the United States. In the 1950s, the adoption of daylight savings time was largely a city option, which produced a bewildering patchwork of different times. My own hometown adopted daylight savings time—"fast time" in local parlance—but the neighboring town, five miles away, did not. I can recall going to that town to watch the Labor Day parade, standing on the curb awaiting its start, and wondering aloud why they had not shifted to fast time. This was clearly a breach of social etiquette, and a local man spoke up and announced it was because they were on God's time. I do not doubt that he believed it and, to me at six or seven years of age, it seemed pretty convincing as well, yet the sheer usefulness of fast time—the swimming pool opened earlier, as did stores and movies—was enough to convince me of the superior wisdom of my own town's city fathers. But the incident does illustrate the ease with which our conventional time zones—created only some sixty years earlier by the railroads for their own scheduling purposes, certainly not accurately aligned with solar time, and initially resisted— had become so ingrained in us that, conceptually, they had become "God's time."

Any time system, whether measuring minutes, hours, days, weeks, months, years, or any of the myriad other temporal possibilities, rapidly becomes part of the normal conceptual order of things that then patterns much of the rest of our activities. Although we think of our temporal order as normal and even God-given, who, how, and why it was initially set up was a political decision. It is not always made by an explicitly political entity, but the consequences are the same; it structures society in ways desired by the originating institution.[8] It is in this sense that time is political—not in terms of what it is, but in how it is structured, how it is used, and who makes these decisions.[9]

Many studies of Mesoamerican calendars assume that they reflect normative time without considering how these calendars are politically motivated or manipulated; such studies do not view time as purposeful or as a context for action. If this political intrusion is, in fact, the case, it becomes evident why Caso's attempt to correlate the Mesoamerican calendars by assuming them to be related but autonomous systems was doomed—they were altered and/or coordinated by polities. Time is not a construct within which political actions are scheduled, once the temporal system has been established. Rather, calendars are created through political actions for political purposes.[10] That this is less than obvious to us today is perhaps the result of operating within a larger calendrical tradition than just that of this particular polity, so that it is not as subject to the unilateral changes of the political elite. But this type of political manipulation can be seen more clearly in the case of the Roman empire, which altered its calendar by renaming the months, changing the number of days in the months, and shifting the beginning of the year to coincide with elections.

Many studies, especially in the case of the Aztecs, treat religion and ideology as self-contained, internally logical, and self-perpetuating systems of belief. It is, after all, most satisfying to feel that one's beliefs are held because they are right, true, natural, and even self-evident, rather than simply to justify one's condition or actions. In any case— and this stance cannot be critiqued internally since such beliefs are held to be causal but not caused—beliefs do have an effect in the world and, at a minimum, they can be assessed in terms of how they are used in the furtherance of other goals. Thus, I may not be able to say what their ideology *meant* to the Aztecs, but I can examine some of what it *did*. But ideology is more than simply a political justifier. After all, it is precisely because it is believed and holds meaning for its adherents that the state can manipulate it so successfully.

Whether or not religious beliefs motivated political actions among the Aztecs, they did structure them. One notable example of this was the 1487 dedication of the Great Temple. Ahuitzotl was chosen to succeed King Tizoc and immediately embarked on the raid that preceded all Aztec coronations. Though this campaign resulted in the conquest of Chiapan, Xilotepec, Cuauhuacan, and Cozcacuauhtenanco,[11] many nominal Aztec tributaries still did not attend Ahuitzotl's coronation because the four to five years of neglect during the reign of his immediate predecessor, King Tizoc, had left the Aztecs appearing weak and indecisive. So Ahuitzotl then undertook a second major campaign into the northeast, conquering many towns[12] and taking a reported 80,400 captives,[13] though other sources put the numbers considerably lower (e.g., the *Codex Telleriano-Remensis* puts the figure at 20,000).[14]

Word of these conquests was spread and his nominal tributaries were then invited to attend the rededication of the Great Temple, where the captives were to be sacrificed, and the leaders of virtually all of the subject towns attended. The issue, then, is how this sacrifice is explained. It has been interpreted as devotion to the gods of Mexico, but the cir-

cumstances strongly suggest that this was a political exercise by Ahuitzotl by which he reasserted control over his wavering tributaries much
more quickly and inexpensively than had he been forced to reconquer
them one by one. In a similar vein, Cortés *may* have been held to be
a god initially; that is, his strange arrival was interpreted consistently
with the Aztec worldview, but that impression quickly faded, whereas
the political goal of deterring him remained constant throughout the
Conquest. Thus beliefs both structured actions and were manipulated
in support of them. The same holds true of the calendar.

Time was a key concept that the Aztec state manipulated. Keeping
time is an expensive enterprise that, in a socially complex but technologically simple society, requires numerous specialists and, in Aztec
society, these were priests. Thus, in such "theocratically" inclined societies,[15] religious-state relations were not predicated simply on the latter operating in accordance with the former. Rather, the state derived
significant advantages from the priesthoods, in legitimating its existence, justifying its actions, and mobilizing popular support for both.
But keeping time was another significant, albeit often ignored, service
the priesthoods performed that was politically useful, which also helps
explain why the state supported them.

Although the calendar may seem to be a relatively self-perpetuating
system, once it has been created and set into motion the disparities
between days and years—which are not evenly divisible by days because of the length of the earth's orbit around the sun—mean that virtually all calendars require some maintenance to deal with the leap
year problem, if nothing else. And if the calendar is tied to astronomical
cycles or occurrences, such as solstices, equinoxes, or lunations,[16] further specialists may be required. In short, all complex calendars require
an intelligentsia to create, maintain, correct, and operate them. Belief
alone will not maintain such systems: they require a political elite to
impose the system and its adjustments. And the longer the cycles involved in the calendar and the more complex the system, the more the
need for the intelligentsia to discern and track it, and the greater the
incentive for elites to emphasize such calendars.

Looking at the state manipulation of beliefs—in this case, time—
does not suggest that belief was uniform, as the strong ideology-as-
action perspective suggests. On the contrary, both belief and reliance
differed, inter alia, by class, gender, ethnicity, and occupation. Among
others, such problems with both a systemic approach to Aztec religion
and our grasp of it as it actually operated call for its reassessment, as
well as a reassessment of the more concrete remnants of Aztec culture.

Perhaps a weaker ideology-as-idiom approach that admits more extra-systemic considerations might have something to offer, so a brief overview of the social context of the Aztec empire is in order.

The Polity

From the overthrow of the Tepanecs in 1428, the Aztecs began the march to empire that Cortés would cut short in 1521, less than a hundred years later. And the Aztecs' political organization, though admirable for a city-state, was not as well adapted to empire, at least not to one that was contested.

The Aztecs were a complex society with a series of classes.[17] At the top was the king (tlatoani; the ruler of a province or town), and below him were the rest of the upper nobles, or lords (teteuctin). These made up the ruling class, and below them were the lower nobles (pipiltin), who were the offspring of the upper nobles. Below these were the eagle nobles (cuauhpipiltin), commoners who had achieved noble status by virtue of their deeds in war.

Below the nobility were the commoners (macehualtin), who formed the bulk of Aztec society. They were organized by wards (calpolli) governed by the ward heads (calpoleque). Below these free commoners was yet another group of commoners (mayeque or tlalmaitin) who were laborers permanently attached to the patrimonial lands of the nobility. And below this serf-like class were the slaves (tlatlacotin), though their owners had limited rights over them, owning mostly their labor.

This class system provided an efficient hierarchical structure running from the king on top to the household on bottom, with everyone answerable to some authority—residential and occupational—all the way up to the king; anyone added to that society—whether by birth or by migration—was immediately fitted into an existing social slot. Other polities—city-states, confederacies, or empires—could not be so easily assimilated, in part because of how they and the Aztecs were organized and in part because of technological limitations on integrating distant groups.

This empire was based on conquest by force and intimidation, with subsequent enforcement through the projection of power; that is, the Aztecs would return and punish the conquered peoples if their wishes were not carried out. They did not alter local social systems, replace local rulers, or station troops in the area to enforce their dictates. Their empire was not one of direct territorial control, but was concerned with a limited range of tributary activities (usually political and economic matters). Because they demanded relatively little from their vassals except tribute and allowed local customs and the local power structure to continue otherwise unaffected, the Aztecs were able to create an empire with a great economy of force. Their expenses in local administration were minimal and the men required for garrison duties were few, with the result that they were able to expand over vast distances because they did not exhaust their forces in directly controlling conquered areas. Though this hegemonic imperial system was efficient, its major fault was that its perpetuation depended on the willingness of the tributaries to comply with Aztec wishes, so any sign of Aztec weakness could undermine their ability to rule. As a result, continual demonstrations of their power were the hallmark of the Aztec empire, and the death of a king left tributaries uncertain about whether or not the next one would be as effective in enforcing his will.[18]

One thing the Aztecs did not do, or try to do, was to integrate the empire ideologically. Most empires stimulate the adoption of imperial wares, practices, and even values, especially among provincial elites. And it is often these shared practical matters of life—linked markets, common calendars, shared units of measure, conventional patterns of behavior—that form the basis for broadly recognized and accepted standards of interaction and hold the polity together more than an official ideology. But this is a matter of emulation, of local elites attempting to associate themselves with power and then having these things filter down through the lower classes, as happened in, say, Roman London (Londinium).[19]

Though three major missionizing religions—Buddhism, Christianity, and Islam—dominate the world today, and proselytizing appears to be a very effective aspect of their success,[20] most religions do not insist on their own exclusive and exclusionary correctness. And this was true of the Aztecs, who, as polytheists, easily accepted gods from other groups. Moreover, though Huitzilopochtli was their special patron, the Aztecs did not force their gods, rites, or social customs on their tributaries. Indeed, Huitzilopochtli had almost no presence beyond the Valley of Mexico, even within the Aztec empire, and the few places where he was found were typically those where Aztecs themselves had resettled.[21] The most widespread gods in Mesoamerica were those tied to natural phenomena, such as rain (Tlaloc) or wind (Ehecatl), whereas those that were not so associated, such as Huitzilopochtli, tended to remain local gods.

Individual Aztecs surely believed in their gods, as did the inhabitants of other cities, and wars were sometimes excused in religious terms, but they were not fought to spread religion. This does not mean there were no religious motivations for going to war; indeed, priests accompanied the army and the temples shared in the tributary spoils. But the motivations did not include forced religious conversion. Even though cities each typically had a patron god, different deities were venerated within the same city by the various wards, occupations, and ethnic groups. Thus the promotion of a particular god or group of gods to tributary cities might have been socially fragmenting even within Tenochtitlan.

The Aztecs appear to have used other people's gods in a socially manipulative way by sometimes seizing the god statues of resisting cities and taking them to Tenochtitlan, where they were housed in a special temple (the Coacalco),[22] but these acts may have been motivated less by religion than immediately seems the case. The economic incentives for seizing these gods were substantial. Removing them to Tenochtitlan meant that the gods' attendant priests had to emigrate as well, and where they went, the wealth from temple lands followed, providing an influx into Tenochtitlan of redirected goods in addition to those demanded directly as tribute. If the goal was a religious one, one would expect gods to be seized from cities throughout the empire; but if the rationale for seizing the gods of recalcitrant tributaries was primarily economic, one would expect this to occur in cities that were relatively close to Tenochtitlan, because the friction of distance would quickly erode the value of goods transported from great distances, and, indeed, the latter seems to have been the case.[23]

Mesoamerican religion was admirably adapted to the cross-cutting ties of urban life, but without supernatural exclusivity or a clear hierarchy of gods, it was ill-suited for imperial integration. It is no accident that the Roman Catholic Church integrated most of Europe through the Middle Ages, effectively overriding the more provincial concerns of the many kingdoms, yet largely lost that role following the Reformation, when different Protestant denominations essentially served as local state religions.

Linking the Empire

By 1519, the eve of the Spanish conquest, the Aztec empire extended from the desert about 100 miles north of Tenochtitlan as far south as Guatemala and from the Gulf of Mexico on the east to the Pacific

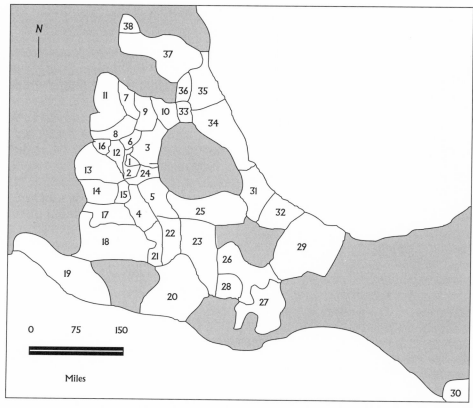

4-1. Aztec empire as of 1519 (from Barlow 1949) [Map from drawing by Doni Fox]

PROVINCES

1. Tlatelolco
2. Petlacalco
3. Acolhuacan
4. Cuauhnahuac
5. Huaztepec
6. Cuauhtitlan
7. Azocopan
8. Atotonilco de Pedraza
9. Huelypochtlan
10. Atotonilco el Grande
11. Zilotepec
12. Cuahuacan
13. Tolocan

14. Ocuilan
15. Malinalco
16. Zocotitlan
17. Tlachco
18. Tepecuacuilco
19. Cihuatlan
20. Tlapan
21. Tlalcocauhititlan
22. Cuiauhteopan
23. Yohualtepec
24. Chalco
25. Tepeyacac
26. Cohuaxtlahuacan

27. Coyolapan
28. Tlachquiauco
29. Tochtepec
30. Xoconochco
31. Cuauhtochco
33. Tlapacoyan
34. Tlatlauhquitepec
35. Tochpan
36. Atlan
37. Tzicoac
38. Oxitipan

Ocean on the west. With hundreds of cities, thousands of towns and villages, and millions of people spread over many thousands of square miles, how were the Aztecs to control such an empire in the absence of wheeled vehicles, draft animals, a state-sponsored road system, or any means of long-distance communication, such as telegraph, telephone, radio, or even heliograph?

There were, of course, ambassadors who plied Mexico's roads,[24] conveying messages of state, but these were few, traveled with large retinues, moved relatively slowly, and were a costly and infrequently employed means of communication. There were also runners who carried messages throughout the empire[25] but, while faster and far less expensive than ambassadors, these would nevertheless have been too costly to be used to link all the cities in the empire on a regular basis. And, there is little evidence that they were so used; in fact, when they are mentioned in historical accounts, it is typically in the wake of some major and unpredictable event—the death of a king or a military triumph that it was politically important to advertise.[26]

In these two circumstances, the very fate of the empire was at stake. The death of a king could provoke a crisis, tempting tributaries to test their obligations, so announcing the death of a king and—more importantly—his chosen successor, so that the subordinate rulers could attend the coronation and repledge their fealty, was a crucial element in maintaining the empire. Similarly, news of a military triumph would be spread by messenger primarily to offset the effect of a previous setback, as with King Axayacatl's victories over Tliliuhqui-Tepec and Zacatlan following his defeat by the Tarascans.[27] Given the size of the Aztec empire, however, the use of messengers for day-to-day matters would have been enormously time-consuming and prohibitively expensive.

Although communication was difficult and costly in Mesoamerica and the Aztecs did not seek close political integration or the spread of their own social practices or religious beliefs, they did spread their calendar. The areas into which it penetrated were characterized by city-states, all of which would have long had their own calendars.

Each city-state needs a relatively sophisticated calendar to coordinate the activities of governance, often adopted from the prevailing religion.[28] Each city-state also had its own priests, who maintained the Mesoamerican calendar they had inherited.[29] But regardless of whether their calendar is created, adapted, or adopted, states require some form of calendar to coordinate large-scale, complex interactions. In the case

of Tenochtitlan, the Aztecs adopted the calendar that prevailed throughout central Mexico, and this provided a more-than-adequate temporal
framework with which to structure the political, economic, religious,
and social affairs of the city, just as it did in the other city-states of
Mesoamerica.

Why, then, would a particular variant of that calendar spread over a
large area if it was not tied to some religious motivation? Since the
Aztecs did not force either social or ideological changes, one answer
might be utility, but whose? Certainly not that of the city-states to
which it spread. Their own calendars were as accurate and reliable as
the Aztecs' and were perfectly adequate to maintain their ritual cycles,
mark major festivals, and schedule their own markets and those of their
surrounding dependencies.[30] An explanation that relies on the inherent
values of a particular calendar system rarely explains its spread.[31]

The Aztecs spread their calendar because it was a political necessity
in light of their imperial organization and the prevailing technological
constraints. Given the high costs of communication and transportation
in Mesoamerica and the lack of Aztec administrative or military per-
sonnel on the ground in vassal cities, the tribute system ultimately depended on the voluntary compliance of subject towns. This was backed
up by Aztec force in the long term, but in the absence of resistance,
tribute assessments were levied and schedules of payment were established and then enforced by local officials.

A self-timed tribute system would seem easy to maintain, but there
were two major difficulties. The first problem was that the tribute
schedule was, from the tributaries' point of view, arbitrary; tribute was
to be paid four times a year in Tenochtitlan at four festivals during the
xihuitl months of Tlacaxipehualiztli, Etzalcualiztli, Ochpaniztli, and
Panquetzaliztli.[32] The Aztecs established this schedule instead of allowing tribute to dribble in throughout the year when it made the most
sense to the tributaries (e.g., after their respective harvests or around
their own ceremonies) mostly in order to impress their vassals both
with the large numbers attending the festivals and with the great ceremonies emphasizing Aztec grandeur and might.

Thus the timing of payments was not evenly spread over the year or,
in particular, tied to harvests, which, in any case, differed by climatic
zone throughout the empire. Nor was the timing based on a natural
occurrence that could be seen and predicted throughout most of central
Mexico, such as solstices, equinoxes, lunations, or the zenith passage
of astronomical bodies. Zenith passages occurred at different times at

different latitudes and so were unsuitable for use in coordinating tribute payments in Tenochtitlan. Furthermore, the triggering event would
need to be anticipated, not merely observed, so that all of the tribute
payers would reach Tenochtitlan at the appropriate time, no matter how
distant their homes and how long their travel time. Thus, the Aztecs
needed a uniform calendar to insure timely compliance with their tribute demands.

The second difficulty with this self-timed system was that the festivals were tied to months based on the Aztec calendar, and while many
tributary cities also celebrated these months, since calendars elsewhere differed in their beginning times, so too did the dates of these
months, the festivals, and the times at which the nemontemi days were
inserted. The Aztecs could have inserted a correction into each local
calendar to adjust for this disparity, but it would have made the calculations more difficult. Instead of ceremonies merely being off by an entire month or multiples thereof, which would have been easily calculated, if the point at which the Aztecs observed their nemontemi days
differed from that of the local calendar, the months of one would have
fallen five days within the months of the other. But this problem, too,
could have been overcome except for the leap year problem.

Mexican calendars had no built-in mechanism that allowed them to
correct for leap years, but since the xihuitl was aligned with the seasons, they must have added days to compensate for this (as would tying
the New Fire ceremony to *any* fixed astronomical marker), though how
and when that happened would have varied by city. Since there was no
mechanism in the Aztec calendar that would allow the insertion of
any days without disrupting the system, the intercalary days must have
been added after the completion of all of the cycles in the 52-year Calendar Round. This is one of the various possibilities recorded by colonial writers[33] which, beyond its logic, is made more compelling by
Jacinto de la Serna's assertion that these 13 days were unnamed, fell
outside both months and years, and were dedicated to Xiuhteuctli, Lord
of Fire and of the Year.[34] But since a 13-day divergence from the solar
year could throw off an ecologically based calendar, I suggest that instead of displacing the xihuitl months by 13 days, the new Calendar
Round did not reset the calendar year to the ecological year, but probably began 6 or 7 days ahead of the seasons so that at 26 years, halfway
through the Calendar Round, the calendar and ecological years came
into alignment and then gradually deviated until, by the end, they once
more diverged by 6 or 7 days. This slight variance would be relatively

unimportant to the calendar's functioning in the short run, would be self-correcting, and would still generate an accurate long-term calendar. Moreover, that the priests would be secretive about the insertion of intercalary days is not unprecedented.[35] And, since many calendrical systems already differed in a number of other respects, whatever correction a city chose—every 4, 13, or 52 years—would further compound the discrepancies between the various calendars.

For the tribute system to work—and this was as much a tributary concern as an Aztec one since the former would bear the brunt of noncompliance—everyone had to know when tribute was to be paid. Because it was due in Tenochtitlan, each tributary city had to know how far in advance to gather tribute from its own dependencies, forward it to the provincial center, and then transport it to the Aztec capital, a duration that differed for every town. Thus, even if it had been feasible to use messengers to notify tributaries when to pay, they would still have been ineffectual because of the different times at which cities would be alerted and the varying distances involved.

The key to a smoothly functioning tribute system was a unified, coordinated calendar system which, because of the necessary leap year corrections, was "set" by the New Fire ceremony. If everyone used the same calendar, the rulers of each tributary town would know when they were to pay their tribute, and they could also calculate the number of days in advance that they would have to begin the process, given their own particular circumstances. Thus, the one ideological construct the Aztecs spread with their empire was their calendar, not because it embodied a specific set of beliefs and values—since gods, rites, and social practices were specifically not imposed—but because it was indispensable to the functioning of a self-mobilizing tribute system, and its imposition depended on centralized political control.[36] The Aztec empire was not only a political entity, it was a synchronous unity.

The tribute system that prevailed at the time of the Spanish conquest was not the original one. Rather, it had been profoundly rationalized; instead of grouping tributary towns together as they were conquered, the Aztecs under King Moteuczoma Xocoyotl reorganized all existing tributary towns into "provinces" based not on duration of Aztec control or on ethnic identity, but on propinquity, creating thirty-eight relatively compact tributary provinces. The king also shifted the schedule of tribute payment. Under the Tepanecs, Tetzcoco had paid tribute yearly; towns in the Cuauhnahuac region had paid tribute to Tetzcoco six times a year during the reigns of Nezahualcoyotl and Nezahualpilli (the latter died in 1515).[37] Whatever the earlier periodicity in the Aztec empire, Moteuczoma Xocoyotl shifted the tribute system to four times per year, keyed to the festivals of Tlacaxipehualiztli, Etzalcualiztli, Ochpaniztli, and Panquetzaliztli, or every 80, 100, 80, and 100 days (except for distant Xoconochco, which paid only twice a year, during the first and third festivals[38]), not only to link the tributaries into a unified payment scheme but to link payment to festivals that emphasized the hegemonic dominance of the empire.

The way the Aztecs harnessed their calendar to imperial goals illustrates the general social and political purposes of time. While the tendency is to view time in terms of its linking of past to present, that may not be its more important role. Linking the past and present is important on a conceptual level, but the past is gone and temporal placement of bygone events can be—and often is—layered for political, religious, and social purposes, as was also the case with the Aztecs. Because the past cannot be directly known, consensus over past dates is more important than historical accuracy, so time's role in maintaining chronological certainty is perhaps not as important as its spatial role. Spreading the calendar so that disparate places can act in synchronous union demands an accuracy that timing the past does not, and this spread creates a temporally based spatial unity that is the calendar's greatest legacy.

Although linear time was used for most political purposes in Aztec society and cyclical time for religious ones, ironically it was the latter that was essential to the orderly functioning of the tribute system. The Aztecs tied their tribute-paying times to religious festivals in the xihuitl, so it was the regular, predictable, annual solar cycle that lent the system its utility. That local groups had to know the Aztec calendar does not mean that it necessarily displaced their own. In areas closest to the Valley of Mexico, and therefore probably under Aztec control the longest, this was generally the case. But elsewhere, the two systems may have been used in tandem, the Aztec for tributary and other imperial purposes and the local for domestic ones.

This sort of calendrical coordination also occurs today, though less from political than from economic domination. The need to coordinate economic behavior internationally, transfer funds, establish mutually enforceable contracts, and so forth, requires an inerrant calendar—which many indigenous systems are not—and the dominant one today is Christian, even though many other calendars may be employed domestically and religiously. For instance, forty-one countries currently use the Christian calendar as the "common" calendar along-side another calendar (e.g., Japanese, Islamic, Jewish, and so forth).[39] But both today and in the Aztec empire, the underlying purpose of the calendrical spread is to coordinate behavior over vast areas and across many cultural traditions. And it was the disseminated Aztec calendar that permitted coordinated political actions over broad expanses and without which the vast tribute system could not have functioned.

The result of this practice is the creation of an imperial zone of relative calendrical homogeneity—relative because of the time required for full assimilation of the Aztec calendar, which argues that it is less likely to be reflected in post-Conquest accounts the more recently the subordination of the areas discussed. It also means that calendrical differences are to be expected beyond the empire, as is demonstrably the case with the Tarascan empire and other independent areas. Thus Caso's idea that Mexican calendars shared synchronicity was not entirely wrong. He saw some unity, which he assumed was the result of an underlying cultural continuity since virtually everyone shared the same fundamental calendar. But this calendrical synchronicity was political rather than ideological, so there were areas of uniformity separated by political divides.

Despite the logic of this calendrical change and its essential role if the tribute system were to work—which it did—how can one be sure the Aztec calendar was actually spread? After all, the same basic calendrical structure of tonalpohualli, xihuitl, and Calendar Rounds was shared throughout central Mexico, and there is no consensus on the coordination of the Christian calendar with any of the indigenous ones through which a shift in year beginnings might be detected. At the level of the tonalpohualli, xihuitl month, or even the entire xihuitl, one cannot tell. But the Aztecs did initiate one calendrical change that marked their system and that, when found elsewhere, establishes the spread of their calendar. They changed the year of the New Fire ceremony.

The Aztecs shifted the New Fire ceremony from 1 Tochtli to 2 Acatl, which is conventionally explained as shifting the start to the birth date of Huitzilopochtli.[40] This association is plausible though tenuous,[41] and is more of a convenient overlay for the shift than a compelling reason to disrupt the calendrical system, especially since the calendar was spread elsewhere but worship of that god was not. Most of those who have dealt with the issue at all have accepted the explanation in the *Codex Telleriano-Remensis*[42] that the shift occurred in 1454 (1 Tochtli), when the New Fire ceremony was moved to 1455 (2 Acatl), because

1454 was a famine year, or that it was moved from 1506 (1 Tochtli) to 1507 (2 Acatl), again because the former was a famine year. And while it is true that 1454 was a major famine year and 1506 a minor one, this is not a plausible reason to shift the New Fire ceremony (though it might be a publicly acceptable rationalization) because the ceremony would begin at midnight before the first day of the succeeding year. That would be in winter (at some date in the first quarter of the year), whereas harvest in the Valley of Mexico was in late summer and early autumn. Thus, although famines did occur in 1454 and 1506, the New Fire ceremony would have been held months earlier before a famine could have even been predicted. Moreover, the effects of the bad harvests in the summer and autumn would still have been suffered throughout the winter and spring of the succeeding years (1455 and 1507), to which the New Fire ceremony was shifted, placing it at an even worse time. Thus, the proposition that the New Fire ceremony was shifted because of famines is unconvincing.

But did the shifted New Fire ceremony remain the initiating point of a recalibrated Calendar Round, or was it now simply considered a commemoration, a convention whose movement had no practical impact on the calendar system and could therefore be repositioned at any point in the year rather than at the beginning? There is evidence on both sides.

Most convincing for the New Fire ceremony as convention is the assertion that it was held on the night when the Pleiades reached its zenith at midnight, which, in Tenochtitlan, would be around October 26 (Julian). But since the New Fire ceremony is recorded as being *both* at the midnight zenith passage of the Pleiades *and* at the end of the 52-year cycle, yet the former is in November and the latter is in February or March, these assertions are irreconcilable. Thus, the issue is how strong the Pleiades zenith passage is as an indicator of the New Fire ceremony.

Shifting the New Fire ceremony by one full year will not affect stellar constellations, as all the stars and constellations will still reach their zeniths at the same time every year. So, moving the position of the New Fire ceremony by a full year would mean little additional distortion of the calendar system. If the Pleiades' midnight zenith passage was truly a marker of the New Fire ceremony, however, it was necessarily an innovation of the new system. The most salient change in the ceremony was its removal to a hilltop; yet a midnight zenith passage could be noted as easily from the Great Temple as from the hill of Huixachtecatl, so moving the New Fire ceremony to a hilltop would not argue for also shifting it to November. In fact, such a spatial move would be entirely irrelevant to its temporal shift. And while a change of any kind opens up the best opportunity for additional alterations, there are reasons to doubt that this was one of them. In fact, if there is any connection between the shift to Huixachtecatl and the Pleiades, it does not lie in the latter's zenith passage at midnight.

Ceremonies atop prominences were common in Aztec Mexico.[43] But why move what is arguably the single most important calendrical ceremony from the Great Temple—the most important pyramid in Tenochtitlan and the symbolic, political, social, religious, and economic center of the world—to a small temple on a distant hilltop? Two reasons come to mind. First, the latter site is visible throughout much of the Valley of Mexico, and a ceremony held there could be seen in all of the major cities.[44] But second, and perhaps more importantly, the relocation of the ceremony was not simply a movement in space, but in time as well—not in months, but in minutes.

In terms of astronomical observations, the primary difference between the Great Temple and the hill of Huixachtecatl is not distance, as the few miles involved are insignificant for this purpose. Rather, it is altitude. The summit of Huixachtecatl is some 900 feet higher than the Great Temple, and that change in elevation translates into a significant difference in time. If the New Fire ceremony was keyed to an astronomical zenith passage, whether the Pleiades or not, this would occur at the same time atop the hill as it did in the capital below, since one can see an object directly overhead as easily on a valley floor as on a hilltop—but it would not have the same timekeeping value.

Without a mechanical means of measuring duration, time was largely a function of the movement of celestial bodies. The sun was used during the day, but at night, the stars, constellations, moon, and planets served that purpose, though they did not do so alone, but in relation to each other or to the horizons. Any celestial body that rose just as the sun set would reach its zenith at midnight. That is, a celestial body that was on the eastern horizon would be at 0° (the ideal eastern horizon), while the sun, on the western horizon, would be at 180°, or directly opposite from the point of view of an observer on earth. When the sun had traveled another quarter of its journey around the earth (adopting a pre-Copernican perspective) and reached 270°, the celestial body that had been on the eastern horizon would now be at 90°, or directly overhead. But these ideals do not work well in the Valley of Mexico because it is ringed with mountains. The eastern and western horizons in the

Valley of Mexico are not at 0° and 180° in Tenochtitlan, but are at approximately 5° and 175° owing to the additional 5° of height supplied by the encircling mountains. As a result, if sunrise occurred at 6 A.M. and sunset at 6 P.M. on the plains, in Tenochtitlan sunrise would be at 6:20 A.M. and sunset at 5:40 P.M. (ignoring the atmospheric diffusion that can actually extend the period of light by up to 40 minutes, though not the observation of celestial bodies). Moving the New Fire ceremony to the top of the hill of Huixachtecatl, however, would produce a truer zenith passage time than that available from the Great Temple. This is important because it is a crucial element of measuring time at night. Just looking at a celestial object in isolation to assess its zenith passage is impossible; such assessment must be done in relation to some other point, and that, I suggest, was the western horizon, which the temple faced. Because the angle between the hilltop temple and the horizon is significantly less than between the Great Temple and the horizon, moving the ceremony to the top of a hill actually shifted it in time by as much as twenty minutes, as the zenith passage of the Pleiades would be coordinated with the setting of the sun as seen from there rather than from the valley floor. Calculating the Pleiades' zenith based on when the sun set on February 1 would yield a zenith at 6 P.M. On the hilltop, this would also be when the sun set, but in Tenochtitlan, it would occur at a difficult-to-determine 20 minutes after sunset (if that constellation would have been visible at all). When the Aztecs shifted the New Fire ceremony from the year 1 Tochtli to 2 Acatl, then, they also took advantage of that change to move the ceremony to a more socially conspicuous location that would produce a more accurate celestial timing for the event and simultaneously reinforce their political action with a supernatural justification would make it more acceptable to the populace and the priesthood.[45]

Moving the New Fire ceremony to Huixachtecatl coordinates the Pleiades' zenith passage precisely with sunset, and its setting at midnight would be marked by descent below the horizon rather than a movement to a difficult-to-determine precise point overhead. This strongly suggests then that the Aztecs used midnight to mark the new day because the New Fire ceremony began at that time, contrary to Caso's suggestion of noon as the beginning, because that would mean the ceremony was either celebrated a full half day after the end of the previous Calendar Round or a full half day before the last Calendar Round ended. Yet the issue remains, at what time of year was the New Fire ceremony held?

The available accounts offer four different times: at the beginning of the new Calendar Round, in December, when the Pleiades reach zenith at midnight, and during the month of Panquetzaliztli. The time I believe is correct, and the one with the most documentary support, is at the beginning of the new 52-year count. The time when this count began differed in Mesoamerica. The Aztecs, people in the other cities in the Valley of Mexico, and their imperial dependencies began the year with the month Atl Cahualo, whereas farther afield, Tlacaxipehualiztli, an older system, began the year.[46] Presumably, this change—which is detectable only from the distributional pattern of year beginnings and not from a historical record of the shift, since changing the year beginning by a full month would leave the same year bearer days intact as well as the year names—accompanied the other Aztec-led calendrical alterations since it also spread with the empire. This shift could happen within the existing calendar system because it moved the year beginning back in time. This shift meant that the year count would begin early, whereas a shift forward would have left a logically impermissible gap in time of twenty days between the end of the last year and the beginning of the next, which also suggests that abandoning the Atl Cahualo system and readopting the Tlacaxipehualiztli system would have been cosmologically difficult.

A number of detailed colonial sources record that the New Fire ceremony was held at the beginning of the new Calendar Round, and many of these same sources note that the year began in February or early March, a date that is also expected from the logic of the New Fire ceremony. Everyone conventionally knew that the world would end, and the logical time for this to occur was after the completion of a Calendar Round. This was the case with the previous four worlds, though which Calendar Round would mark the end was made uncertain by the shift to the 5-Sun belief, and no one could be certain whether the sun would emerge after the completion of a Calendar Round, so there was considerable anxiety. But if the New Fire ceremony had been torn free of its year-starting position, there would be little need for a ceremony and no anxiety over the beginning of another Calendar Round cycle since a November or December date would mean that the cycle had already been under way for fifteen xihuitl months.

A February or March New Fire date is also supported by the behavior of the Aztec kings. King Moteuczoma Ilhuicamina is recorded as having taken Huaxtec captives thirty days prior to the New Fire ceremony.[47] And, since the war season began in early December and extended into April, this fact, plus the logic of the New Fire ceremony, forcefully argues for the event taking place in the first quarter of the Christian year. Nevertheless, three other dates for the New Fire ceremony have been proposed, and all have some support in chronicles or codices.

The major alternative date for the New Fire ceremony is in the month of Panquetzaliztli, an interpretation that is primarily based on the flag on folio 34 of the *Codex Borbonicus*. This folio, which is taken to illustrate the New Fire ceremony, is part of a sequential listing of monthly festivals and is also in the appropriate position for Panquetza-liztli, and thus convincingly illustrates that month.[48] From this, it is concluded that the New Fire ceremony was held in the year 2 Acatl, which is widely attested in other historical sources, and in the month of Panquetzaliztli, which Caso puts at November 20–December 9 (for 1521).

December is also mentioned by Torquemada and the *Crónica mexicana* as the date for the New Fire ceremony, which may support the Pan-quetzaliztli interpretation. Both of these sources are relatively late—early-seventeenth and late-sixteenth centuries, respectively—there is a possibility of error since they discuss a ceremony that had last been celebrated almost a century earlier. But both postdate the Gregorian reform, so early December dates in the revised calendar would have been ten days earlier—in late November in the Julian system, which was in place until 1582—so these anomalous dates may simply be two other attestations of a November New Fire date. However, since there is no other documentary support for these dates and considerable contrary evidence, if the conventional interpretation of the *Codex Borbonicus* fails, so do they.

But another line of evidence argues in favor of Panquetzaliztli. A November date, though not explicitly listed in the historical accounts, arises from an extrapolation from descriptions of the New Fire ceremony. The beginning of that ceremony was when the Pleiades reached zenith at midnight. Though none of the historical sources date this midnight zenith, with today's knowledge, it is a simple matter to calculate back, which would put the Pleiades' zenith at midnight on October 26 (Julian; November 6 Gregorian). There is no other time that the Pleiades reaches its zenith at midnight in the Tenochtitlan area, and it is largely from the scientific certainty of this fact that a late October date for the New Fire ceremony has been supported.

But there are four problems with this seemingly incontestable dating. First, as discussed earlier, without a mechanical clock, the Aztecs had little means of determining when midnight was in the sense of the sun reaching a point that was 180° from the zenith. Instead, they used astronomical positions as the time rather than actually timing astronomical positions, and this is especially evident for the Pleiades, whose zenith they noted with trumpets and regarded as midnight, no matter when it occurred. So whereas today we can determine precisely when the Pleiades reaches zenith at midnight, the Aztecs could not, so placing the New Fire ceremony at a date that we have deduced from colonial records by lending them a meaning they never had is insupportable. Second, even if this line of reasoning were defensible, these dates do not fall in December or even in Panquetzaliztli, but in the month of Quecholli. So, the seemingly strongest data that are the least dependent upon the vagaries of Spanish records and possible misunderstandings do not, in fact, support the Panquetzaliztli interpretation. Third, on October 26, 1507, when the New Fire ceremony would have occurred in this interpretation, there was a waning gibbous moon over three-fourths full that rose at 8:44 P.M. and was thus only some 40° off the zenith at midnight; thus the Pleiades would have been difficult to see then if it was visible at all. And fourth, this calculation depends on today's precision falsely projected into the past. Since naked-eye observations cannot distinguish astronomical locations within several degrees, and the Pleiades is a cluster rather than a discrete body, it would have been difficult, if not impossible, to distinguish on which of several nights that constellation actually reached its zenith. Instead, a calendrically dictated date would more likely have been selected as knowable and certain, and then whatever astronomical event was propitious would have been used. Yet despite the ostensible impossibility of the October timing for a New Fire ceremony, the seemingly transparent folio 34 with its depiction of the New Fire ceremony, its 2 Acatl year glyph, and its flag and sequential placement in the month of Panquetzaliztli are difficult to ignore.

An examination of folio 34 alone largely substantiates the general interpretation of this scene as the New Fire ceremony in 2 Acatl. But a broader focus suggests problems. Folios 3–20 of the codex depict 18 of the 20 trecenas of the tonalpohualli, followed by the 52 xihuitl years of the Calendar Round (21–22), then the monthly festival cycle (23–37), and finally the last 52 sequential xihuitl years (37–38). Thus, the codex follows a logical ordering of the Aztec calendar as a whole. Yet if folios 23–37 depict the monthly festival cycle, why would every month show its monthly festival except Panquetzaliztli? Why would Panquetzaliztli show not the monthly festival, but a ceremony that took place only once every 52 years? After all, the New Fire ceremony as depicted in the *Codex Borgia* (which is pre-Conquest and from central Mexico, although probably from an area outside the Aztec empire) does not bear a year glyph and is not among monthly ceremonies.[49] The answer, in short, is that it does not.

There are a number of descriptions of the monthly festivals in other accounts.[50] Each is in sequence and each depicts a monthly ceremony. Moreover, that depicted for Panquetzaliztli bears marked similarities to the more elaborate *Codex Borbonicus* example.[51] While there are differences between the version in the *Codex Borbonicus* and the example in the *Primeros Memoriales*, both show a temple with a flag, both show Huitzilopochtli in a temple at the top of the page, and both show the burning of a bundle of sticks in a center temple. What is being depicted is the same ceremony, yet neither here nor in any other depictions in xihuitl festival sequences is there a 2 Acatl year glyph in that month. And it is primarily that glyph that has led to the interpretation of the *Codex Borbonicus* Panquetzaliztli depiction as the New Fire ceremony rather than the monthly festival that all the cognate manuscripts reveal it to be.

If folio 34 of the *Codex Borbonicus* does not show the New Fire ceremony, what festival does it depict? The New Fire ceremony was Huitzilopochtli's most important festival, but Panquetzaliztli was the only month in which he was honored alone, so the Panquetzaliztli festival was a commemoration of that more important event, incorporated into the monthly festival. Thus, in the *Codex Borbonicus*, many of the elements of the New Fire ceremony can be seen, just as in the *Primeros Memoriales* version, but not all. There is no sacrifice of a man on Huixachtlan; indeed, there is no Huixachtlan depicted that can be identified as such with certainty. There is a temple with a flag and Huitzilopochtli in front, but that may simply indicate his temple; and there is a place glyph with a fire drill and a tree, which indicates Huixachtecatl, but not the temple. There are people in houses and a woman hidden in a granary, as happens during the New Fire ceremony, and the people all have masks, which are presumably of woven maguey. Moreover, the 2 Acatl glyph has no accompanying New Fire glyph. Thus the festival is a recapitulation of the New Fire ceremony, linking this celebration of Huitzilopochtli to his most important festival, but this reenactment has important differences from the real event held every 52 years. Yet, if it is merely a monthly festival, as all the other descriptions of the Panquetzaliztli festival indicate, why is there a 2 Acatl glyph on that page?

4-1. Festival celebration of the xihuitl month of Panquetzaliztli. Folio 252v, detail, Códice Matritense del Palacio Real (Courtesy of the Palacio Real, Madrid)

The festival section of the *Codex Borbonicus* is a set of monthly celebrations, but it also has year glyphs at the top of three pages— 1 Tochtli on folio 23 with the first Izcalli, 2 Acatl on folio 34 with Panquetzaliztli, and 3 Tecpatl on folio 37 with the second Izcalli feast. These year glyphs constitute the first three years of the last section of the codex, the calendrical sequence. Thus, the first Izcalli bears the 1 Tochtli glyph to show that it is the last month of that year, followed by Atl Cahualo, the first month of the next year, which should logically be 2 Acatl, and which is confirmed subsequently by that glyph's presence later in the monthly sequence, in Panquetzaliztli. The months follow sequentially until the last, Izcalli, which should conclude the xihuitl year. That folio, 37, also bears the 3 Tecpatl glyph, which would mean that the annual monthly cycle has concluded and this is the last month of the next year, which would deviate from all other listings of the monthly cycle or, as I believe, the year glyph is placed there to emphasize the new Atl Cahualo initial year system and as a conceptual lead-in to the rest of the year count that begins immediately thereafter.[52] Since the initial month of the year was shifted in the Aztec calendar from Tlacaxipehualiztli to Atl Cahualo (making Izcalli the last month, rather than Atl Cahualo), and since it was important, for reasons discussed below, that the month of Panquetzaliztli be marked with the year glyph 2 Acatl, the only way to indicate that Izcalli was unambiguously the last month of the year was to include one at both the start and at the end, each marked with its own year glyph.[53] The final folios then continue the year count through 2 Acatl, which also has a New Fire ceremony glyph. But the inclusion of year glyphs on the three ceremonies of the monthly cycle, and the continuation of those year glyphs in an uninterrupted sequence until the next New Fire ceremony, demonstrates that the monthly festivals presented in this codex, unlike all the other examples, are not generic festivals, but historically specific ones.

As the *Codex Telleriano-Remensis* records, the New Fire ceremony was moved from 1 Tochtli to 2 Acatl, which I argue occurred *after* the 1454 ceremony. Because such a ceremony is the culmination of 52 years, it cannot simply be switched at will. Although 1507 was probably the first formally shifted ceremony celebration, it necessarily depended on a buildup of year counts for the previous 52 years, because a New Fire ceremony links the past 52-year cycle to the next and therefore requires a full count before its celebration. Thus, although no New Fire commemoration may have been held at that time (1455), the 52-

year count would necessarily have begun then. Moreover, the 1506–07 New Fire ceremony would also be a double Calendar Round, in which the Venus cycle would also correlate, so it may have been a more propitious time to shift the ceremony than 1454–55.[54] In any case, it is this shifting of the New Fire ceremony from a 1 Tochtli to a 2 Acatl date plus the 52-year buildup that is recorded in the *Codex Borbonicus*. After all, the 52-year Calendar Round was already chronicled on folios 21 and 22, so the year count on folios 37–40 need not be included for that purpose. And though it is laid out like the years in a historical chronicle, it notes only the New Fire ceremony in 1507. If the codex were simply a generic record of how the calendar worked, no year dates would have been needed on the monthly festivals, and there would have been no reason to stop the annual year count that ends the codex at 2 Acatl. After all, the codex was most likely written shortly after the Conquest, so the year count should have continued for an additional fourteen years at a minimum. But it does not. It stops on the New Fire year of 2 Acatl, which is 1507. Moreover, by counting back from that year in which the New Fire ceremony was celebrated, it is evident that the monthly festival cycle begins with Izcalli in 1454 (1 Tochtli), the earliest Calendar Round beginning when the hill of Huixachtecatl was under Aztec control, so that Panquetzaliztli falls in 1455 (2 Acatl). That is the year the new count would have to begin, yet by depicting the first Izcalli with a year glyph to point out its new year-ending position and to show the absence of a New Fire ceremony at the end of that year, the codex demonstrates that the 2 Acatl shift had not yet occurred. The reason for that, I suggest, is that the formal New Fire ceremony was held in 1454 (1 Tochtli). And because the Great Temple underwent a major expansion in 1454,[55] suggesting that it would have been the site of the New Fire ceremony at that time, it was celebrated that year, 1 Tochtli. Moreover, a February 1, 1454 New Fire ceremony was feasible in relation to the moon, which was only a sliver, had already set at 8:05 P.M., and would thus not obscure the zenith. In contrast, on February 1, 1455, the moon was full (.9747°) and reached its zenith at 10:31 P.M., so the midnight zenith of any constellation would not have been visible, making a New Fire ceremony at that time problematic. But if the New Fire ceremony was celebrated in 1454 rather than 1455, why does the 1 Tochtli year date on the first monthly festival not have an attached New Fire glyph? The answer is that no New Fire glyph was attached because the 1 Tochtli date was not intended to signify an entire year. Rather, it was associated with Izcalli and meant to date that last month of the year. The New Fire ceremony had already been held earlier in the year at the beginning of the month of Atl Cahualo, so the date on Izcalli is intended both to indicate only the last month of the previous year and to initiate the following year, which is the focus of the codex. And the fact that the year date in Panquetzaliztli does not have an attached New Fire glyph indicates the absence of a formal ceremony. But that month and year are nevertheless important because that is when the New Fire recapitulation ceremony began to be held in Panquetzaliztli so that the full count could be completed for the formal shift of the ceremony from 1 Tochtli, as it had been in 1454, to 2 Acatl, and as it would be in 1507. This reading accounts for the ceremony in Panquetzaliztli as a normal monthly festival rather than an anomalous 52-year festival, brings the *Codex Borbonicus* in line with the other depictions of the monthly festivals, and explains the continuation of the next full 52-year cycle on the final folios and its ending with the 1507 New Fire ceremony. Moreover, if the New Fire ceremony were actually celebrated in Panquetzaliztli, and if it were sufficiently important that that month depicted a once-every-52-years ceremony rather than its monthly festival, it seems anomalous that the distant province of Xoconochco would have been compelled to bring its tribute in Tlacaxipehualiztli and Ochpaniztli, yet be excused in Etzalcualiztli and Panquetzaliztli.

There is further evidence in the *Codex Borbonicus* that would support this interpretation when the manuscript is read from this perspective. For instance, the first year of the 52-year cycle (fol. 21) is paired with Mictlan-Teuctli, the fifth Lord of the Night. As the initial date of the count of the Calendar Round (though not of the new functional Calendar Round, which was thereafter altered to begin on 2 Acatl), all cycles—9, 13, and 20 day, months, and years—should start at the beginning of their respective series. Yet the Lord of the Night paired with the first year, 1 Tochtli, is not the first of its series. There is no satisfactory explanation of this if the Lords of the Night cycle began on the first day of the new Calendar Round. But it cannot have done so and produced this result. What can account for it, however, is if the Lords of the Night cycle ran without regard to the days inserted to correct for the accumulated leap year errors, though with the last (or first) Lord of the Night doubled. Then the fifth Lord of the Night would be the initial one for the year, 1 Tochtli, after 13 intercalary days had been added (i.e., 9 Lords of the Night would have been counted plus 4 more for the 13 additional days, pairing the first day of the first year of the new Calendar Round with the fifth Lord of the Night). Despite the pains taken to have all the tonalpohualli cycles end simultaneously, the Lords of the Night cycle is the likeliest to be used in this fashion since only it is not also tied to the xihuitl cycle and would thus be free to continue running at its completion. The depiction of Lords of the Night accompanying xihuitl years is very unusual, but is necessary to indicate an entire trecena shift that would otherwise be invisible in the Lords of the Day cycle, since these always begin with the same number and lord. Moreover, the first Lord of the Night of the intercalary-day spans—and who would therefore dominate the series—would be Xiuhteuctli, providing some corroboration of Serna's claim that the added days were dedicated to this god. In any case, though still imperfectly understood, the *Codex Borbonicus* is not simply a normative description of the Aztec calendar, but also an explanation of the calendrical shift that was crucial to the functioning of the empire.

But why would the Aztecs have made a change in the calendar that pushed the New Fire ceremony ahead by an entire year, creating logical difficulties in how the Calendar Rounds were counted, instead of simply moving it a few days or months? The answer, discussed in further detail later, lies in the way annals are recorded (by year), so that if a change were to be made and it needed to be evident in the calendar, an entire year shift was required. But did this occur in 1454–55 or 1506–07, as there is evidence for each?

The documentary sources are muddled on this issue, but the expansion of the Great Temple in 1454 supports the thesis that the first 2 Acatl New Fire ceremony was celebrated in 1507, as do two other major archaeological indicators. One is the Teocalli de la Guerra Sagrada, which clearly places the New Fire ceremony in 1507 (2 Acatl) and, although earlier commemorative sculptures might have been carved for their respective New Fire ceremonies, none that directly relate the ceremony to a year have been found for the Aztecs, suggesting that this monument is particularly unusual and important. The second is the construction of a temple atop the hill of Huixachtecatl, ordered for the 1507 New Fire ceremony by King Moteuczoma Xocoyotl.

But is there further evidence for a 1455 shift to set up the 52-year cycle for a completion in 1507, given the 1454 dating of the Templo Mayor expansion? Yes, though not unequivocally so, in two of Chimalpahin's relations. He states that the New Fire ceremony was held in 1455 atop Huixachtecatl.[56] And since he is silent on the ceremony or its location during the previous Calendar Round cycle, it would appear that 1455 was its first occurrence there, which accords with other lines of evidence. But how does this fit with 1507 being the first 2 Acatl New Fire ceremony, as commemorated on the Teocalli? In discussions of the 1455 ceremony, Chimalpahin refers only to Huixachtecatl (the hill), but regarding the 1507 ceremony, he states that it was held at Huixachtlan (the temple) on Huixachtecatl (the hill).[57] Whatever took place on Huixachtecatl in 1455, there appears not to have been a New Fire temple there, and so, if there was a ceremony held there that year, it was a more rudimentary one, perhaps of the sort I suggest, to follow the formal one commemorated at the Templo Mayor in 1454, in an effort to reinitiate the altered Calendar Round count in 1455.

What effect did the Aztec shift of the New Fire ceremony have on such ceremonies elsewhere? Every city would have marked the passage from one Calendar Round to the next, but a New Fire ceremony does not appear to have been a necessary or integral part of that, and none of the cities of the Valley of Mexico other than Tenochtitlan[58] celebrated it because, while the ceremonies were couched in calendrical terms, they were primarily political events. Their major purpose was to assert temporal control and subordinate all of the towns sharing that system. As a result, towns within the Aztec empire did not conduct their own New Fire ceremonies but instead participated in Tenochtitlan's, which set their calendrical cycle. The area covered by the Aztec calendar was extensive, and relays of runners carried the new fire to distant towns.[59] Smaller independent towns with few vassal communities had no need to hold New Fire ceremonies; only other complex polities with subject towns requiring calendrical coordination were apt to have these,[60] as was the case in Tlaxcallan, which held its own New Fire ceremony.[61] This marked it and its subordinates as independent by creating a similar zone of temporal coordination, but with a different initiating point from that of the Aztec empire. The same may have been true of Tetzcoco[62] and Chalco in 1454, before the former lost its parity with Tenochtitlan (and under whose New Fire ceremony it fell in 1507) and when the latter was still unconquered.[63]

In the Aztec world, this ceremony was also a celebration of Huitzilopochtli, yet, if this enormous ritual and political emphasis was placed on that god alone by the Aztecs, why was parity given to Tlaloc in the Great Temple? A symbolic interpretation of ritual structures does have benefits. For instance, one can look at a medieval French cathedral and recognize the symbolism of the west-facing front, with the altar in the east, reflective of the resurrection.[64] And such ritual significance may well be why certain architectural forms and orientations are selected and may usefully inform one about the nature of the symbolic relationships of forms and orientations. However, unfettered by the world, such interpretations often ignore inconsistent data, arguing that the symbolism is structural rather than empirical, and they do little to explain how those notions became important in the first place or why the cathedral was built when and where it was. The same is true of the Great Temple.

An alternative approach to the dual pyramid structure may be sought in its history. When the Aztecs arrived in the Valley of Mexico, they were an unimportant, relatively backward group. Moreover, their tutelary god, Huitzilopochtli, was unimportant and not worshiped or even recognized by any other group in the region. While each town, and even each calpolli, had its own god who might not be worshiped by any other town in the area, I suggest that linking Huitzilopochtli to Tlaloc was a conscious attempt on the part of the Aztecs to tie their provincial god to the most widely venerated deity in Mesoamerica. Thus, the creation of the twin pyramid was a political move designed to speed the acceptance of the Aztecs and their tutelary god by tying him to a widely accepted deity. And while it is tricky to appeal to later evidence to support earlier actions, the tributary offerings found in the caches of the Great Temple suggest that distant tributaries gave their offerings overwhelmingly to Tlaloc. It has been argued that the paucity of Huitzilopochtli's offerings reflects the fact that they were composed of perishable matter, like the images of the god himself, but there is little evidence to support this notion, and I believe that the more plausible explanation is that dedications in the caches were brought into Tenochtitlan by tributary groups and, to these, Tlaloc was either the only god of the two, or decidedly the more important, and their offerings reflect that. But at the same time, the greater emphasis on Huitzilopochtli reflected in the construction of the pyramid, which the Aztecs controlled, contrasts markedly with the pattern of offerings, which reflects non-Aztec orientations. I believe the Aztecs placed Huitzilopochtli on Tlaloc's level in the Great Temple to hitch their tribal god to a pan-Mesoamerican god in an effort to increase the importance of their own—but how might such an interpretation be confirmed?

One interpretation that focuses on the Great Temple expansion, inaugurated in 1487, claims that it had 13 vertical levels because it was constructed in four stepped platforms; since the pyramid base was square, that meant that the three lowest parts each had four faces (3 × 4

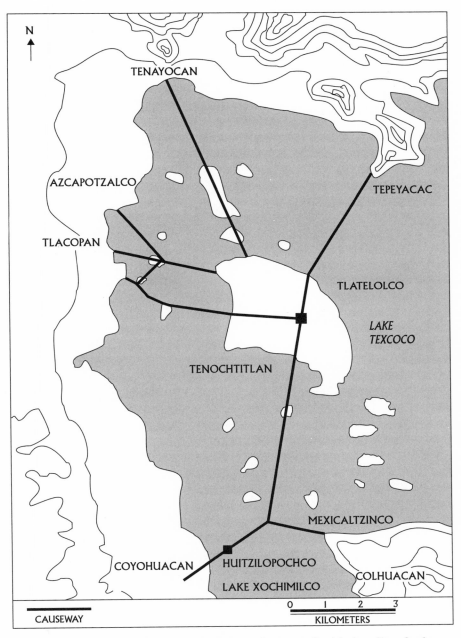

N

TENAYOCAN

AZCAPOTZALCO

TLACOPAN

TEPEYACAC

TLATELOLCO

LAKE TEXCOCO

TENOCHTITLAN

MEXICALTZINCO

COYOHUACAN

HUITZILOPOCHCO

COLHUACAN

LAKE XOCHIMILCO

CAUSEWAY

0   1   2   3
KILOMETERS

4-2. Tenochtitlan and the causeways connecting to the surrounding lakeshore (from Sanders, Parsons, and Santley 1979) (Map from drawing by Doni Fox)

= 12), which, combined with the topmost level where the twin temples sat, made 13.[65] But this analysis assumed the accuracy of the post-Conquest descriptions, which could not have been written by eyewitnesses (there was at least one subsequent expansion) and are therefore questionable; this interpretation also assumed a 13-level Topan at this earlier time, which probably was not the case. Moreover, it ignores the other incarnations of that temple, both earlier and later. One would assume that each would have to reflect the same basic structure, but the destruction to the Great Temple was such that this cannot be ascertained from the remains, and the other extant examples of dual pyramids—Tenayuca, Tlatelolco, Santa Cecilia (Acatitlan), and Teopanzolco—show considerable variation in structural styles, suggesting that extrapolating from a written description of an unobserved, earlier structure to still earlier or later ones is questionable.

Even if the 13 levels of Topan and the 9 levels of Mictlan can be applied to an analysis of the Great Temple, why could these not be applied to any building? After all, the Great Temple does not possess 13 levels, 13 stairs, or any multiple thereof that could convincingly be claimed as evidence of such an interpretation, and there are absolutely no subterranean levels to represent the claimed 9 levels of Mictlan. Thus, once the symbolic interpretation is torn free of the physical structure of the Great Temple, the assessment loses its force, since a similar interpretation can be projected onto absolutely any building— or none at all. These difficulties in sustaining a symbolic interpretation based on physical structure aside, there are several discoveries made at or about the Great Temple that throw this assessment into further doubt.

First, if the Great Temple is the axis of the world, as claimed, one would expect this axis to be centered on the structure, with the east-west axis passing midway between the two temples. But this centrality can be sustained only by taking the pyramid as the definitional center. If it is judged in relation to all of the other constructions in the city or in the ceremonial precinct, it does not appear to be bilaterally symmetrical. The ceremonial precinct was bounded by a high wall and entered by any of four gates that bisected the four sides and that connected it to the four major roads—to the north, the road became the Tenayocan causeway, to the west, the Tlacopan causeway, to the south, the Coyohuacan/Iztlapalapan causeway, and to the east, it ran to the lake edge. These four roads formed the axis of the ceremonial precinct and should logically divide the Great Temple, or at least the east-west axis should bisect it. But they do not. The pyramid is located eccentric to that axis, with the east-west axis running through the temple of Huitzilopochtli, rather than bisecting the pyramid as a whole.[66]

Second, there is an inequality between the two gods in the location of the date glyphs commemorating the pyramid's construction. Not all of the presumed date glyphs have been located; the destruction of the temple was progressively worse in later constructions (later phases encompassed earlier ones and were therefore larger, and the temple was leveled, leaving a series of truncations, and proportionally more of the later, larger phases were destroyed). Nevertheless, three date glyphs survive—4 Acatl (1431), 1 Tochtli (1454), and 3 Calli (1469), and perhaps a fourth, 2 Tochtli (1390)—and all of these were found on the Huitzilopochtli side of the pyramid, none on Tlaloc's.[67]

Third, the Great Temple was the burial site for many of Tenochtitlan's political elite. Cremation was the preferred form of burial, especially for nobles,[68] and several burial urns were recovered from the temple.[69] The finely crafted urns and their placement within the Great Temple indicate the great status of the deceased. Yet all of the urns that have been recovered were found on the Huitzilopochtli side in the upper temple, not on Tlaloc's.[70]

Fourth, the symbolic equivalence of Tlaloc and Huitzilopochtli suggests that the pyramid itself was bilateral with two equal temples on top. However, this, too, seems not to have been the case. Although the bases of only the Stage II temples survive, and that for Huitzilopochtli only incompletely, his temple is not a twin of Tlaloc's, but is, in fact, larger. And for that and most of the subsequent stages, the width of the stairways leading to Huitzilopochtli's temple is consistently larger. Archaeological reconstruction is inexact, and it might be argued that these were errors in restoration. But for those stages where the stairs were divided, the same relationship holds at the other three surviving Valley of Mexico dual pyramids—Tenayuca, Tlatelolco, and Santa Cecilia Acatitlan. At the different stages for each of these, the stairs on the Huitzilopochtli side are either equal or wider. This is also true at the major extant example beyond the Valley of Mexico—Teopanzolco—but there, the temple bases survive and Huitzilopochtli's was also significantly larger than Tlaloc's, something that cannot be assessed in the four other cases.[71] The same relationship is often true in pictorial manuscripts, showing Huitzilopochtli's temple to be larger than Tlaloc's,[72] and in written accounts—for the now gone dual pyramid in Tetzcoco, Huitzilopochtli's side was explicitly described as larger than Tlaloc's.[73] In short, the dual pyramids are not bilaterally symmetrical at all: Huitzilopochtli's side is equal to Tlaloc's or is larger, never smaller.[74]

If the pyramid were primarily ritual or symbolic, one might expect its enlargement to correspond to ritually important cycles, but the construction phases reflect kingly reigns rather than 52-year periods. In short, they were keyed primarily to political events, not religious or calendrical ones.

Is there any further corroboration of this assessment? I believe so, in the Teocalli de la Guerra Sagrada, though this again requires a reinterpretation. Fortunately, two major reassessments of this monument have led the way to what I see as a less symbolic and more practical interpretation.

In 1979, Richard Townsend argued that, although monumental art featured religious iconography, its primary purpose was to legitimate Aztec rule and to integrate the empire ideologically.[75] Thus, Townsend directly confronted Caso's interpretation, which stressed the myth of sacrificial genesis as the basis of Aztec ideology and emphasized religion as the main impetus of Aztec civilization. Instead, he argued that

[i]t is quite unlikely that the Mexica were somehow compelled to an unquestioning repetition of mythological archetypes, for myths could be adapted, regenerated, or created anew according to the policies of imperial states. While a sense of divine mission surely lent impetus and inspiration to conquest, such convictions must also have been visualized and forcefully promoted by powerful rulers wishing to unite a nation in imperial endeavors.[76]

This approach contradicted Caso's interpretation that the sacrifices required to create the present era established a blood debt that conferred upon the Aztecs the responsibility to continue sacrifice as an exchange of vitality and that warfare was therefore an ongoing, sacred necessity.[77] In Townsend's reanalysis, religion alone did not motivate Aztec rulers or impel them toward conquest. "Religion was simply the language, the vehicle, for a spectrum of ambitions and endeavors that were authenticated by a sense of participation in the transcendent reality of the cosmos."[78] In short, religion was used by the rulers to legitimate and reflect imperial ambitions and policies.

This shift in interpretive emphasis does not discard everything Caso proposed. For instance, the 13 steps of the Teocalli may reflect the 13 levels of heaven, the 1 Tochtli and 2 Acatl glyphs may indicate the dates of the beginning of the present era, and the platform does depict the earth monster. Moreover, Townsend accepts the identification of the figures flanking the sun disc as Huitzilopochtli and Tezcatlipoca, though he identifies the latter's accompanying glyph as alluding to Tetzcoco and its political alliance with Tenochtitlan. He likewise accepts the reading of the atl-tlachinolli glyphs and, tentatively, Caso's identification of the four gods on the sides, though he suggests that they may represent priests of their cults during the New Fire ceremony rather than the gods themselves.

In emphasizing the political as well as the religious, and seeing the former as expressed through the latter, Townsend stresses three themes in the Teocalli and other Aztec monuments: the universe as a sacred structure, the social and imperial orders as reflecting this sacred structure, and Tenochtitlan as the legitimate successor to past civilizations. In short, he views Aztec monumental sculpture as reflecting Aztec history and social organization, and as validating it in terms of the larger cosmological universe.[79]

In 1981, Emily Umberger also reassessed the Teocalli monument from a more explicitly historical perspective,[80] producing a reading of the iconography that differs even more significantly from Caso's. Though she still saw it as fundamentally focused on human sacrifice to the sun, Umberger dated the monument at 1507, based partly on the 2 Acatl glyph.

Much of her iconographic interpretation followed Caso's and concurred with the designation of Huitzilopochtli on the front left, but identified that on the right as Moteuczoma Xocoyotl based on the name glyph above and before him, which she convincingly established as his.[81] The back of the monument held a symbolic depiction of Tenochtitlan, and the 2 Calli glyph atop the monument referred to 1325, the date of the city's founding.

Most importantly, Umberger interpreted the monument as a small throne (momoztli) associated with Tezcatlipoca, upon which Moteuczoma sat in the guise of that god. With the king thus seated, "Sitting on the earth symbolized his dominion over the land; wearing the solar disc on his back represented his sacred duty to carry the sun."[82] She also focused on the dates on the monument, noting that three of the four—2 Acatl, 1 Miquiztli, and 1 Tecpatl—were associated with the New Fire ceremony and were found together on stone year bundles. The two glyphs on the front—1 Tochtli and 2 Acatl—she identified as the first two years of the present era, when the earth was formed and when Tezcatlipoca invented fire, respectively. Moreover, they indicated the years when the New Fire ceremony was changed—1506 and 1507. Thus, Umberger interpreted the iconography as supernatural when there were no apparent historical referents, but historical whenever possible, as in her readings of the 1 Tochtli, 2 Acatl, and Moteuczoma Xocoyotl glyphs. Moreover, she placed the reigning king on the monument and gave it an even greater political role than Townsend had. In short, she not only reinterpreted many of the personages and objects on the monument, shifting away from myth and toward history, she explicitly reassessed the date glyphs in linear (historical), rather than cyclical (ritual) terms.

I am convinced by much of the previous iconographic interpretations of the Teocalli and, while the monument clearly has ritual and supernatural implications, in light of the way I have reinterpreted the New Fire ceremony in the Aztec political world, I see it in even more historical and political terms than either Townsend or Umberger (but in discussing my interpretations, I will deal primarily with the points of difference). The pairs of figures on the two sides of the monument have been interpreted as gods—probably soundly as Tlaloc and Tlahuizcalpan-Teuctli on the left side, but less certainly on the right, which defy definite identification.[83] These two figures are quite similar, being posed the same and wearing the same garb, except for the slight differences in their sandals, facial decoration, and headbands and drops. The front figure is interpreted as a god primarily because of the exposed teeth. However, this portion of the sculpture is abraded, and the suggestion that he has exposed teeth, which indicate gods or the dead, arises from the great symmetry among the four figures. But if he is not a god, who is he? The answer, I believe, is in his headgear. That figure is wearing the crown of an Aztec king and, if he is alive, as the lack of exposed teeth would suggest, he must be Moteuczoma Xocoyotl, who is also depicted on the front of the monument. Who, then, is the rear figure? Because neither figure on the right side of the monument displays non-human facial features, like the pair on the left, and because the two figures appear so similar, if the one in front is a person, then they must both be human, albeit one alive and one dead. And the most likely candidate to appear strikingly similar to the reigning king, yet be dead, is a prior Aztec king, and most probably not Moteuczoma's immediate predecessor, Ahuitzotl, but his father, King Axayacatl, from whom his own claim to the throne derived. So I suggest that this is a depiction of the legitimacy of royal succession, similar to that found depicted in the Lower Temple of the Jaguars at Chichen Itza.[84]

Another striking feature of the Teocalli is that, while it honors Huitzilopochtli, its structure is quite unlike other such temples. When Huitzilopochtli is honored, as at the Great Temple (or Teopanzolco, Santa Cecilia Acatitlan, Tenayuca, or Tlatelolco), it is always on a dual-stairway pyramid atop which are temples to both Tlaloc and Huitzilopochtli.[85] Here, there is only one stairway and Tlaloc has been reduced in significance by being pushed around the side of the monument, though still on the left (north) side, as is normal (calculated as though the monument were facing west). The upper portion of the monument still holds two figures, but instead of being two gods, they are one god— the primary Aztec deity Huitzilopochtli—moved to the left (north), and the Aztec king on the right (south). Moreover, the left side is flanked by two other gods, whereas the king side is flanked by the king and his predecessor (or perhaps two predecessors, if the identification of the first as Moteuczoma is not sustained).

Further buttressing this division of the monument into god and royal halves are the pairs of shields, flags, and projectiles on the lower platform. The set below Huitzilopochtli includes atlatl darts (suggested by the double fletching, which would not hinder an atlatl dart); these are associated with the supernatural, as it was the god Opochtli who invented the atlatl, whereas that below Moteuczoma includes arrows (indicated by the single fletching and nock), which have no supernatural association.

Moreover, I concur with César Sáenz's assessment[86] that the year glyphs on the front are not incidental dates, but are meant to commemorate the date shift of the New Fire ceremony and are thus largely the point of the monument. In other constructions, such as the Great Temple, date glyphs are added to building phases, but these are generally placed at the rear of the structure and are relatively small in relation to the overall building. In the case of the Teocalli, however, both glyphs are in front and are large and quite prominent, suggesting a role greater than merely year dates, which are typically found in isolation. In fact, the 1 Tochtli (1506) and 2 Acatl (1507) glyphs do not merely indicate the last year of the 52-year Calendar Round and the first of the next, or denote the celebration itself, but commemorate the shift of the New Fire ceremony from 1 Tochtli to 2 Acatl. To denote the celebration itself, the 2 Acatl glyph alone would have been sufficient. And, while it has been noted that the two day glyphs on the upper portion of the Teocalli (1 Miquiztli and 1 Tecpatl) begin trecenas, this is true of all 20 day symbols that begin with 1. So although they may have been depicted for that purpose as well, trecenas are not generally recorded because they are logically included in more comprehensive dates. Instead, I suggest that these two days, which are also found on the stone year bundles, represent the 13-day leap year correction essential to the maintenance of the new Calendar Round, as these two dates fall 13 days apart in the tonalpohualli and xihuitl counts, and their function in this role requires that they be explicitly recorded.

All six figures, plus the two anthropomorphized day name glyphs, have glyphs emerging from their mouths that have been interpreted as the atl-tlachinolli glyph. This glyph means water and burned-over land and, as interpreted by Caso, signifies sacred war in which the object is to take captives for sacrifice in order to insure the perpetuation of the world. There are, however, some difficulties with this reading. First, what he refers to as a sacred war is the flower war (xochiyaoyotl), which has long been interpreted as a ritual war for the purposes described. But this interpretation results from looking at only the initial phases of a flower war. What began as a relatively stylized battle was, in fact, only the first part of a protracted struggle in which the Aztecs sought to subdue strong opponents, first through a demonstration battle that might yield voluntary submission and, if that failed, an escalation of the conflict until it became a war of attrition leading to outright conquest.[87]

Caso also follows the etymological and iconographic analyses of Seler,[88] who claims that the atl-tlachinolli glyph consists of a stream of water and a fire strip intertwined with it, though he identifies glyphs of water and fire lying side by side as the atl-tlachinolli as well. The surface of the fire strip is divided and filled with hooks or dots, which he associates with similar markings on glyphs for towns, earth, and fields; the ends of these strips often have a butterfly glyph. The hooks are used in other depictions to denote something loose, detached, or curly.[89] Seler argues that tlachinolli actually means "what is burned" and claims that the war implication derives from the word "atlatl," or throwing stick, or that the "atl" of atl-tlachinolli derives from an ancient notion of village, as does "altepetl," so that the term meant "burnt village."[90] He is rather expansive in his notion of what glyphs depict atl-tlachinolli or just tlachinolli alone, going so far as to include pictographs of burned grass in the Codex Borgia.[91] In fact, atl-tlachinolli translates as "water and scorched land."[92]

An excellent example of an atl-tlachinolli is in the Códice de Huamantla,[93] which separates two warring factions armed with shields (macuahuitls) and bows and arrows. Bows and arrows were not used initially in classic ritual war encounters, but were only used later, after the xochiyaoyotl escalated into a normal war of attrition.[94] Thus, the symbol indicates at least ordinary war, in which captives may or may not be taken for sacrifice,[95] and whether or not it also refers to ritual war, it is clear that it is a larger, more generic term meaning simply war.

That Seler emphasized the atl-tlachinolli as a ritual war is consistent with his ahistorical, symbolic approach to Mesoamerican iconography, but the fact that Caso followed this problematic reading does not refute his interpretation of this monument. It can be argued that the other martial elements on the Teocalli support a ritual war reading, since both Tezcatlipoca and Huitzilopochtli are gods of war; thus no further connection to the shields need be established. But the traditional

4-2. Atl-Tlachinolli glyph from the *Códice de Huamantla* and Atl-Tletl glyph from the Teocalli de la Guerra Sagrada (Drawing by Doni Fox)

atl-tlachinolli sign is an interweaving of the water sign with that of burned-over land in a sort of martial caduceus, whereas all of the glyphs on the Teocalli are distinctly separate and can better be interpreted not as a single atl-tlachinolli glyph, but as water (atl) and fire (tletl). It might be argued that the glyphs here are merely variants of the more common interwoven atl-tlachinolli glyph, though the interweaving seems to be an inherent part of that glyph. Moreover, there is another reason to suggest an altered reading of these glyphs.

The carving on the back of the Teocalli represents Tenochtitlan, whose founding is dated by the 2 Calli glyph on top of the monument. Sahagún notes, however, that Tenochtitlan was founded in a swampy area, at a spring called tleatl (the compound form of tletl, atl [fire, water]), at the place where there is burning on the water (possibly a reference to swamp gas [methane]), so that the glyphs emanating from all eight mouths reflect not bloodlust, but a reaffirmation of Tenochtitlan, the center of power, and the legitimation of that capital, as the back panel clearly does as well. A further complication in the reading of the "atl-tlachinolli" glyph is introduced by the fact that on the upper front panel, Moteuczoma is shown holding a ritual maguey puncturer with the tletl (fire) symbol alone protruding from its end, and Huitzilopochtli holds something similar, although his is detached (whether for artistic reasons, to permit the unobstructed depiction of his xiuhcoatl foot, or some other significance, is unclear).

This reassessment is not intended to eliminate the supernatural elements on the monument, for clearly they are there in abundance. Rather, it suggests that, while invoking ritual associations, the monument also addresses a number of secular concerns. First, it commemorates the importance and legitimacy of Tenochtitlan as capital of the empire. Second, it celebrates the elevation of the Aztec kings to co-equal status with the gods and ties the current ruler into a legitimate line of divinely blessed succession. Third, it elevates the specifically Aztec patron god, Huitzilopochtli, over Tlaloc, the more widely venerated Mesoamerican god. And fourth, it commemorates the ideological shifts that appear to have been introduced by the Aztecs in recent years—(1) a fifth sun rather than the earlier Mesoamerican notion of only four suns (commemorated in the 4 Olin glyph in the center of the sun disc), (2) 13 levels of heaven (Topan) rather than the previous 9 (commemorated in the 13 steps on the Teocalli, but this is not reflected in any of the dual-stairway pyramids, nor would it be expected, as many early versions would have been built before this ideological shift), and

(3) the shift of the New Fire ceremony from 1 Tochtli to 2 Acatl, which was first celebrated at this time (commemorated in the two large year glyphs and two day glyphs, 1 Miquiztli and 1 Tecpatl, which indicate the 13-day leap year correction). In sum, then, a practical reassessment of these codical, architectural, and monumental evidences of Aztec belief has produced an alternative interpretation of their significance.

Chapter 5

The Ripples of Time

The political purposes of the calendrical change are apparent, but the impact of this shift should also be seen elsewhere in Aztec society. The shift of the New Fire ceremony and the Aztec emphasis on linear time in historical accounts throw a different light on a variety of traditional interpretations. One of these is how the codices are understood.

Time and History

One place a more linear view of time is evident in Aztec society is their histories. Aztec histories were not comprehensive, but primarily chronicled political events, with supernatural occurrences being notable primarily by their absence. Although no examples survive, various groups apparently maintained their own historical accounts that reflected what was significant to them, but not necessarily to the rest of society. Thus, while merchants (pochteca), for example, played little, if any, role in the historical codices, they recorded their own history by kingly reigns in the accounts written by Sahagún. This did not reflect the same political concern in imperial expansion as the historical codices but, rather, illustrated their own interests in terms of what new merchandise was available as a result and who the leading merchants were at that time. In this case, exotic feathers were the most valuable commodity and served not merely as a record of the objects themselves, but as an indicator of the range and quality of the goods available during each king's reign.[1] Other interest groups, such as occupational guilds and certainly various priesthoods, doubtless kept their own histories as well, though the records of the native priests were consigned to the fires by which the Spanish priests cleansed the world of Mexican "devil-worshiping" books.[2]

The official histories were political creations, chronicling the events of state, rulers, and nature, but cause was not a concern and explanations were not sought. Rather, the historical codices were written in the style of annals in which the notable events of the year were recorded[3] without explanation of their importance, cause, or consequence. Nevertheless, some notion of what the Aztecs thought was significant is revealed in what was recorded: the coronation of kings,[4] their deaths and those of other high political officials,[5] the conquest of cities,[6] major temple expansions and other significant public works,[7] unusual astronomical events such as solar eclipses and the appearance of comets,[8] and disastrous acts of nature, such as earthquakes,[9] severe freezes,[10] droughts,[11] and crop-destroying insect and rodent infestations.[12] In short, what was important were the acts of kings and other political functionaries, natural setbacks that affected the state and to which it had to respond, and astronomical omens which, given the focus of the rest of the historical chronicles, were probably included because of their influence on political decision making.

But the chronicles omit other events that lack direct political impact: the deaths of anyone other than a king or high political official, virtually all marriages, the role of families, even royal ones, intellectual achievements, the construction or expansion of cities other than political or religious structures, and the role of any commoner or occupational group. Historical codices in the Aztec world were strictly political annals, and their compilers were clearly in the service of the king.[13]

Not all of the Aztec past is historical; part is myth, although it is not clear whether the Aztecs themselves drew such a distinction. In the mythical past, before the creation of the fifth Sun, the gods existed and acted, though they did so outside of time.[14] But once the fifth Sun was created, the calendar began again and, from that point on, when the gods interacted with humans, they did so at specific times. Such events typically took place in a dated though temporally unanchored past, a point in history that, even if a day or year was given, it was not tied to a Calendar Round that would give it a place in linear history. Rather, such temporal designations were in ritual time and occupied a position only in the context of its unspecified repetitiveness. Such commemorated events referred not to actual occurrences but were, instead, atemporal, mythical explanations for the Mesoamerican cultural baseline. For example, the atlatl is an ancient device in Mesoamerica dating back to at least 4000 B.C.,[15] so the Aztec story of Opochtli's invention is a cultural, mythical way of accounting for what is, not an attempt to explain a historical change at a specific time and place. And none of these mythical accounts—dated or not—find their way into the historical codices. Thus, they, like us, distinguished such myths from history, no matter how uncertain aspects of that history may have been. Gods interacted with people directly in myth (and doubtless in their religious lives as well), but not usually in history.[16] In the Aztec migration legend, however, from their departure from Aztlan (1 Tecpatl)[17] through the founding of Tenochtitlan in 1325 (2 Calli), Aztec history merged uneasily with myth, increasingly so as one goes back in time.[18]

Whether or not Aztlan was based on a real place, the legendary origin place of all the major central Mexican groups, Chicomoztoc (Seven-Caves-Place), from which the Aztecs also came (in 2 Acatl, 1194),[19] certainly was not, yet departures from both places have been given specific dates within the sequential series of Calendar Rounds that continued well into the Spanish colonial period. Moreover, specifically Aztec gods appear, such as Huitzilopochtli, Coatl-Icue, and Coyolxauhqui, at dated times (e.g., 1 Tecpatl) and specified locations (e.g., Colhuacan),[20] though whether these were always gods or were important personages who were deified over time is uncertain. In the migration histories, the Aztecs are recorded as staying at Coatepec for twenty-eight years.[21] But did they? There is no way of verifying this, and their migration accounts often conveniently fit with Calendar Rounds (wholes, halves, or quarters), which suggests a temporal shoehorning of the journey such that a stay of twenty-eight years does not necessarily reflect a specific length of time, but a relative duration compared to those recorded as shorter or longer. As the Aztecs get closer to the founding of Tenochtitlan, the role of the gods declines. But it is only with the origin of kings that history as a human endeavor emerges, because it is now that political history and time take on a meaning other than duration. With the emergence of kings at the beginning of the reign of their first, Acamapichtli, in 1372 (8 Acatl),[22] year dates lose their timelessness. Year counts are continued, of course, but kingly reigns become the periods of significance—conquests, disasters, constructions, and even the deaths of other rulers—all take place within the reign of this or that Aztec king, and each is specific, of different durations, and datable by year.[23] But it is the continuity of the reign that provides the temporal unity that the calendar merely dates.

There are no certain surviving pre-Columbian historical codices from central Mexico (although there are from Oaxaca[24]), and much of what we know of Aztec history is supplemented by the written accounts of early colonial chroniclers, since even the colonial historical codices in the native tradition offer a skeletal history at best. But more elaborate accounts, such as Durán's,[25] adopt the Europeanized views of history in vogue at that time, in contrast to the written style that follows the annal more closely, such as the accounts of Chimalpahin.[26] That there was a more elaborate explanation of events available to Durán, however, suggests that the historical codices were intended to be mnemonic devices that would allow learned individuals to expand on those histories.

Aztec historical codices use the calendar but reflect an ongoing linear temporality. Events occur sequentially and produce an ever-changing world. In contrast, ritual codices also invoke the calendar, but they do so in the endlessly repetitive cosmic time that is without duration and that admits of no unique happenings that alter matters in any fundamental way. Moreover, whereas religious events are datable in days and months, as one would expect in a cyclical account, the historical codices rarely note days, but focus instead on years, as befits a linear account.

As Donald Brown[27] has argued, societies with open social systems of stratification have strong historiographical traditions of critical analysis and constant revision, whereas closed systems have traditions that merely validate the extant social system. Aztec society was dynamic, royal lines vied for power, social mobility was not only possible, it was valued, and in such a society, a timeless justification of the status quo has little role except in religion. In civil society, history was real, ongoing, and contested, at least at a societal level if not by individuals or classes, as evidenced by King Itzcoatl's burning of the codices and rewriting of history after the Aztecs became an empire.

One thing that is common to most historical codices is the depiction of New Fire ceremonies, stretching back to 1143, albeit with some omissions[28] and some disparities in years among sources (attributable to mistakes in applying the Christian calendar, not the Aztec).[29] There are also emendations, such as one depiction of a New Fire ceremony under 2 Acatl (1247) in the *Codex Telleriano-Remensis* with a line attaching it to the year to the left, 1 Tochtli (1246),[30] which suggests some uncertainty regarding the date in the indigenous system. But overall, the New Fire ceremonies consistently fell on the year 2 Acatl as far back as the historical chronicles depict, which would seem to suggest an error in the thesis that the New Fire ceremony moved from 1 Tochtli to 2 Acatl in 1506–07.

This record of New Fire ceremonies in the year 2 Acatl going back to the beginning of recorded Aztec history is consistent in most of the codices. But in the *Codex Telleriano-Remensis*, the Spanish commentary notes for the year 1 Tochtli (1506), "In this year they were to bind the years according to their count, and because it was always a difficult year for them, Moteuczoma changed it to two reeds."[31]

If the authors of the *Codex Telleriano-Remensis* knew that the date of the New Fire ceremony had been changed from 1 Tochtli to 2 Acatl, one would assume that many, if not all, of the other scribes and ritual specialists would have as well. So why did they record the ceremony in 2 Acatl all the way back to the twelfth century if they knew that earlier New Fire ceremonies occurred in the years 1 Tochtli, instead listing them all—not just the one in 1507—as happening in 2 Acatl?

The answer lies in the fact that, whereas all the other incidents recorded in the historical codices are actual events that occurred in their respective years, the New Fire ceremonies are not and cannot be real events, or at least not real events that occurred in the years to which they are attributed. At the time of the earliest recorded New Fire ceremonies, the Aztecs were still a semibarbaric migratory group in the north, so it is doubtful that they were yet familiar with the Mesoamerican calendar or, if they were, whether they understood its functioning enough to use it accurately.[32]

The New Fire glyphs are alone in being consistently and regularly repeated in the historical codices; all other events are, or seem to be, random and unpredictable, such as the death of kings, the conquest of cities, severe frosts, the appearance of comets, and earthquakes. But, I argue, they did not, in fact, all occur in the years to which they are attributed and, in the earlier years of the historical record, they most likely did not take place at all.

It might be argued that the regular record of the New Fire ceremony stretching back some four hundred years simply reflects the crucial ceremonial and cosmological importance of the commemoration to the Aztecs—which I do not dispute. But that does not adequately address the issue of why they should record the ceremony in years in which they knew it did not actually occur, or in periods when it most likely did not take place at all. The confusion lies, I argue, in seeing the New Fire glyphs as indicative of actual events.

Alfonso Caso suggested, to mixed reception, that a pair of sculptured serpent heads found in Tenochtitlan that had a bar and three dots (indicating the number 8) and an accompanying 2 Acatl glyph recorded the Aztecs' eighth New Fire ceremony since leaving Aztlan.[33] Whether he was correct about these particular carvings and what they commemorate (and these have been assailed as not in the Aztec style,[34] though they have been explained as commemorative of the Xochicalan style[35]), his fundamental argument is well founded: the Aztecs did know how many New Fire ceremonies had been celebrated.[36] This is not reflected iconographically in the historical codices[37]—that is, the ceremonies are not numbered—but it is a frequent point of comment in the written histories compiled shortly after the Conquest and was thus something of which the chroniclers were very much aware. But why should this matter? The enumeration of New Fire ceremonies is significant not because it is important to know how many have occurred for their own sake, but because this enumeration is crucial to the Aztec notion of time and history.

It is a commonplace to contrast the Maya calendar, whose zero-date of 3114 B.C.[38] initiated its continuous long count, with the Aztec system of endless, yet discontinuous, 52-year cycles and to see the latter

5-1. Serpent head with the numeral 8 and the 2 Acatl glyph (Drawing by Doni Fox)

especially as producing a defining cultural notion of cyclical time and endlessly repetitive history. Because the Aztec calendar lacked a zero date, it is often argued, the Aztecs lacked a linear history.[39]

While it is frequently pointed out that an Aztec date that is not part of a Calendar Round sequence cannot be located with certainty, much like a specific Fourth of July cannot be located without a year date attached, the corollary of this idea is that only by recording complete runs of back-to-back Calendar Rounds can a long-term history be achieved. Any gap in recorded years leaves the detached portion hanging in an undatable past. If the Aztecs had actually possessed a cyclical notion of history, such a sequential layout of Calendar Rounds to achieve linear history would not have been needed, nor would the serial enumeration of the New Fire ceremonies. After all, if the New Fire ceremony is merely the commemoration of an event in cyclical time, why record the number of repetitions instead of the ceremony itself? Perhaps the answer lies in reconceiving the New Fire ceremony and the accompanying Binding of the Years (Toximmolpilia), which was directly associated with the New Fire ceremony.[40]

The Binding of the Years is commemorated by stone year bundles.[41] These bundles are considered to symbolize the bundling or completion of 52 years of the ending Calendar Round, which are tied and burned in their wooden manifestation.[42] The extant carved stone bundles never contain 52 sticks, however, but always more or fewer, based on counts of the visible ends of the sticks' carvings or on the number of sticks depicted on the bundle's exterior and extrapolating to a total. While it is true that these stone bundles may merely be symbolic of 52 sticks rather than being an accurate stone reproduction, if they were as important as they would seem to be, a more accurate stick count would be expected. After all, in the historical codices, each individual year is depicted, even when it is only one in a group. But the term "Toximmolpilia" does not necessarily mean that the past 52 years have been bound together. Linguistically, Toximmolpilia just indicates years and does not specify past years, and I suggest that it refers to the tying of the past 52 years to the next 52 years; the ceremony signals a tying together of otherwise largely independent cycles broken by a leap year correction to create continuous linear time. After all, at the New Fire ceremony, the previous 52 years are already finished and the year bundles under the traditional interpretation would serve no more than a commemorative function, but a linking of the 52-year cycle just ended with that just beginning serves vital calendrical, if not ritual, purposes. And

5-2. Stone year bundle with 2 Acatl glyph commemorating the Binding of the Years (Drawing by Doni Fox)

in 1507, if the New Fire ceremony had been moved from 1 Tochtli to 2 Acatl, this year "jump" from the traditional New Fire ceremony time may have rendered the year bundles particularly significant.

The late importance of the commemorative stone year bundles, that is, when the New Fire ceremony began to be celebrated in 2 Acatl, seems to be borne out. Most of the extant examples have the year glyph 2 Acatl and those with day glyphs have 1 Tecpatl and 1 Miquiztli,[43] the same glyphs found on the Teocalli de la Guerra Sagrada and the dates of the birth and death of Huitzilopochtli (and thus they would not have been important before the rise of the Aztec empire). All of this suggests that the stone year bundles were either a 1507 innovation or became particularly important at that New Fire ceremony.

This reinterpretation of the Binding of the Years not as the commemoration of the completion of the past 52 years, but as the linkage of the ending and beginning Calendar Rounds, dovetails nicely with the New Fire glyphs depicted in the historical codices. These glyphs are attached to the wrong years before 1507 (i.e., to 2 Acatl rather than 1 Tochtli), and knowingly so at least in the case of the *Codex Telleriano-Remensis*.[44] But how can these ceremonies be so important, especially in their cyclical time role, if they are dated incorrectly on purpose?

That question assumes the traditional interpretation is true, that these are intended to reflect actual events that transpired in those years. But the historical chronicles of most other Mesoamerican groups, including the Maya, Zapotecs, and Mixtecs, do not mark the New Fire ceremony.[45] And while tentative indications of New Fire ceremonies have been suggested for other calendars, including those of the Olmecs, the Maya, and the Mixtecs,[46] no one has compellingly demonstrated that they are actually New Fire ceremonies or, if they are, that they play the same role as in the Aztec calendar.[47] The New Fire ceremony becomes important in non-zero-date calendars where there are no cycles larger than the Calendar Round because it commemorates the linkage of the old and new 52-year cycles. Such a festival would be relatively unimportant in zero-date calendar systems, since larger temporal cycles overlapped the Calendar Rounds and no temporal break would be apparent or cause concern.

But not only was the New Fire ceremony not a universal characteristic of non-zero-date calendars, it was observed only in political centers which controlled the calendar. Thus, Tenochtitlan celebrated the New Fire ceremony, but its subordinate cities did not, as the ceremony was more a marker of political dominance than of calendrical necessity. Commemorative stone year bundles have been found in Tenochtitlan and, if everyone else were freely celebrating the adjusted New Fire ceremony, one would expect to find them distributed widely. Yet they are not. While stone year bundles were discovered in Tenochtitlan's skull racks, they were not found at either Cholula, which has no pyramid dedicated to Huitzilopochtli, or at Tenayuca, which does. Caso[48] argues that year bundles must have been there because he views the calendar as reflective of general ideology, and he rationalizes the absence of year bundles by arguing that these examples were probably made of real reeds that have since rotted away. Stone year bundles *might* be found elsewhere, but their presence in the capital and their absence elsewhere, I would argue, more likely reflect the political nature of time and the calendar. Year bundles with 2 Acatl, 1 Tecpatl, and 1 Miquiztli glyphs reflect Tenochtitlan's control of that specific calendrical time, and since the New Fire ceremony was celebrated only by the political center, I would expect to find them only as indicators of political allegiance to that center. Consequently, projecting the classic New Fire ceremony as described for Tenochtitlan to other times and other places is generally unwarranted; the ceremony was both a requisite of non-zero-date calendars and a political corollary of state-level calendrical control.

Moreover, the New Fire glyphs in the historical codices only incidentally marked actual ceremonies. Rather than being commemorative of actual events, the New Fire glyphs served merely as temporal markers that denoted 52-year periods, as their enumeration in written chronicles substantiates. They mark abstract temporal durations of 52 years, as can be seen in the whole, half, and quarter Calendar Rounds that appear so often in historical events shown in codices since the Aztecs' departure from Aztlan,[49] yet the fact that that departure is not marked by the New Fire ceremony argues for the New Fire ceremony glyphs as primarily counting devices rather than rituals. Indeed, marking the New Fire ceremony is unnecessary since the way the year count operates, going sequentially through the 4 year symbols and 13 year numbers four times in each a Calendar Round of 52 years should be indicator enough.

A similar situation is found in ancient Greece. There, each city-state's history was initially tied to the reign of its own kings, a chronological system that functioned adequately as long as the concern was domestic. But with expansion and foreign contacts, local histories were inadequate to incorporate the chronicles of other groups in a meaningful fashion.[50] To overcome the problem created by a plethora of local histories and idiosyncratic chronologies, the Greek historians used olympiads—the sequence of athletic gatherings that took place every four years and that thus provided a chronologically abstract, content-free temporal yardstick against which events everywhere could be placed and therefore coordinated.[51] This creation of an abstract time unrelated to domestic events allowed the Greeks, for the first time, to bring the histories of other peoples into their own chronological construct. History was no longer just the events of this city or that, lacking any coordination with comparable events elsewhere. The abstract Calendar Round served the same purpose. It allowed the expanding Aztecs to relate the events of other peoples to their own historical chronology.

The creation of this abstract time marker based on a 52-year cycle, rather than on kingly reigns, allowed the Aztecs to create a broader history, just as the use of olympiads allowed the ancient Greeks to do the same, albeit in a somewhat different fashion. The Greeks did not spread the use of olympiads as a historiographical device to other peoples. The Aztecs, by contrast, did spread their calendar but accomplished much the same thing historiographically. If the 1 Tochtli to 2 Acatl shift was merely an adjustment in the time of a ceremony, however, it should have been recorded as a historical occurrence that took place in 2 Acatl, as of 1507, but in 1 Tochtli in earlier years; the fact that it was not strongly supports the interpretation that something more significant was involved.

That the New Fire glyphs do not fall on the actual years in which the ceremonies were celebrated prior to 1507 is wholly irrelevant. Commemorating actual ceremonies was not their purpose, and it is only so assuming that creates the problem in codex interpretation. Indeed, it is the fact that the New Fire glyphs in the historical codices are not events but abstract time markers that allows the 1 Tochtli to 2 Acatl shift to go entirely without comment in all but the *Codex Telleriano-Remensis*, and there only in the Spanish gloss. Even then, the codex did not commemorate the change as an important event, but merely a shift in forms of measurement, much like the change from the Julian calendar to the Gregorian passed without lingering effects, and we now project the Gregorian dates back to Julian times, generally without comment.

This trend toward a more cosmopolitan history can be clearly seen in the historical codices and, after the Aztecs began their empire, political events elsewhere (notably the death and succession of kings[52]) are noted in Tenochtitlan's history, which had earlier been inward looking. At the same time, the Aztecs spread their own calendar with its distinct 2 Acatl New Fire ceremonies among those it conquered[53] so that their histories, too, now reflected not just local events, but also the deaths and successions of Aztec kings, though not typically those of other rulers.

That the Aztec historical codices then projected this new chronological system based on 2 Acatl back in time, and not just forward, is entirely typical of calendrical reforms. The Christian calendar is nominally based on the birth of Jesus, yet this chronology contains a number of logical problems. First, the actual birth of Jesus appears to have been in 8 to 4 B.C., not A.D. 1.[54] Second, if the nativity was, as conventionally celebrated, on December 25, the year that nominally begins with Jesus' birth actually started almost a full twelve months prematurely. In fact, the celebration of Christmas was actually timed to correspond with the Roman sun festival at the winter solstice.[55] And third, although we may date the invasion of Rome by the Visigoths at A.D. 410[56] and the earliest celebration of Christmas occurred in A.D. 336,[57] the first use of an A.D. date appears in 525, with B.C. not being used until the seventeenth century,[58] yet we unhesitatingly project it back in time, just as have other groups with their own calendrical traditions, including Muslims, Jews, Maya, and Aztecs, as well as the Imperial Chinese in 114 B.C., when Emperor Wu-ti retroactively renamed years based on the beginning of his reign.[59]

It is the fact that the New Fire glyphs are regular and repetitive that has accentuated their supposed cyclical role and obscured their actual linear functions. The Aztecs—at least the intelligentsia—knew the number of New Fire ceremonies that had been celebrated since their legendary departure from Aztlan (eight), with the result that they had over four hundred years of continuous, linear history, rather than just an untethered endlessly repetitive cycle of 52 years. A zero date is not crucial to a concept of linear time or secular history. What is needed is a *sense* of linear time and, in the Aztec case, this was event-focused, not time-focused. The Aztecs used their myth of the migration from Aztlan as the beginning point from which they sketched their history forward,[60] though it has also been argued that after the Aztecs shifted the New Fire ceremony, they adjusted their history to fit the new patterns.[61] But Aztec years did not need to be absolutely located in time, like Maya dates. It was enough that they be located in sequential time. Moreover, using the New Fire ceremony as a "zero" date can be added to any existing Mexican calendar without upsetting the system. In this respect, it is similar to the central Mexican glyphs that are not tied directly to a specific language, as are the Maya syllabaries, but can be used throughout the region with an ethnically and linguistically heterogeneous population. A change, such as that made by the Aztecs, may require adjusting the calendar a bit, but it can all be accommodated within the logic of the system, whereas a change in the Maya calendar would require a total restart or a falsification of past dates. Consequently, the Mexican calendar is a more useful system for purposes of political integration. That this was not much commented upon by the Spaniards may reflect the fact that the 52-year periods had no associated gods and thus did not offend them. Furthermore, centuries as explicitly recognized temporal units, such as the sixteenth century, were not even used in Europe at that time[62]: the sequential numbering of years had been practiced in Europe since the sixth century[63] and there were de facto centuries in their calendrical system, but they were not yet explicitly conceived as temporal units.

How does this reinterpretation of the calendar and the role of the New Fire ceremony affect the prevailing view of the ceremony's shift as the result of an inauspicious famine year? The timing of the New Fire ceremony within the calendar year in relation to the occurrence of a famine has already been discussed as historically improbable. And if the year count continued as usual after the shift to the 2 Acatl New Fire ceremony (which it did), and the change involved only the movement of a ceremony but nothing else about the calendar, the ritual importance of the New Fire ceremony is undermined. It might be argued that such a shift was entirely feasible if the New Fire ceremony was, and always had been, only a time marker, but that idea ignores the importance placed on it and its role in the continuation of time and the world as chronicled by numerous historical accounts. Furthermore, moving the event to a point within the year greatly diminishes its role as a year counter. These considerations, which present significant problems for an ideological interpretation, are overcome by viewing the New Fire ceremony in a political light, as establishing a new, distinctive calendar that is spread throughout the empire to control the flow of tribute; creating a new year date for the New Fire ceremony was an ideal means of keeping all of the dispersed calendars synchronized because it established a distinct system within a shared tradition.

Time and Religion

Although the overt changes the Aztecs made in the calendar by shifting the New Fire ceremony were minimal, the impact elsewhere was nevertheless significant beyond its political purposes. Other than the local rulers, the group most directly affected was the priesthood, both foreign and domestic. In the Aztec world, as in many other cultures, time was the province of the clergy. It was they who maintained the calendars, oversaw the cycle of rituals that tied it to the world, and marked the divisions of day and night.

But in addition to their importance supernaturally, the various cults were intimately tied to the Aztec state. Priests were trained in the same schools (the calmecac) as the political elite, they accompanied the army on campaigns, and they officiated at many public functions that had political purposes.[64] All of these ties to power are open and obvious; the less apparent connection between the priesthoods and the state—through the former's control of the calendar—has been largely overlooked.

State and public functions, such as periodic markets, must be coordinated; political officials must meet, hold dedications, and convene courts; social gatherings must be scheduled; and labor drafts and large-scale enterprises must be planned. To do this, the state and other social apparatuses took advantage of the regulation of time emanating from the priesthood, just as they had in medieval Europe. This parasitic use of religious time for other purposes does not make it political, but state manipulation for its own purposes does.

Given the close association between church and state in Aztec society, it is likely that the state's manipulation of the calendar was neither resisted nor resented. Rather, it was likely seen as almost no alteration in the existing relationship in which the state already relied on the priesthoods to maintain the calendars by which it scheduled its wars, regulated the flow of tribute, and patterned its markets. If anything, the state's manipulation of the calendar increased the importance of the Aztec priests, for now the calendar they controlled was spread throughout the empire.

A complementary effect can be presumed among foreign priests. The imposition of a foreign calendar could have caused resentment and resistance, even though the Aztec calendar was a cognate of other central Mexican versions. But minimizing friction in hegemonically controlled tributary cities may have been one consideration underlying the Aztec practice of nonintervention in local social and religious practices. And while the Aztec calendar did spread, there is no evidence that it was imposed; moreover, such imposition would have been counter to all other Aztec imperial practices. What was demanded, however, was that tribute be paid four times a year, with each occasion tied to a religious festival set according to the Aztec calendar. Local priesthoods could—and, in many cases, very likely did—maintain their own calendars, but the Aztecs' political demands meant that, as a practical matter, someone had to understand and keep that calendar as well, and this task fell to the priests. So the new calendar may not have been actively resented, since it need not have affected life locally, at least in the short term. In addition, because of the local priests' grasp of the workings of the new calendar, they actually gained ground, becoming politically indispensable to the local rulers. Thus, the calendar may well have been embraced rather than resented, at least by the priests.

The spread of the Aztec calendar, either displacing local variants or being maintained in tandem, did not, however, create a vast expanse of totally uniform time. The elite in major centers might all know what day it was in the Aztec system, but the difficulties in timekeeping would likely have limited the calendar's spread.

Regulating the calendar, making astronomical observations, and planning the normal rituals tied to the various temporal cycles must have consumed the attention of many highly trained priests, but the seemingly simple matter of marking the hours of day and night without some mechanized means of timekeeping also required considerable manpower, even though much of this was provided by novices. Nevertheless, timekeeping was important for the priesthoods. Being able to calculate temporal divisions more precisely allows them both to fix the points of daily rituals better and to demand stricter observance from the faithful, from which the cults would presumably profit in greater or more frequent giving. But whereas the hour-keeping enterprise could be maintained in Mexican cities, where there were numerous priests, the same was not true of the countryside.

Mesoamerican religious behaviors, rituals, and priestly organizations as described in the literature overwhelmingly reflect urban patterns. These descriptions and studies provide a picture of the most sophisticated, elaborate, and full religious life, but the majority of Mexicans lived in towns, villages, and hamlets, not cities, and even in the densely urbanized Valley of Mexico, at least half of the population was rural.[65] Except when these rural dwellers journeyed into cities for major festivals, Aztec religion as typically described would not significantly reflect the religious experience in the countryside.

Not all towns or villages worshiped the same gods, and most would honor far fewer than in cities. Consequently, not only would their rituals have been simpler, but their religious calendar would probably have been somewhat gap-toothed. The smaller scale of their priesthoods would also prevent their keeping the more time-consuming measurements (e.g., marking the "hours") and thus further restrict their ceremonialism by hindering the observance of temporally sensitive festivals. Moreover, rural priests would likely have been more lax in the demands they could make on the observant.

Equating the typical pre-Conquest Mexican religious experience with what is usually described in historical accounts is like equating the Catholicism in a rural Mexican village today with that of Rome.[66] So rather than assuming that religion in cities was the full pattern while that in the countryside was simplified and scaled down, as the historical accounts lead us to believe, it may be more useful to see religion as practiced in villages and towns in central Mexico as the norm, and the practices in large cities, and especially Tenochtitlan, as hyperdeveloped and elaborated as a result of size and scale, such that the latter should be taken as the exception. In effect, the scale and complexity of the priesthoods required to maintain an urban level of time marking meant that cities were pockets of temporally synchronized behavior surrounded by timeless wilderness. Nevertheless, temporal complexity is not likely to arise just in large cities as a result of urban scale, but primarily in politically dominant centers.

Empires encourage travel over great distances, and this often brings awareness of temporal variations that are not apparent from a single location. That time shifts with longitudinal change is well known from studies of the difficulties in developing clocks for shipboard use[67] and, more contemporarily, from jet lag. But before the invention of mechanical clocks and with the constraints of slow animal transport, such time shifts would not be apparent and, in the case of Mesoamerica, the longitudinal expanse is relatively small. Latitude is a different matter, but these changes do not produce time variations. Noon is still noon, no matter how far north or south one goes, but the duration of the day differs, as does the occurrence of solstices; the Mesoamericans recognized this variation,[68] which gave greater impetus to a centralized calendar as empires expanded.

Earlier and Elsewhere

Is this view of time and the calendar as politically manipulated applicable only to the Aztecs? If so, theirs must be seen as a unique case. If not, this pattern may have broader implications for the study of pre-Columbian Mesoamerica. Thus I will briefly and tentatively assess the political uses of time elsewhere and elsewhen.

Little can be said for pre-state societies in Mesoamerica, owing to the dearth of information. But given the role and importance of calendars later, the early stirrings of complex chronological awareness most likely had political purposes as well, even if not exclusively so. The centers of less complex polities were sites of major ceremonial events, and however the initial patterns of attendance by the people of distant settlements began, this sort of ritual coordination could easily have set the stage for creating a spatially expansive political entity. Normatively based attendance could easily become politically mandated as well. And the greater the frequency of these events and the shorter their duration, the more (and finer) the temporal coordination required, which, because of its growing complexity, becomes an elite function and spurs greater centralized control, especially as timing becomes more complex and breaks free of such easily observable astronomical events as solstices, equinoxes, and lunations. Thus, the formal calendar may have originated less as a ritual system that could be turned to political ends than a political tool from the outset, and one guaranteed to stimulate greater centralization of power.

Calendrical studies in Mesoamerica necessarily tend to focus on later periods in cultural development, concentrate on individual examples, and emphasize identifying the glyphs used and how they functioned. Such studies thus tend to be heavily descriptive, synchronic, and to focus on the Conquest era because of the great number of colonial descriptions of the various calendars, though there are studies of archaeologically known examples as well, including those of the Olmecs,[69] Teotihuacan,[70] Zapotec,[71] and Xochicalco.[72]

Among the few studies that seek some chronological or developmental dynamic are those by Alfonso Caso[73] and Munro Edmonson.[74] Caso's study makes little attempt to explain sequential developments in and of themselves, though some chronological changes are apparent. By contrast, Edmonson explicitly seeks to link and explain the evolution of the calendar from the original Olmec invention. His basic assumption is that a calendar system like the Aztecs' can be traced back to its Olmec beginnings, and he sees its development as the result of a series of evolutionary shifts. Assuming that Mesoamerican calendars were largely continuous over time has enabled researchers to generate a branching genealogical tree of shifting day symbols and year bearers.

Since the basic Mesoamerican calendar was widely shared,[75] regardless of the shift between mother and daughter calendars, the various examples can always be linked together if the focus is not on historically specific alterations, about which we are generally ignorant, but on how the calendrical system functions. Thus, if systemic shifts are assumed, only a change to a completely different calendar would show up in the record as evolutionarily inexplicable. But calendars change for historical reasons that cannot be as neatly defined or predicted as genetic changes. Indeed, the Aztec case provides an excellent example of calendrical change that could not be anticipated either as to timing or nature because it occurred for political reasons that cannot be detected by examining the internal workings of the calendar as a system.

For example, while knowing how our calendar works, I can easily calculate back to last October 12 and establish the day of the week on which it fell, simply from the logic of the system. And if someone asked me to calculate back to October 12, 1492 and determine the day of the week on which Columbus first made landfall in the New World, I could similarly produce an answer. When Columbus sailed, however, the Christian calendar was based on the Julian calendar, established by Julius Caesar, which calculated a mean year length of 365.25 days. Since practical calendars operate on whole days, the Julian calendar added an extra day—an intercalated day—every fourth year, so although each whole-day year deviated slightly from astronomical reality, the quarter day per year variation was quaternarily corrected for with little practical inconvenience. But the actual mean length of the solar year is 365.2422 days, not 365.25. This meant that adding a day every four years led to a slight overcorrection and, in the sixteen centuries during which the Julian calendar was in force in Western Europe, the calendar had advanced almost eleven days more than required to maintain its alignment with astronomical reality. And because of the problems this caused for the Christian ritual cycle—notably in the timing of Easter and the festivals keyed to it—Pope Gregory instituted a correction in which ten days were skipped over to realign the calendar with the vernal equinox. Thus, midnight of Thursday, October 4, 1582 was followed the next day by Friday, October 15, 1582. Thereafter, an intercalated day was not added to any centurial years (e.g., 1700, 1800, and 1900), which would have had them in the Julian system except those that were multiples of 400 (e.g., 1600 and 2000).[76] Even though it was a technical improvement dictated by astronomical reality, the adoption or nonadoption of this calendar was politically influenced. Most Roman Catholic countries adopted the Gregorian calendar immediately but, because of religious animosities, other Christian countries rejected it, only accepting it much later—1752 in England and not until 1917 in Russia.[77]

This change was a political alteration whose occurrence, nature, and timing are entirely unpredictable in the absence of historical records. This means that, without knowing that the calendar had been thus manipulated, and guided by the prevailing assumption in calendrical studies, I would have used the internal logic of the system to arrive at my answer for Columbus's arrival. My calculations could have been arithmetically flawless, but I would nevertheless be wrong. Columbus recorded landfall in the New World on Friday, October 12, 1492, but beginning from today's date and calculating back based on the logic of the calendar system—yet without knowing that a calendrical reform had been instituted in 1582—my calculation for October 12, 1492, would yield an erroneous Tuesday.

The same situation applies to the Mesoamerican world. There is nothing inherent in calendars as systems suggesting that they should change, or how. Changes that do occur in the Mesoamerican calendrical system depend on events and conditions entirely extraneous to the calendar itself. So Mesoamerican calendrical studies can demonstrate structural continuity but not necessarily strict chronological continuity; they simply assume it and use that assumption to structure their interpretation without regard for the changes that demonstrate the historically contingent nature of calendrical shifts. Taking the logic of any calendrical system and projecting it backward to interpret dates and systems assumes a continuity that is not demonstrated and requires a leap of faith that is unwarranted. It demands an assumption of no intervention in the calendar except those that were gradual, incremental, and logical, whereas the history of calendars elsewhere in the world suggests quite strongly that this is rarely, if ever, the case over such time spans. What, then, are the implications of abrupt calendrical change for our understanding of past Mesoamerican calendars?

The Mesoamerican calendar is generally attributed to Olmec[78] or, less likely, Maya origins, and certainly the massive structural parallels convincingly indicate a common beginning, but some fundamental early split divided it into the zero-date Maya calendar and the Mexican calendars, which functioned without such a fixed starting point.[79] The notion that there is a basic continuity in the calendar since its inception is buttressed by the significant parallels between earlier and later calendars, as evidenced by the presence of tonalpohualli, Lords of the Day, and xihuitl cycles, as well as year bearers that span many languages and even more societies. But because the evidence for specific early calendars is incomplete for any of them and the gaps between them are so large—often centuries—how they are reconstructed depends, to a great extent, on how much calendrical knowledge from the sixteenth century one is willing to read into the earlier scraps of data and how much cultural continuity is assumed.

Given the ubiquity of the Mesoamerican calendar, how and why did it spread? The social and ritual uses are so obvious for complex societies that the calendar's dissemination seems to need no explanation, and, indeed, its spread in Mesoamerica was early, pervasive, and coterminous with the state. But because keeping it requires a cadre of specialists, areas beyond the state, non-urban areas tributary to the state, and areas predating or postdating the state were unable to maintain the calendar, but also had little need to do so.

In any case, Mesoamerican states all presumably had the calendar, which was located and maintained in the city, where the core of the priesthood was found. But the surviving evidence suggests that calendars are more uniform when there are empires and more varied when there are only city-states.[80] Moreover, as the Aztecs spread their calendar for primarily political purposes, not ideology, and as it was an effective way of coordinating their tributaries in the absence of more efficient means of communication, I suggest that the same pattern probably held during earlier empires, since the same basic constraints on communication prevailed. Thus, the pattern in which there appear to be the fewest different calendars during empires and the most calendars between empires is not explained by a natural evolution of systems proliferating by gradual changes or culturally dictated increments. Rather, with no fixed starting point and no definitively established leap year intercalation to compensate for the .2422 days a year the solar year gains over the calendar year, each city's Mexican calendar would gradually deviate from the astronomical year and require correction. But leap year corrections occur locally and have a centrifugal effect on the overall coordination of calendars, since each one will most likely differ in the time at which such alterations are inserted and in how often and how many days are intercalated.

Astronomical considerations aside, maintaining an independent calendar is often a conscious act of asserting self-identity. For example, countries in East Asia equated independence with their own calendar era names, although they used the same calendrical system, so countries under the suzerainty of another used the era name of the suzerain country.[81] Without a shared (and centrally controlled) ideological basis for integration, which was weak or absent in Mesoamerica, with transportation too slow and inefficient to engender an area of coordinated time based on urban need, and with no overarching polity to maintain control, multicalendricality would have been the norm in pre-Hispanic Mexico. It is not just natural differentiation that changes Mexican calendars—space, separation, and the constant need to realign the calendar with the solar year would naturally achieve that—it is also, and most dramatically, their episodic unity. And that was the result of imperial expansion, the incorporation of tributary states into a single chronicity with the timing being determined by the priesthood in the imperial capital. Thus, Mexican prehistory was characterized by repeated imperial expansion and calendrical unification followed by political collapse and calendrical diversification.

What does this pattern mean for archaeology? The grand historical patterns of the rise and fall of Mesoamerican civilizations are already known, albeit debated. And since unified calendars characterize imperial periods, sustained calendrical unity can be taken as an indicator of political integration, even without other evidence of direct imperial control. After all, given the hegemonic nature of Mexican empires, there is often little evidence of domination in tributary towns based solely on traditional archaeological evidence of political control or other forms of social uniformity. Such was certainly the case with the Aztec empire. Thus, a shared calendar on an imperial or even regional scale should serve as an indicator of political integration.

How difficult would it be to impose a foreign calendar on conquered cities? In part, this depends on the power disparity involved, though adoption may have been eased by allowing the maintenance of both local and imperial calendars. But the greater the effort required, the more imposing a calendar undermined the empire's hegemonic control.

Virtually all of Mesoamerica used the same calendar in its essential outlines, which allowed the spread of the imperial version with minimal disruption. As a result, although the earliest empire may have had to spread its calendar into calendrically virgin territory, subsequent empires would have found these same regions preadapted to this type of tributary control. Indeed, the absence of a complex calendar in the desert north may be added to the lack of a complex political hierarchy and fixed settlements as reasons the Mesoamerican empires were relatively unsuccessful in their expansionary efforts there. But in addition to noncalendrical areas, were there other barriers to this sort of imperial control?

The major calendrical division in Mesoamerica is between those with a fixed-zero date, such as the Maya, and those without, which was the case in the Mexican area. Because Mexican calendars were not tied to a fixed starting date, an imperial demand that the local system conform to the centralized one would have caused only minor disruptions as the tributaries shifted the months slightly.[82] But a similar demand would have serious repercussions for a zero-date calendar. Dual systems could, of course, be maintained, but the decreased efficiency makes control, if not conquest, more difficult, more costly, and a constant source of cultural friction. Perhaps in the Mexican areas, with their great degree of linguistic, cultural, and ethnic diversity, there was no common event, real or mythical, that could have served as a zero date, so the free-floating calendars that emerged there were more suited to sharing by multiethnic communities. The extent to which this flexible chronicity affected the expansionary plans of Mexican empires is uncertain, but they definitely had to deal with it, as the displacement of the Maya calendar and the adoption of a Mexican one at Mexicanized Chichen Itza makes clear.[83] In the Aztec case, imperial expansion had largely halted at the lowland Maya periphery (although it did continue into the Guatemala highlands, where Mexican calendars had been adopted); this was probably an accident of Cortés's timing, however, rather than a function of the difficulty of controlling any tributaries at that distance.

In addition to the loss of political and economic control, the demise of empires also freed local calendars. This may have meant reversion to the local calendar in some cases, though where areas had long adhered to the imperial version, the latter were most likely retained. But even if they were, the imperial version of the calendar was no longer centrally controlled, and each city would be forced to establish its own system of calendar year/solar year realignment, which would result in the differentiation of what had previously been a unified system. This may well account for post-Teotihuacan Xochicalco, where some sort of calendrical correction was indeed made. And if any cities harbored their own political ambitions, establishing a strong, independent calendar was a prerequisite to establishing their own tributary systems if they were to attain any size.

Once empires relax their grip or collapse, the calendar system continues among the autonomous priesthoods of the various cities—rituals still need to be maintained and the state retains an interest in social coordination such that each city has its own need to maintain the calendar—but in the absence of some pan-regional basis or integration, be it political or ideological, each center is free to adjust the calendar as best suits its own needs, and the synchronicity that characterizes empires lapses. Coordination ceases, but the calendar is maintained and the persistence of this common calendar effectively preadapts the region to calendrical control if and when a new empire emerges.

The cyclical pattern of imperial rise and calendrical coordination, and then demise and calendrical fragmentation into semi-autonomous city-state systems that characterized Mexico, with its non-zero-date calendars, is suggestive when contrasted with the relative stability of the zero-date Maya area. Calendrical spread would seem to be easier in the latter, where everyone already shares a common calendar and starting point, than in the former.

What empires can do better, however, is establish new starting dates for the calendar and impose them on others. For example, the Roman calendar introduced by Julius Caesar on January 1, 45 B.C. was spread into "barbarian" lands with the legions.[84] Empires are—and must be—dominant,[85] and a shift to the imperial calendar, at least to its adjusted starting point, is a recognition of its supremacy and one's own sub-ordination.

While my main focus has been on Mexican calendars, this altered view of them has implications for the zero-date Maya calendar as well. If an area of homogeneous calendars suggests an empire, how can the classic Maya be understood? Their calendar apparently shares both uni-formity throughout the region and great continuity over many hun-dreds of years because of its zero date, and both these characteristics are widely considered to make this the superior system. But is the ca-lendrical uniformity touted for the classic Maya lowlands real? In the Aztec case, the calendar was manipulated for political purpose, which meant, among other things, that one cannot necessarily begin at a given date and calculate backward to reach an accurate earlier date. A logical extrapolation can be made, but historical perturbations may in-tervene, as they do in our calendar with the Gregorian Reforms, and these are invisible at a logical, system, level. Did such an unrecorded alteration occur in the Maya calendar, and, if so, how could it be de-tected? Or, perhaps more to the point, how can we know that such an event did *not* occur so that we can maintain our confidence in our read-ings of the Maya Long Count dates?

The Maya calendar, despite its apparent complexity, required no ad-justments and seems to have progressed from its starting date in an uninterrupted series of cumulative and increasing cycles, though the Maya did not celebrate the 52-year cycle.[86] As it needed no adjustments and was thus simple to maintain, the Maya calendar required fewer specialists in any given center. But while the uniformity of the calendar system in the Maya lowlands suggests integration, other evidence of political unity is largely lacking.[87] So could the presence of a common calendar suggest no more than an ideological linkage?

Medieval Western Europe used the same calendar through the Ref-ormation, spanning many different, and often competing, polities: the same type of religious unity that held Western Europe together calen-drically could also have held the Maya calendar together despite the many independent city-states. But there is little other evidence of such an ideological unity or of a missionizing religion that would promote it. In short, although either political or ideological unity can promote a common calendar, neither form of integration was particularly evident among the classic lowland Maya.

Nevertheless, there are two other possible explanations for this ap-parent calendrical unity. First, since the operation of the Maya Long

Count calendar was relatively easy, perhaps it simply spread like other cultural practices without requiring regional integration of some sort. After all, priestly organization, class structure, and the type and rights of kings throughout Mesoamerica were all widely shared yet imply little beyond an underlying cultural similarity. Even in Mexico, the basic form of the calendar was shared. But, second, the Maya calendrical unity was more apparent than real. How do we know that the Maya all used the same calendrical count that would yield the same dates for the same days? The evidence indicates that they all used the same calendar system, with the same internal structure, that calculates back to the same starting date. Unfortunately for this line of reasoning, the Western calendar and the Eastern Orthodox calendar would produce precisely the same types of evidence despite the fact that one is Gregorian and the other was Julian into the twentieth century[88]; they share the same essential structure in the form of twelve months with the same names, the same number of days in each (except on every fourth centurial year, which would be virtually undetectable archaeologically), and the same year enumerations, and they both ostensibly calculate back to the same zero point. Yet these two systems do not yield the same calendrical date for the same physical day. This difference is the result of a correction in the Julian system that produced the Gregorian, but which would be undetectable if one simply calculated back from the present. How can it be determined whether or not similar changes were introduced into the Maya calendar by any of the many cities that used it?

The only evidence for the uniformity of Maya dates other than the shared calendar system is stratigraphic analysis, which places the dated objects in an archaeologically determined span of years, but these are inevitably too broad to assess differences in dates of only days, months, or perhaps even a few years. There is, of course, no known third calendar, such as the Christian, by which different date glyphs can be independently correlated and then compared to other, similarly established dates. Consequently, this leaves only the prospect of finding a single unambiguous event—say, a total solar eclipse, the destruction of a city, or the death or accession of a king—that was recorded to the day in two different politically independent Maya locations to assess whether, for these two places at least, a common dating system was actually used rather than merely a common calendar system. But I know of no such paired set of precisely dated monuments.

In the absence of political or ideological integration, a shared calendar among the classic lowland Maya remains only an assumption based on the presence of an apparently common calendar system. A shift from one calendar system to another apparently happened at Chichen Itza, which may be excused as resulting from a Mexican intrusion.[89] But the Maya calendar system of the Terminal Classic and Postclassic also underwent some shift, as its dates differ from those of the Classic.[90] Perhaps the *lack* of evidence of differences has been too eagerly embraced as the *presence* of a common calendar, despite the fact that the same uniformity does not prevail later, when the evidence is better, nor does it hold elsewhere in Mesoamerica. And political practices elsewhere in the world suggest that, as Maya cities achieved independence or as upstart lineages ousted rulers of traditional ones, there would be sufficient reasons to alter their calendars to assert independence or to establish the legitimacy of new royal lines. For example, after their revolution, the French introduced a new calendar in 1792 of twelve months with 30 days each, which were also divided into three weeks of 10 days each, to which 5 days were added to the end of the year. This system met with little acceptance elsewhere, and even the French abandoned it in 1806,[91] as they also did their attempt to establish a "metric" clock of ten hours of 100 minutes per day.[92]

Uncertain factors, notably political, foster calendrical changes. After all, the original Mesoamerican calendar presumably possessed a zero date, yet the Mexican area abandoned it. There has been a tendency to feel that the Mexicans "lost" the zero date and thus had an inferior, watered-down version of the Mesoamerican calendar. But this perspective is flawed. The Maya calendar had a zero date from which the calendar built up by the accretion of ever-larger cycles. Because of this, it is held that establishing new starting dates was not permissible. Yet we know that new polities and even dynasties within old polities elsewhere in the world often restart the calendar, beginning with their ascendancy to power. Moreover, the Maya did not incorporate a leap year correction, which still remains true today,[93] so although their system could nominally be used to figure dates absolutely, these gradually fell out of alignment with the ecological year. As Pedro Carrasco notes,[94] the only major source describing Maya calendrical ceremonies is de Landa's,[95] which makes clear that these were not tied to seasons.

Because most scholars have been primarily concerned with how the Maya calendar allows the dating of monuments, that has been the analytical focus as well as the primary contrast with the Mexican area, where this cannot be done. But ignored in all of this is what the calendar could do for the people who used it.

The Olmec/Maya zero-date calendar had shortcomings that had to be overcome in imperial systems. Because the Maya Long Count calendar did not correct for leap years, even though it could theoretically establish a fixed date as far back as 3114 B.C., it was not in sync with the solar year. Every four years, it fell one day further behind, and the disparity was cumulative starting with the nominal beginning of the count. At an everyday level, then, the practical cyclical element was absent. The Maya could not declare a set of fixed calendrical points that would repeat accurately year after year, as the Aztecs had with their four tribute festivals. Furthermore, such points are not, and cannot be, completely arbitrary, but must be tied to social behavior. In the Aztec case, it was the harvest and war season that were dictated by the ecological cycle.[96] Specific ceremonies could be designated in the Maya calendar, too, but because it did not correct for leap years, they would gradually fall back, further and further away from the ecologically dependent social behavior on which they would be based. Such differences can be calculated, of course, but the likelihood of error within a large region is great, and keeping the points fixed to the ecological year deprives them of the social importance attached to the attendant festivals. So while the Maya calendar is a model of logic in which lesser cycles combine to generate ever-greater cycles, it did not adjust for leap years, which would throw off the mathematical logic of increasing cycles with the result that the calendar was not well adapted to the cycle that was most important socially, the solar/ecological cycle. Thus, it did not produce a means of predictably controlling preplanned behavior via the calendar, by which an empire might be regulated over long time spans.

The converse of these criticisms of the Maya calendar offer some insight into why the Mexicans adopted the system they did, however. The non-zero-date calendars of Mexico sacrificed the logical purity and precise linear calculability of the zero-date calendars in exchange for a predictable annual cycle. With the insertion of a leap year correction, festivals in the 365-day xihuitl cycle can be tied both to the calendar cycle and to the solar cycle, which means that they can be used to coordinate behavior over a wide area.

This calendar could be used to establish regular, predictable, and ecologically tied tribute dates over long periods of time, with the result that it could be used as an efficient administrative tool for regulating an empire that exercised control through indirect rule. Moreover, the non-zero-date calendar allowed the creation of its own sort of zero date through the New Fire ceremonies, which could be tied to politically auspicious events or rulers. As a result, the non-zero-date calendars offered a tool that made political expansion significantly easier and less costly than that available to polities using zero-date systems. So, the Mexicans did not have a calendar that was inferior to that of the Maya; the latter's one advantage was that it established fixed linear dates. This single advantage, though, was matched by the Mexicans in the arena of practicality: the Mexican calendar both facilitated the administration of empire and permitted the integration of larger spatial areas, which the zero-date calendars did not. Though the system lacked an absolutely fixed date, Calendar Rounds were counted and formed the basis for a supra-Calendar Round—a calendrical starting point which, albeit floating, was tied to political events of importance to the central power.

Chapter 6

The Colonial Transition

Mexico's calendrical complexity did not collapse immediately following the Spanish conquest in 1521. But the Spanish invasion did set the stage for a conflict between the Christian calendar and the Mexican. What followed was both confrontation and accommodation.

The spiritual conquest of Mexico has long been a staple of histories, and the Spanish imposition of Christianity is a much-discussed feature. Conversion was easiest among the young, who were now being instructed by Spanish priests,[1] and among political elites, who may have believed in the new faith, but who also underwent conversion in an effort to retain positions and privileges that were now subject to Spanish control.[2] Typically, however, the conversion process has been presented in terms of ideological shifts, with indigenous beliefs being displaced by Christianity—often fitfully, sometimes partially, other times only cosmetically, frequently conflictually, and almost always syncretically.[3] The Spaniards had initially planned to train Indians for the religious life,[4] but this experiment was cut short, and they were barred from priestly roles in the Church.[5] This reversal has been explained on doctrinal grounds: Christian orthodoxy might be contaminated by them. But focusing exclusively on belief systems does not capture the totality of the religious shifts taking place in what was now New Spain.

The substitution of Christianity for indigenous religion also meant massive cosmological shifts. The flat earth over which the sun god, Tonatiuh, journeyed each day was replaced with a round world whose rotation made the natural object which was the sun seem to move. The 5 Suns were replaced by the various ages of medieval thought.[6] The world that perhaps faced its end at the completion of each 52-year period now faced only one end, at the Second Coming, but rather than being the end of everyone, the faithful, and only the faithful, would be saved.[7] The multiple, nonexclusive gods were replaced by the Trinity and a multitude of saints. And to regulate it all, the Christian calendar was introduced and maintained by the Roman Catholic Church and its clerics.

Shifting Religion, Time, and History

The Christian calendar owed its imposition not to technical superiority, but to politics, though several related factors eased its adoption. Once the Aztecs fell, the imperial political control that maintained a unified calendar no longer existed. But there was also no longer any need for calendrical control over a broad expanse and thus no agency attempted to reestablish this. Instead, each town's priests managed their own calendar, which served local purposes admirably. Even had other rulers wished to reestablish a unified calendar, the political leadership of city-states was also subordinated.[8] Some were killed, but most were simply left in position, though in weakened condition, and often had more concern for their own future prerogatives than with the well-being of the regions over which they no longer actually ruled.

Once in power, the Spaniards employed their own calendar, and their priests spread it with special vehemence, since it was intimately connected to the ritual cycle of the Church and since the extirpation of heathenism, which was intimately tied to the ritual cycle of the Aztec calendar, was a major goal of the Spanish priests. In a famous statement, fray Diego Durán[9] argued that Spanish priests had an obligation to learn the Aztec calendar—not for its own sake, but to root out hidden idolatry. He cited an example in which some natives claimed to have converted to Christianity and wished to adopt the saint of a specific day as their patron; in fact, that day was the festival day of the town's pagan god, and they were attempting to hide their continued veneration of this idol behind the ostensible worship of a Christian saint.[10] But not content merely to foster the spread of their own faith, the Spaniards also destroyed the elite cadre that could understand, amend, and disseminate the calendar in its full complexity.

Beyond the religious changes, this shift in calendars directly affected how Indians used time and recorded their history. With the lapse of a central Indian authority to maintain the unified calendar upon which linear time depended, Spanish chronologies gradually displaced native ones. Pre-Conquest, the indigenous annals recorded the year's events beginning in February or March and running to the following February or March of the Christian calendar, in keeping with the later starting time of the Mexican year. Indigenous annal records continued to be kept by Indian chroniclers and to use the native year designations during the colonial period even though they typically did so in tandem with Christian numerical dates. But this demonstrates the ideological perpetuation of the indigenous calendar rather than the practical, as the year that was actually reflected in the annals had shifted the recording period away from the indigenous February/March through February/March cycle and to the Christian January through December sequence. Thus, events in January that should have been recorded at the end of one indigenous year (for example, an event in January of 1560 should be listed under 2 Acatl) were "wrongly" included in the next indigenous year (3 Tecpatl), though in the proper Christian one (1560), illustrating the priority of the latter calendar.[11] A long count was no longer maintained by an educated indigenous elite. Rather, local histories merely used year notations involving four repetitions of the 13 year numbers and thirteen repetitions of the 4 year bearer symbols to produce the 52-year sequence, and tied this to the Christian year count, without having to generate that cycle from the ground up, or to correct for leap years, since these were built into the Spanish system. The Spaniards seem to have made little attempt to eradicate native year designations; these were probably considered innocuous as they were not directly associated with native gods or rites, unlike days, trecenas, and months. Moreover, some synchronization was needed to tie Mexican history into European.[12] History for the Aztecs, as formally maintained in the codices, slowly came to a halt, though the paucity of pre-Columbian central Mexican historical codices makes it difficult to assess the immediate effect of the Conquest on these records. Pictographic annals with year signs and depictions were now often augmented with brief accompanying Nahuatl statements written in Latin script, but most such records trailed off in the latter half of the sixteenth century and increasingly became town accounts in which Spanish actions at the national but not local level dominated.

At the time of the Conquest, the European idea of history was still heavily influenced by the notion of God's plan working out in the world and the fusing of ancient models with contemporary events, but the humanist approach of making people and their actions the center was making inroads.[13] By the mid-sixteenth century, a more secular view of the world had emerged, and, though it was still a minority perspective, it was the intellectual forebear of subsequent historiographical trends.[14] But in indigenous histories, the same year-annal style of nondivine, causeless major events persisted, though it no longer reflected an independent intellectual tradition.

Politics and Change

When empires had expanded and spread their calendars, the replacement, though not immediate, was apparently virtually complete because the local calendar and that of the empire were quite similar. Their differences were not with the overall system, but with starting points and perhaps the emphasis placed on different festivals, and the slide from one calendar to the other was easy. The Christian calendar, by contrast, was radically different from that of the Aztecs, and offered an alternative cosmology and perception of the world and people's relation to time and astrology.[15] As a result, no simple slide from Aztec to Christian was likely, and simplified native calendars persisted in resistance to that of the Spaniards.

Part of the purpose in destroying the native calendar was to foster religious conversion, which dovetailed nicely with Spanish efforts at political control. With the calendars fragmented and left without central control, there was little likelihood of coordinated Indian resistance to Spanish domination. There was a unified calendar, of course, but it was Christian and remained in Spanish hands. One consideration in prohibiting the training of Indians as Catholic priests, though, might have been the fear that creating an Indian cadre that could use the calendar at an elite level could offer indigenous rebels an opportunity to achieve regional integration and threaten Spanish control. Relinquishing such a means of coordinating native actions over vast spaces was unthinkable. Thus, in addition to other means of destroying indigenous control above the village level, communities were kept isolated and no indigenous supracommunity organizations were allowed to exist.

The Spanish push to replace the native calendar was also aided by the decline of the indigenous priesthood. Before the Conquest, priests trained in formal schools drew support from the various cults and the state. But with the Conquest, the economic underpinnings of the cults virtually vanished. Indigenous priests had drawn funds from the performance of ritual duties, such as marriages and burials, and from cult lands,[16] much of which was received as tribute from distant conquered territories. With Christianity, many of these ritual duties were no longer performed by native priests, but by Spaniards. Moreover, the arrival of the Spaniards meant the reassignment of many lands, if not to Spanish *encomenderos*, then back to the towns originally owning them, which eliminated the bulk of the priestly finances. Unable to prop up their institutions in the face of such financial distress and overt Spanish hostility and destruction, the indigenous priests rapidly declined. Thus, the Spaniards pushed to eliminate the calendar, but the loss of the native priesthood also meant that no one remained who could fully comprehend and maintain the system.[17] As a result, it increasingly fell into the hands of folk practitioners who emphasized its divinatory and astrological aspects, and while various calendars continued to be used,[18] the native calendar now focused largely on the short-cycle tonalpohualli or an agrarian-focused xihuitl with no linear historical role.[19] Its historical functions declined, its political role largely evaporated, and what was left was primarily its ritual, astrological, and divinatory uses as folk practices.[20] And in 1559, when it was time for the next New Fire ceremony, it had lost its importance and was not celebrated.[21]

The Time That Was Left Behind

European notions of time did not accompany the Spaniards into Mexico immediately. Throughout the Conquest itself, there is no indication that the Spaniards relied on uniquely Western notions of time, other than the calendar, which they did keep. Lesser divisions, such as hours or minutes, are mentioned in the conquistador accounts, but there is little evidence that these emerge from the use of clocks, sundials, hourglasses, or other mechanical means of time assessment;

these are merely used as conventional descriptive duration markers rather than technical ones. Throughout the Conquest, it was the movements of large Indian forces that were significant and that dictated the timing, not Cortés's small party. The Spaniards, accordingly, relied on the same duration markers as the Indians—days, sunrise, noon, sunset, and so forth—which they used effectively.

From the destruction of the native calendars and the imposition of the Christian, however superficially it may have been grasped, a new, more detailed notion of time emerged. The concept of "hours" in Mesoamerica before the Conquest was not the one we use today and, in fact, should probably not be applied to pre-Columbian Mexico at all, if abstract periodization is meant. Instead, there were divisions of day and night, but these differed in length between night and day, and also varied with the seasons. Indeed, these "hours" likely served as markers of duration between significant points in the day that were not—and could not have been—of equal duration.

Ritual periodization had probably been important in Aztec Mexico for religious matters, as it had been in Europe,[22] and various temples announced the "time" by drums, conch-shell trumpets, and fires at night, though these apparently indicated significant points or events in the day and night rather than precise durations.[23] Daily time divisions for the bulk of Aztec society were based on the rhythm of social life—daybreak, eating, sunset, and so forth—with ritual time divisions playing little role. In other words, social practices dictated durational periods,[24] and as a result, Aztec "hours" differed markedly from those introduced by the Spaniards, though these were relatively new even in Europe.

European hours before the fourteenth century were remarkably similar to Aztec hours. They marked important points in the day, but they varied in length throughout the year.[25] Indeed, there were precious few mechanical devices to measure time in an abstract fashion. Candles could be used, but they do not burn for equal durations and depend upon someone being constantly alert to light the next candle as needed.[26] Water clocks provide some accuracy, but they also require tending and serve only problematically in the colder northern climate, where freezing is a common occurrence.[27] Sundials offer considerable accuracy, but they do not function at night or even during the day in countries such as England that experience prolonged periods of rain and overcast skies.[28] In short, before the mechanical clock, time was inherently uneven, so noting abstract periods of short duration was not particularly useful or necessary. Life was task oriented, not time oriented, at least not for periods shorter than a day.[29] Indeed, before the Industrial Revolution, there was virtually no awareness of hour time.[30] Oddly, that most rudimentary of time-keeping devices, the hourglass, did not exist until the early fourteenth century; it embodies the concept of a fixed hour of arbitrary initiation, which only arose with the invention of the mechanical clock.[31]

How clocks emerged in Europe, and for what purpose, is debated, with three different perspectives vying for dominance. One holds that clocks were invented by or for monasteries where the observance of designated hours throughout the day and especially the night served a ritual purpose, and there would have been a major impetus to create a more reliable and accurate measure.[32] A second holds that clocks emerged from the needs of the rising mercantile class to regulate commerce and contracts.[33] The third traces the development to astronomers and astrologers, who, being concerned with the motion of the heavens, both needed, and effectively already had, a means of measuring time.[34] Why mechanical clocks actually emerged need not detain us here but, by the Conquest, time in Europe had been thoroughly commodified, with hours and minutes marching in regular order and for uniform durations. With the creation of abstract time, timekeeping was no longer tied to the sun.[35] It is these hours—twenty-four to the day/night cycle and sixty minutes to the hour, never varying, day or night, winter or summer, year in and year out—that the Spaniards used when they came to the Americas.

Although the Aztec calendar measured the same phenomena as the Christian calendar, albeit with different religious implications, it was displaced. European hours had no precise counterpart in the Aztec world. Life was dictated by work rhythms, and the relatively imprecise Aztec "hours" did not pattern life in a fashion analogous to that of European hours. This conceptual vacuum could quickly and easily have been filled by the Spanish hours. But it was not.

The Spaniards were not greatly concerned about imposing Western hours since Aztec life did not revolve around them. They relied on natural time markers, such as dawn, noon, and dusk, to coordinate short-term public interaction. So there was little impetus to replace native patterns with mechanical clocks, which permit more finely tuned interactions, such as a meeting at 10:30 A.M., which has no ready or precise natural correlate.

To use preestablished times for coordinating activities requires prior notice and is not adequate for everything. Signaling devices, such as trumpets, drums, or signal fires, could be used when the need to coordinate was immediate, much as small-town volunteer fire departments in the United States used to employ a central siren to summon their members. But these devices are not functionally analogous to clocks, as there are significant differences between signaling an immediate need and using some natural time indicator to trigger a preestablished gathering.

Immediate needs demand an immediate response by everyone at the same time. And while a central signal will alert everyone within range at the same time, their responses will necessarily differ by their distances from the response point. As a result, the larger the expanse involved, the more the response will be staggered according to arrival time. A preset time, by contrast, enables everyone to begin journeying toward an established place at different times to compensate for their varying distances, producing a common arrival to the central place.

Introducing clocks and the precision these permitted would, in effect, build an entirely new social edifice around which any practice could be structured. Calendars are useful in exercising political control over a large expanse because the durations in question are days. Hours, on the other hand, are not as useful for broad-expanse political control under the technological constraints of the day. But they could coordinate and control political activity within short expanses for at least local purposes. Any Indian capacity to mobilize themselves in a coordinated way concerned the Spaniards, and public clocks were not widely used.

Of the various time-keeping mechanisms introduced by the Spaniards, one of the simplest was the sundial. Sundials are accurate and relatively simple to construct, once the mathematical principles are understood. But they had little impact on social patterns in Mexico owing to a series of drawbacks. Sundials cannot serve the great public function that clocks can because they have to be situated to cast the sun's shadow across their face, which limits their positioning. If placed horizontally, they cannot be seen from a distance, whereas if they are placed vertically, they are more visible but cannot be seen from all directions. Thus, they do not serve well as public timekeepers for great expanses. Moreover, sundials are accurate only relative to the sun. That is, they measure the sun's position in relation to a fixed point, but any shift in longitude effectively means a shift in time, so two towns separated by as little as five miles will record noon at two different times.

Thus, while sundials are accurate for given locations, they do not measure time in a way that is useful over a large spatial expanse.

The most familiar example of the need to coordinate time over space is the emergence of time zones in the United States. In the mid-nineteenth century, each town maintained its own clock and, in the absence of any means of linking these spatially dispersed timekeepers, the sun provided the sole means of regulating them. But longitudinal differences meant that each town was effectively in its own time zone, as the sun would reach its zenith at a slightly different time in every community.[36] This geographical difference, exacerbated by the mechanical uncertainties of the clocks, in addition to human observational error, created a temporal patchwork across the country. This lack of uniformity, however, had little practical importance since town clocks regulated local time and activities. Travel, even by the swiftest stagecoach, was too slow and uncertain to create significant scheduling difficulties. But all this changed with two innovations, the railroad and the telegraph.

Railroads quickly achieved the speed and reliability that demanded accurate schedules,[37] especially where more than one railroad company intersected or shared lines, which instantaneous telegraph linkage permitted.[38] But in the United States, the government failed to address the need to measure time uniformly (the first institutions that measured time accurately and provided it to paying subscribers were commercial businesses[39]). And as long as coordinated times were not possible, each railroad operated according to its own time, creating a nightmare of coordination where railroads intersected.[40] To solve this problem in the face of government inaction, the heads of the railroads met in 1883 and adopted a standardized time system in which the country was divided into time zones.[41] Social and political considerations did play a part in creating the time zones, but the basic idea was to extend the Greenwich time system to the United States, based on the logic that, since there are 24 hours in a day and the earth, as a sphere, has 360°, then each 15° of east-west travel is a different hour.[42] This created uniform zones within each of which the relation to the sun was only general; that is, the sun may be up in the eastern portion of a time zone while it is still dark in the western portions at the same 6 A.M. hour. But the compensating virtue of this distortion was that it created a region of uniform time within which coordinating social behavior was much easier.

Sundials cannot coordinate time over vast expanses, though at the

6-1. Bell tower and sundial atop the west side of the cloister to show the A.M. hours in Convento de Churubusco, Mexico City [Photo by Ross Hassig]

technological level of sixteenth-century Mexico, there was little likelihood that anyone could travel quickly enough that the disparity in time would have been meaningful. Nevertheless, sundials are best at socially integrating a small area, and at least those that survive from colonial Mexico tend to be located within church cloisters and served as timekeepers not for the public, but for the internal purposes of the religious, which is evident from their locations, facing into internal courtyards and often located on east and west walls, with the western sundial marking the morning hours and the eastern one the afternoon.[43] For instance, the Convento de Churubusco in Mexico City has two sundials set internally on the eastern and western sides of its cloister; the inward facing western sundial marks the morning hours and the inward-facing eastern one marks the afternoon hours.

One non-clock timekeeper that was introduced into Mexico by the Spaniards, and that had pre-Columbian parallels, was bells.[44] These served to punctuate the day and to serve notice of immediate activities, notably masses, in the same fashion as trumpets and drums had before the Conquest. At a more subtle level, these bells—which were far larger than the pre-Columbian examples—also served as a reminder of Spanish control.

Bells had long been an indicator of religious as well as secular functions, but they had commonly been joined by clocks in any European town that could afford them.[45] The church bell is virtually the sole remnant of a period in early medieval Europe when bells unrelated to clocks created social time. These emerged in monasteries and churches as early as the fifth century to mark hours.[46] Although hours were then of uncertain beginnings and durations, bells nevertheless marked points in time that could be used by everyone within aural range. And early in this millennium, church bells were joined by a competing host of secular bells that pealed to mark municipal events, such as public assemblies, fires, and wars. But with the elaboration of bell ringing to include storms, funerals, punishments, guild activities, and work schedules, cities became cacophonous and strict regulations on bell ringing were imposed.[47]

An alternative or—more likely, complementary—explanation for the reliance on bells in New Spain rather than clocks lay in labor control. If clocks were publicly accessible, the duration of the Indians' various labor obligations could have been generally known and timed, much like laborers in the eighteenth century bought pocket watches to insure the reliability of factory clocks, which were believed to be deliberately slowed during working hours to extract additional labor from the employees.[48] The signaling of public time by bells under the control of Spanish religious or political leaders made time manipulation easy for the Spaniards to accomplish and difficult for the Indians to challenge, even as it increasingly intruded into their lives.

Bells alone predominated in the vast majority of early colonial Mexican churches, as there was no pre-Hispanic public timekeeper with which the European notions of time had to compete. As public indicators, bells emphasized public meetings—usually religious—but created only isolated pockets of socially coordinated activity, with each town relying on its own bells, which roughly ordered the lives of everyone within earshot.[49]

Mechanical clocks, however, offered greater precision and accuracy that were unaffected by seasonal fluctuations or climatic change. Moreover, they simultaneously offered both greater public coordination, as they could be seen from towers for considerable distances, and private coordination, as they did not necessarily announce an activity.[50] And this lack of official control may have been a key reason they were not employed. Bells, on the other hand, rang only as needed by Spanish authorities; they could not be used by Indians for their own purposes and thus buttressed Spanish control.

Early clocks in Europe were often associated with churches and monasteries, though towns soon began building clock towers as expressions of civic pride as well as useful social devices. The same held true for Mexico, though to a much lesser degree. In fact, the earliest record of a mechanical clock in Mexico was one ordered for the Casa de la Audiencia in 1530, although Carlos V sent a clock from the cathedral of Segovia to Cortés for his house in Cuernavaca in the early years after the Conquest.[51] By the mid-sixteenth century, clocks were reported in a number of important public buildings.[52] But despite a few prominent examples in large cities, clocks did not dominate churches in sixteenth-century Mexico.

Expense and a lack of expertise were both hindrances to building clocks in early colonial Mexico, though a few clock makers had settled in Mexico City by the latter half of the sixteenth century.[53] A study of the 440 artisans in Mexico City in 1525–55 found no clock makers.[54] And in response to a 1595 order of the Real Audiencia to send Matias del Monte back to Castille to be married, the city council of Mexico City resisted, arguing that he was the only clock maker in the city or country and that he was sorely needed there.[55] Part of the reason for the absence of clock makers in Mexico was undoubtedly cost, but a major factor was also the absence of an indigenous pattern that clocks were needed to displace. Life in small towns and rural areas continued largely as before, with the pace dictated by daily cycles and social patterns rather than by hours and minutes. Clocks primarily affected the Indians only when they were forced into contact with Spanish officialdom.[56] Courts, city councils, and other bureaucratic authorities had hours set by the clock, and Indians seeking to plead their cases or seek assistance were forced to conform; predictably, this occurred most often in cities.[57] The countryside, however, continued to be a vast, untimed wilderness.[58]

Lest it be thought that Europeans did not generally spread clocks beyond their home continent, or that the Roman Catholic Church opposed it, consider Japan and China. The Portuguese brought clocks into Japan in 1542,[59] and a Jesuit, Matteo Ricci, introduced them into China in 1577 as gifts to further Christian missionization.[60] Moreover, these clocks were meant for the use of the Japanese and Chinese for their own purposes, rather than just for the Europeans. It might be argued that the

Japanese and Chinese were able to use the European clocks because both groups were more technologically advanced than the Aztecs; they were already marking temporal subdivisions of days. However, the difference in the introduction of clocks was largely political. Whereas Japan and China were independent polities that had to be enticed to admit Europeans and their trade, Mexico had been conquered. Since the Spaniards had settled among the Indians to dominate them, and the introduction of clocks and hours served no practical purpose in supporting their rule, they were not introduced. Nor were they needed in a missionizing role. Indeed, the Spanish use of sundials and clocks meant that even a single rural priest could tell time in a way that would have taken many indigenous priests to accomplish. Thus the Christian religious could have a greater degree of temporally based ritual complexity than pre-Hispanic indigenous priests.

The Demise of the Practical Calendar

Before the Conquest, when empires contracted and collapsed, the impact on the calendar was gradual and basically amounted to a lessening of external control, which was largely manifested in an imposed starting date. Freeing local calendars from centralized control resulted in calendrical fragmentation as each city instituted its own leap year corrections. But with the Conquest, the impact on the calendar was sudden and devastating. The calendar that replaced the Aztecs' was radically different, and would not, on its own merits, have replaced the indigenous system. For one thing, the Spaniards brought the Julian calendar, which had already been recognized by the Church as inadequate. Furthermore, the Spanish calendar did not relate to the Aztecs' ritual life. Finally, the new calendar began not with the culturally important migration from Aztlan, but with the birth of Jesus. The birth of Jesus, of course, had no significance for the Indians of Mexico—but that is precisely why this starting point was imposed: it reflected the Christian ritual cycle.

The Spaniards sought to control the Indians by fragmenting them into semi-autonomous villages and eliminating their ability to exercise political control at regional or higher levels.[61] Eliminating supra-regional indigenous political organization was the proximate cause of this social fragmentation, but destroying the indigenous calendar was a key element in how this was accomplished. While displacing the in-

digenous calendar with the Christian one was a self-conscious Spanish policy, at least for the priests, there were few or no secular actions
aimed at destroying the indigenous calendar.

Did the Spaniards recognize the political nature of the Aztec calendar? Perhaps not. After all, the Conquest destroyed its central role, and
the experiential baseline of even the earliest Spanish priests and colo-
nists was not of the empire, which had been destroyed, but of separate
cities, each with its own calendar. None of these calendars, by that
time, would have had more than a domestic political role. Indeed, perhaps an indigenous calendar might have reemerged, but the vigorous
attack of the Spanish priests, for their own religious purposes, largely
forestalled that possibility. The wholesale calendrical substitution apparently sped conversions, as it was not merely a shift in how one
counted days and years, but in what festivals and associated deities and
saints were celebrated. Furthermore, aside from altering the cycle of
ritual observances,[62] the shift to a Christian calendar—and especially
to a 7-day week from the Aztec 5—changed marketing patterns.[63]

In addition to the changes in market schedules, shifting periodic
markets from a 5-day indigenous week to a 7-day Christian one,[64] and
the ripple effect of bigger markets seizing better and more days while
displacing smaller ones,[65] market schedules are also tied to the material constraints of transport and spoilage, which also changed with the
Spanish conquest.[66] Since spoilage increases with time, the new, longer
periodicity of markets increased that risk, as did the newly introduced
European domesticates. Chickens were readily adopted, not merely because they had indigenous parallels in turkeys or were examples of
"penny capitalism" within the grasp of commoners, but because they
fit extant patterns of preservation until use. Large animals, such as
cattle, sheep, and goats, however, were not only more costly to pur-
chase and maintain but also could not be consumed by a single household at a single setting, as could a turkey or chicken. Furthermore, marketing them entailed a significantly greater risk because they had to be
butchered and sold in lots, all of which might not sell but all of which
was nevertheless subject to immediate spoilage. Thus a longer time between markets would have worked against Indians raising and selling
large livestock. The Indians would probably have regarded large animals like fish and game rather than like domesticated animals, and
their sale would have been aimed at urban markets, which met more
frequently and had greater demand. Thus the sale of large animals was
an urban-focused industry, whereas most Indians concentrated on lo-

cal, village, and other rural markets with a smaller demand for meat; so theirs was a small-livestock industry. And even if large livestock had been raised for both markets, it would have been at radically different scales. These practical matters were patterned on the new market periodicity, which in turn was based on the Christian calendar. The natives had little choice but to conform, and the new system was quickly learned and assimilated.

The practicalities of coordination once one major market adopted the 7-day weekly schedule forced others to shift in order to avoid conflict.[67] And it was primarily practicality, not ideology per se, that forced the change. The Spanish colonial government formally allowed the continuation of 5-day markets (based on the indigenous calendar) well into the sixteenth century,[68] perhaps because the 5-day week did not have directly associated gods or religious festivals. But part of the success of the conversion effort was owed to the shift in economic and political dominance.

Once the permanence of the Spanish presence was relatively certain, native temples were destroyed,[69] marking not only the decline of the indigenous gods and the ascendancy of the Spaniards' religion, but also entailing a profound economic reorientation. With lands now being distributed among the Spaniards and with the various regular orders requiring some economic support (and seculars requiring vastly more),[70] many of the temple lands were forfeit. As a consequence, the finances necessary to sustain the indigenous priesthoods were greatly reduced or cut off, and the cults withered. So conversion was not simply a battle between competing belief systems that Christianity won by virtue of a superior orthodoxy; rather, the indigenous system was economically strangled. The number of trained priests rapidly dwindled, leaving indigenous beliefs in tatters, tended by folk practitioners whose grasp of the complexity of indigenous religious thought was a mere skeleton of the original, lacking the ability to reproduce itself fully.[71]

Perhaps these changes could have been resisted—certainly the Spaniards feared an Indian revolt for years following the Conquest.[72] However, no Indian revolt materialized in early colonial central Mexico, though there was a black slave revolt in 1537.[73] And no indigenous leader emerged at a national level, despite the fact that former elites continued to occupy traditional, though now subordinated, political offices.[74] Part of their failure to act overtly may be explained by their political subordination and part by their scramble to salvage whatever personal advantages they could from their now diminished positions;

concern for the overall welfare of their followers was not paramount.[75] In addition, though, as time went on, they had less likelihood of successfully revolting, partly because of the calendrical change. With the imposition of the Christian calendar, Spanish priests displaced indigenous ones as the guardians of time. Regional coordination was now in Spanish hands and indigenous leaders lacked the means to mobilize resistance at anything above the local level, where such actions would be small, limited, regionally uncoordinated, and thus easily suppressed if they became violent. The only coordinated time was Spanish, and even if most towns still retained indigenous calendars, they were rapidly falling out of sync with each other in the absence of an indigenous centralizing force.

The political impact of the Christian calendar was less apparent to the Spaniards, who were already accustomed to it, than to the Indians, who experienced its dislocations. They could not readily see the role of the indigenous calendar in Indian society—just as they could not see the Indians' reliance on that calendar through the wreckage of native society. And, the Christian calendar was spread throughout Mexico much like the imperial calendars of earlier eras, though the driving force now was not just politics but missionizing ideology.

Aztec notions of time and history depended upon sophisticated political and religious organizations that did not long survive the Conquest, leaving little more than folk history and folk calendars in the colonial period. Moreover, with the demise of the indigenous specialists, calendrical knowledge became conventional and standardized. The focus was on year dates, and all questions about the 2 Acatl New Fire ceremony were lost. Indigenous dates were used primarily to legitimate the records, and issues of how they functioned or changed were swept aside as unknown, unknowable, or completely irrelevant to their new authenticating role. In the eighteenth-century Techialoyan manuscripts, which were falsified sixteenth-century codices used to sustain land claims,[76] place glyphs and name glyphs survived, but not date glyphs.[77] And while indigenous histories continued, at least through the colonial period, they largely lost their linear temporal component, as one would predict, and focused on shorter, cyclical histories[78] that bear only superficial similarities to the historical and temporal structures of the indigenous imperial past.

Chapter 7

Time and Analysis

In Mesoamerican studies, the ideology-as-action approach has generally held sway, especially in the interpretation of time, history, and religion.[1] This tendency holds more prominently in religious studies and art history,[2] where the emphasis tends to be on ideological factors, than in history and anthropology.[3] But if there is ample evidence that the Aztecs emphasized a linear notion of time in their calendar and histories, as demonstrated in the foregoing chapters, why has the idea arisen and persisted so strongly that they possessed a cyclical notion of time? Three things have fostered such a view: fundamental theoretical orientations, how time is analyzed, and the types of data available and their traditional interpretation.

Much of the conventional interpretation reflects the centrality of religion in Mesoamerican life, as it is presented in recorded accounts. As the most salient form of ideology, religion is often the most publicly accessible. It offers a meaningful world in an evolving intellectual framework that anchors people to their past traditions, while constantly incorporating novelty in a way consistent with extant beliefs. That is not to say that religion cannot obstruct innovation—a Galileo can be threatened with torture for espousing empirically verifiable facts that run counter to established Church teachings.[4] But religion can also ease the transition between the old and the new, and where it obstructs, it is more often religious structure as political force than religion as faith.

Ideology makes past, present, and future both intelligible and meaningful. Old actions, current dilemmas, and novel situations are all eased by assessing them in familiar terms, hence the astonishing persistence of cultures that we in the West often see as based on immediately dismissable ideological premises. The image of a highly trained and skilled Indian physicist venerating an elephant-headed god may strike many of us as odd, just as transubstantiation probably does to him. But his tradition provides a meaningful way to see the world and its events no less useful to him than our own is to us. The issue, however, is not whose ideology best reflects the world, since none of us has direct access to it; each of us necessarily understands the world in light of our own cultural background. Rather, the issue is whether an ideology can provide comfort, sense, and purpose; for these goals, the fit with the observable world, though significant, is less important than the fit with one's cultural tradition. Thus, we cannot dismiss the worship of Huitzilopochtli or Tlaloc as a quaint but meaningless custom, for it is not, any more than our own beliefs and worship are meaningless. So it is reasonable to assume that one can find the reflection of fundamental beliefs in the practices and constructions of Aztec society.

Interpreting actions and events in light of prevailing ideological notions, however, is a far cry from interpreting them as caused by these beliefs. For instance, if I say that something has been this way since Adam, does this mean that I literally believe that something can be traced genealogically back to the Adam of the Genesis creation, or do I simply mean that something has been this way for a very long time? In short, how can ideology-as-idiom be distinguished from ideology-as-action? It might be argued that distinguishing these is unnecessary since they both relate cultural interpretations to actions and events. But, in fact, they lead to profoundly different explanations.

If ideology is taken to be causal, it is presumed that everyone in a society more or less shares the same ideology or that culture would not have been produced. It is only when ideology is seen as an effect, as a culturally consistent interpretation of conditions, that one would not expect uniformity and when the lack of cultural unity ceases to be problematic. Thus, I can make reference to something as a Garden of Eden to evoke a widely shared image and all it implies without believing in the literal reality of such a place. And the same may well have been true of the Aztecs. Legends, myths, and history form the common currency of social interaction, a type of shorthand that allows rapid dissemination of shared perspectives, yet it need not imply belief either in their absolute reality or in their uniformity.

This does not mean that religious beliefs are a form of cultural caprice, with one being as acceptable as any other: religion must be consistent with the world as understood in that culture. Its explanations may be mythical, but these often do not relate to the direct physical world around us and, unless they manifestly clash with reality, how accurately they describe the world is not an issue. Instead, the religious perspective influences how we *see* the world, though this must be congruent with reality as experienced by ordinary people or lapse into desuetude.[5]

The difficulty in this approach is in distinguishing between the natives' meaning(s) and our own. All too often analysts project their desired meanings onto the objects being assessed, and, since objects are inherently polysemic, this approach often yields an entirely plausible interpretation. But since meanings are many and varied, how compelling is an ideological explanation of behavior? Interpreting behavior as the direct outgrowth of an ideological motivation appears to offer direct access to the individual actor—at an academic level because it presumes to link action to motivation, and at a personal level because we perceive our own actions as stemming from conscious motivations. For example, an ecological explanation may convincingly tie a society's patterns of behavior to the ecology of the region, but this explanation inevitably arises ex post facto because any given type of ecological regime has given rise to a wide range of different adaptations around the world. So while ecology sets limits, it does not explain what actions will be taken or what choices will be made. The cultural tradition—the ideology—exercises a dominant influence, so a direct ecological (or economic, social, or so on) explanation is inherently insufficient. It lacks an account of the element of choice. And it is here where ideological explanations are superior. Or, at least, they are presumed to be superior. But an ideological approach shares the same epistemological weakness as other explanations. Just as with ecological, or any other choice, ideological choices are not foreordained and a wide range is available. However people act, the explanation of an action in terms of ideology is always made after the fact, just as ecological explanations are. Because they are direct motivations, however, whatever ideological choice is preferred appears more satisfactory on its face, and the many alternative ideological explanations typically are not considered, or at least not as often or as vigorously as they are for other types of explanations. Ideological explanations in any sociological sense are no more satisfactory than non-ideological ones. That is, they offer the appearance of getting at why people do what they do, but in terms of their explanatory logic, it can rarely be demonstrated that they actually account for the behavior as claimed. Thus, in terms of their explanatory logic, they occupy precisely the same epistemological position as other approaches: they are inherently ex post facto and only one of a host of possible alternatives.

Sahlins's explanation of Cook's death grasps part of the puzzle. It shows how actions, whether or not they have the motivation assumed, are explained, rationalized, and made consistent with cultural values, though Sahlins's interpretation represents only one of many culturally consistent ways in which this mapping could have been done in relation to Cook. And Obeyesekere's radically different assessment is also probably correct—it was the political act of the chief. But his explanation does not speak to the issue of how the actions were rationalized and made culturally intelligible, which goes to the question of how support, or at least acceptance, is generated, any more than Sahlins's focus on the latter goes toward the question of the action's political purposes. It is Wolf's focus on power in social relations that links these two halves of the analysis.

The ideology-as-action approach takes beliefs themselves as the cause of the actions, whereas the ideology-as-idiom approach argues that actions are motivated by culturally congruent practical reasons rather than by primarily ideological ones. That is, achieving a specific understanding of actual motivation may not be possible—or at least not convincingly so to others. But achieving a culturally consistent pattern of observable behaviors and ideological justifications is, and in the context of a hierarchical political structure, and a complex society with an inevitable diversity of interests, the political manipulation of legitimizing ideology for partisan purposes is likely, if not inevitable. Thus, what is of interest in the analysis of religion, not as a thing-in-itself but as a part of the wider social world, is how it is manipulated by various interest groups for their own purposes. This manipulation is seldom acknowledged as such; instead, different political, economic, or social positions are supported in public debate in terms of the same basic religious tenets. These positions not only mask political ambitions, they serve to make the underlying policy palatable to those who must live under it.

That religion is manipulated does not address the issue of whether the manipulators believe in the truth of the positions they espouse.[6] Ideology is always contested in complex societies; if not by heretics and radicals, then certainly by occupation, class, gender, generational, ethnic, or residential groups. Different interests are inevitable in complex societies; pointing to these and the differential impact of an ideological shift is not inherent evidence of self-conscious manipulation by one group against another.

Whether or not manipulators actually share a common ideology with the bulk of their society, they may well convince themselves that their partisan aims are consonant with those beliefs.[7] If political elites are to achieve support for their actions, however good or evil, honest or duplicitous, their actions must be couched in terms accessible to, and nominally accepted by, most of the populace. This, of course, is a long way from claiming that people act as they do because they believe in the official tenets of their religion. But it is evident that rulers do use religion for their own political purposes.[8] And while hypocrisy may well play a role in this, simply interpreting political actions taken under the guise of religious purposes as entirely self-serving does not encompass the complexity of the phenomenon.

Both commoners and nobles may make decisions on a religious or individual basis by considering issues on their merits, but leaders are rarely in a position for such simple calculations. The decisions leaders face are complex and have vast implications because of the variety of interests that are brought to bear and the range of people they affect. As a result, even issues that are ostensibly religious may be decided on terms that seem driven primarily by economic or political considerations. But issues that seem simple and straightforward at the individual level, where relatively few competing interests vie for attention, are inherently complex at the highest levels, with the king having to balance many religious, social, political, and economic interests because any imperial action has consequences for all of these realms. He may (or may not) personally share the religious orientation of the commoners on the issue in question, but his is not an individual decision. Rather, his job is to make decisions that balance all the interests (which assuredly include his own), and the more he can align—or the more that are powerful—the greater his support and the less endangered his position. So when the king acts contrary to the interests of a commoner, he is not necessarily being hypocritical; rather, he sees the world differently, many factors affect his decision, and, essentially, he

makes seemingly incongruent decisions because he and the commoners are not facing the same questions at all. In any event, the central
fact of the political use of religion is that it masks the self-interested
acts of principals in the rhetoric of morality and the supernatural.

But curiously, blatant manipulation of political and economic incentives for state purposes provokes less reaction than does ideological
manipulation for the same end. The reason lies in the degree of congru-
ence between stated purpose and action. The logic of following a direct political compulsion, such as threatened punishment for failure to
comply with the edicts of the state, or a somewhat less immediate economic incentive, such as being paid to provide a state-mandated service, is apparent. The state goals require no commitment on the part of
the participants because their motivations can be understood in more
immediate terms.[9] Political penalties and economic incentives both
rely on an individual's assessment, but they do not demand a motivational embrace of ends, whereas religious motivations do. Political
power requires expenditure for implementing force—whether used or
merely threatened—and economic incentives demand either political
control or the outlay of financing, but successful religious appeals rely
to a great degree on the internal motivation of adherents. As a result,
ideology may motivate even beyond the reach of political control or
economic incentives, though the future of an ideology where these are
not congruent is bleak. While virtually everyone within Tenochtitlan
shared in its political and economic benefits to some extent, elsewhere
in the empire, these gains accrued to fewer people (e.g., the elite), yet
phrasing state dictates in the idiom of religion could still motivate
those less driven by economic or political concerns.

But ideology alone, or even as primary motivator, has significant limits. Religion may be a shared idiom among antagonistic polities, even
when there is a clear religious hierarchy that could or should regulate
such conflicts, as is evident in warring medieval Europe.[10] Religion and
ideology do not seem to be particularly effective in integrating complex societies[11] because that very complexity produces diverse perspectives, such that only by purging dissidents (e.g., with an inquisition) can
homogeneity be accomplished, or seem to be. But even when achieved,
the accomplishment is a fleeting one as the centrifugal forces of increasing complexity make this a losing battle. The integrative accomplishment of religion is thus not so much to link people to people but,
rather, to connect people to their past and future by providing a framework for interpretation, a way of making sense of the past, present, and

future. A diachronic focus makes it clearer that individuals are pivotal in religious continuity because they are surely linked to that past and future; a synchronic analysis focuses on the society as a whole, yet the contemporaneous linkage between its members is a presumption rather than a certainty.

The undeniable power of ideological motivations has made religious interpretations of Aztec behavior common. Such assessments may be accurate, but this is more often assumed than demonstrated, which is explicable partly by theoretical predisposition and partly by the lack of evidence left by internal motivations compared to political or economic incentives. But a further difficulty is distinguishing a genuinely religiously motivated act by both elites and commoners from one that is genuinely motivated among the commoners but disingenuously instigated by the elite. This is a difficult task because actions can be most easily motivated if they are carried out in a manner consistent with extant beliefs, practices, and interests. Thus, ideological motivations are rarely evident in isolation: the corporate nature of motivations greases the way for interpretive bias.

Theoretical predisposition aside, at a more practical level, the typical analytical approach also pushes the interpretation of Aztec notions of time and history toward cyclicity. Under the standard interpretation, there is ample reason to believe that the Aztecs viewed their world in terms of cyclical time that structured their history, despite countervailing evidence. Their calendar was composed of multiple interlocking cycles of days, building into still larger cycles, until the culmination of 52 years, which itself repeated endlessly, giving their history a cyclical cast. Yet evidence of a linear aspect to their time was largely ignored, partly because of the difficulty in distinguishing linear time from cyclical.

Time can be logically analyzed as either cyclical or linear, and a cyclical approach is most revealing for studying social configurations, such as households as recurring systems. But if the focus is on the life of one individual, a linear approach is more revealing. Yet merely adopting one or the other perspective and finding positive results does not mean that was the type of time believed to exist by the people themselves. Thus, one needs to distinguish between analytical approach and belief of the people being studied.

Focusing on the internal temporal structure of the time system, rather than on the social practices related to it, also skews the outcome toward cyclicity. Focusing on the temporal structure as embodied in the calendar will inevitably produce a cyclical view of time. As a result, behavior that is tied to the calendar will generally be seen as cyclically patterned, irrespective of the beliefs of the subjects. By contrast, a societal focus yields an interpretation of the calendar based on the social uses to which it is put, not its internal logic. These practices are seen to structure the temporal pattern, to which calendrical dates may then be attached, with results that may or may not be cyclical.

The third factor promoting a cyclical view of time is the nature of the data on which it is based. A major—and perhaps the main—reason scholars have emphasized the cyclical nature of Aztec time and history lies in the original data on which their interpretations are based. Much of what survives about Aztec culture was written by Spaniards, notably by priests. And among the main concerns of such men was converting the Indians from heathenism to Christianity.[12] Accordingly, much of their writing does not reflect an open intellectual curiosity about this new and strange culture, but rather was geared to informing the religious so they could carry out the task of conversion more effectively.

In many of the indigenous rituals, the Spaniards saw reflections of their own practices.[13] Moreover, they did not deny the power of indigenous rituals and practices that they encountered.[14] But from their perspective, if native religious practitioners could perform supernatural acts and yet were not Christians, they had to be invoking the devil.[15] Thus, in making native practices intelligible to themselves, the Spaniards promoted syncretism—perhaps as a reasonable trade-off for easing conversions—by relabeling the native gods and creating the very devil they nominally sought to defeat.

An excellent example of this reinterpretation of native practices in terms that would be meaningful to Christians is found in Córdoba's *Doctrina Cristiana* (as modified by Bishop Zumárraga for use in Mexico).[16] It discusses the seven sacraments of orthodox Roman Catholicism, for each of which an indigenous parallel can be found in Sahagún's *Florentine Codex*. Baptism appeared among the Aztecs as a bathing ceremony for infants, four days after the birth.[17] Confirmation was paralleled by the Aztec dedication of children to temple schools to become priests.[18] Penance was also sought by the Aztecs by praying to the goddess Tlazolteotl.[19] The Eucharist, in which Christian priests changed the bread into the body of Christ through transubstantiation before communion, was echoed in the Aztec practice of fashioning idols of Huitzilopochtli and Omacatl from amaranth dough and then eating them.[20] Extreme Unction also had ceremonial parallels among the Aztecs, though their notion of sin was different.[21] Holy Orders were found in the Aztec practice of training priests who were dedicated to specific gods.[22] And Holy Matrimony, though apparently involving priests less than in Catholic ceremonies, was celebrated on portentous days and festivals for the gods.[23]

To the Spaniards, native practices that paralleled those of the Roman Catholic Church could only be reinterpreted as an attempt at mockery, as in a black mass. Thus, the religious needed an in-depth knowledge of indigenous beliefs to insure that they were not hidden in the guise of Christian orthodoxy. For example it was claimed that the Indians sought to fool the priests by burying idols under crosses which they venerated while seeming to worship the cross.[24] And fray Diego Durán[25] explicitly states that he is explaining the native calendar because some natives have claimed to give up their old gods and accept a new Catholic patron saint when, in fact, they have sought out the patron saint in the Christian calendar for the date of their heathen god in their traditional calendar; they are doing no more than substituting an acceptable name for an indigenous god, which they continue to worship in a different guise.

The calendar posed a particular problem for religious conversion. As with the native calendar, the Catholic calendar laid heavy emphasis on the ritual cycle. Every day had one or more patron saints, as did the native calendar, there were movable feasts,[26] as there were in the native calendar, and the focus was on the endless repetition of holy festivals in ritual time, as it was in the native calendar. The two ritual calendars—Christian and Aztec—shared many features in common, and a conflation of the two was an ever present danger as the Spaniards sought to convert the natives to Christianity. As a result of the close parallels between Christian and Aztec religious practices and the ritual use of their respective calendars, the Spanish priests especially emphasized the religious role of the Aztec calendar, largely ignoring its more secular functions.

The New Fire ceremony also loomed large in the accounts of Spanish priests. Whatever functions that ceremony might have had in the secular world (after all, it is consistently recorded in the historical codices that otherwise largely ignore religious activities) were swamped by the Spanish priests' emphasis on its religious ones. Perhaps the concern arose from its parallels to the millennial concerns of the Church, which also promised an end of time, or at least of this age.[27]

Indeed, cyclical aspects of the native calendar were the Spanish priests' primary concern. But the New Fire ceremony aside, the priests expressed little interest above the level of sub-year cycles. In fact, since years do not possess associated gods, the priests paid them little attention, and numerous historical annals using indigenous year counts continued through the colonial period.[28] The imposition of Spanish ideology was political, but no more blatantly so than it had been under the Aztecs. The religious enforced changes, but civil officials were far less concerned, presumably because they possessed more efficient means of integrating New Spain politically than had been available to the Aztecs. Hence, annals continued, the use of Spanish hours and minutes was not imposed, native markets based on their own calendars were tolerated, and only enough alterations to bring the Indians into behavioral conformity with Spanish officialdom were imposed. All else fell to the priests, whose preoccupation with conversion led them to place particular emphasis on the Aztec calendar in their writings, making it a centerpiece of their analyses because it so closely paralleled the Catholic calendar in both form and function. To convert the Indians to Christianity, they had to understand the calendar in its ritual role and then root it out so it would not be conflated with the Christian one and perpetuate heathenism in disguise. But as an unintended consequence of their priestly concerns, our modern understanding of the calendar has been skewed toward its cyclicity—which one expects in rituals—to the detriment of its more linear aspects. Consequently, our own interpretations have been less than even handed as they continue along the lines of the early Spanish clerics'.

Modern theoretical biases have reinforced this inheritance from the colonial perspective.[29] These stem from the way many researchers have used the calendar to open up the Mesoamerican past, and the absence of a zero date in the Aztec system.

For many researchers, understanding indigenous belief systems is the primary concern, and focusing on the calendar is a common approach to understanding the ideology of various Mesoamerican groups.[30] Because the calendar is expressed in arithmetical terms (with a limited number of month and day symbols) and is related to the physical world, whose cycles we already understand and upon which we can map Mesoamerican calendars, it seems like the perfect entree into a world whose other components are often poorly understood. It provides a structure in which we have a great deal of confidence and against which less sure data can be arrayed and assessed. This was particularly true of the Maya, whose glyphs largely resisted decipherment until they slowly began to yield in the 1950s.[31] Before that, their writing may not have been under-stood but their calendar was, and thus the entire span of Maya history was opened, even if only partially, by tying people, places, and events to the dates obtained from the already-understood calendar.[32]

A major difference between Maya and Mexican calendars is the pres-ence of a zero date among the Maya, so that their calendar endlessly unfolds in increasingly larger cycles from an original starting point. The Mexican calendars did not have such a starting point, and this was taken as proof that the Mexican calendars were *only* cyclical. After all, without a starting date and only operating as a series of endless 52-year repetitions, how could they be anything else?

Moreover, the cyclical view of the calendar presented by the early Spanish chroniclers was reinforced in the twentieth century by such ideologically driven perspectives on time and ritual as that of Mircea Eliade.[33] The answers, we are told, are all there in the calendar, ours to unfold. And once it was established—or at least believed—that the Indians held a cyclical view of time as reflected in their calendar, the system was self-perpetuating. It ran itself—certainly forward, which was the primary indigenous interest, but also backward, which has been the scholarly concern. Declare the reality of cyclical time and all else is interpretation; empirical research plays only a secondary role.

Emphasizing cyclical time allowed scholars to make arguably reli-able assertions beyond the evidence; if time was cyclical, then it was less important that not all of the pertinent evidence was available since the missing parts could be logically inferred. Cyclical time promised the researcher a hidden dynamic that could be studied in microcosm and then projected onto the macrocosm. A linear notion of time would not permit this intuitive leap and was thus not as appealing to scholars, even if they considered it.

The calendar became the touchstone for interpreting the past, and because of its current importance in Mesoamerican studies, it was also felt that its centrality was not just ours, but the natives' as well. After all, if it was that important to us, then surely it was that important to them too. Thus, the dates on Maya stelae were taken as measures of the Maya concern with time[34] even though they contained far fewer dates than comparable monuments in contemporary society, dated cor-nerstones, and certainly any graveyard—yet few argue that we are simi-larly obsessed by time. The calendar system was assumed to be crucial to the Maya because it was understood first and best, and because it played such an important role in how we interpreted Mesoamerican cultures, not because of any compelling evidence of such centrality in their own perspective.

Modern studies of the colonial period, too, often emphasize cyclicity, and there is evidence that temporal cycles dominated indigenous calendrical perspectives.[35] This was not, however, a strict continuation of pre-Hispanic practices, but rather the scaled-down remnants of the earlier, more sophisticated system. So while historical studies can accurately interpret colonial ritual activities as patterned by cyclical notions of time, this patterning reflects few links to pre-Columbian practices or cosmology. The Aztecs no longer possessed their own regional political system and had thus lost their longer term, more linear temporal structures.[36]

The same principle holds for the colonial period as for the pre-Conquest period: no study is satisfactory if a set of commonly accepted but not empirically supported beliefs is taken as given. The pre-Conquest example requires not only careful analysis, but the historicization of materials that one might be tempted to collapse into a generic, timeless social past. Post-Conquest studies have typically focused exclusively on the colonial situation, without considering what the colonizers faced. Yet studies of the post-Conquest world depend on our understanding of pre-Conquest practices; thus uncritical acceptance of the conventional view of the pre-Conquest world yields a poor foundation for studying the colonial world. Colonial evidence of the indigenous past is not an adequate baseline from which post-Conquest developments can then be seen diverging, as it is inescapably contaminated with European or Westernized concepts and perspectives. For example, in his translation of Nahuatl religious incantations, fray Hernando Ruiz de Alarcón interpreted *Ceteotl* as "The One God."[37] But *Ceteotl* is actually an instance of the assimilation of a consonant and should be *Centeotl*, "Ear-of-maize-god," from *centli*, "dried ear of maize," and *teotl*, "god." Ruiz de Alarcón's interpretation is a clear projection of Christian monotheism. The bulk of the evidence on which both pre- and post-Conquest studies rest is colonial.

This uncritical acceptance of a colonial baseline has persisted into contemporary analysis. Studies of the modern period also often invoke pre-Conquest calendars to structure current histories. Not only do the concerns of stripped-down calendars of the colonial period remain,[38] but misunderstandings of the original calendar are often projected onto modern data,[39] yielding interesting, though sometimes questionable, interpretations that rest on flawed views of the original calendrical systems or on colonial remnants that were typically merged with Christian cosmology.

The historical analysis of ideology anywhere is difficult and it is assuredly so in Mexico. What is recorded is scattershot, typically urban, and permeated with European preconceptions. Even to assess the colonial period alone, the pre-Columbian period must be thoroughly reassessed to minimize the likelihood of taking colonial distortions of indigenous beliefs as the baseline for documenting later deviations.

Instead of seeing the pre-Conquest calendar as an ideological imperative and assessing its impact accordingly, adopting an ideology-as-idiom perspective frees the interpretation to pursue more political avenues common to the control of time elsewhere. Moreover, such an approach makes sense of heretofore anomalous matters. For example, in the absence of an imperative for a 1 Tochtli Calendar Round versus a 2 Acatl one, or an Aztec sense of time versus a Spanish one, why and how were these changes successfully implemented? All aspects of the time system were meaningful to those accustomed to them, and all new ones became familiar with time. The 2 Acatl system held no functional superiority over the 1 Tochtli one, nor did the Spanish calendar, especially as adopted in its Julian form. Those aspects of it that were superior—the noting of regular hours and minutes—were precisely the points the Spaniards made the least effort to impose. So while there is little internal basis for preferring one perspective over another, such that an ideological interpretation seems adequate when dealing with a temporal system at one point in time, changes, whether internal like the 1 Tochtli to 2 Acatl alteration, or external like the imposition of the Christian calendar, require going beyond the system itself. Politics determines calendars, and viewing these chronological systems against the political dynamics of the day, plus the historical developments involved, renders more intelligible Aztec and colonial notions of time and history.

Appendix
Pronunciation Guide

In this study I have attempted to conform to a standardized Nahuatl orthography as far as possible, following J. Richard Andrews's *Introduction to Classical Nahuatl*, though neither length marks nor vowel length have been shown.

Letter	*Pronunciation*
c + a/o	as in *can*
qu + e/i	like *k* in *kit*
c + e/i	as in *cease*
z + a/o	like *s* in *sod*
ch	as in *church*
chu	like *ckw* in *backward*
cu/uc	like *qu* in *quick*
h	as in *hill* (but, strictly, a glottal stop)
hu	like *w* in *wake*
uh	like *wh* in *wheel*
tl	similar to *tl* in *settler*, but a single sound
tz	like *ts* in *hats*
x	like *sh* in *ship*

All other letters are pronounced with standard Latin values.

In general I have not tampered with the form of the Nahuatl words; however, I have used the anglicized "s" for pluralization, even though in Nahuatl, a word that refers to an entity not considered to be animate lacks marked pluralization. I have used the term "Aztec," rather than "Mexica," on the assumption that it is more widely recognized.

To clarify the names of kings and gods in this work, I have omitted the honorific suffix -*tzin*. Sometimes the omission was unnecessary, because the names are commonly offered in both forms, such as Ahuitzotl and Ahuitzotzin, or Nanahuatl and Nanahuatzin. I have also shortened other names, even though they are almost never given without the honorific. Thus, Moteuczoma Xocoyotzin appears as Moteuczoma Xocoyotl.

Notes

Preface

1. Hassig 1985:3–150.
2. E.g., Broda 1969; Caso 1967; Edmonson 1988; Séjourné 1981, 1987.
3. E.g., León-Portilla 1971, 1992.
4. E.g., Florescano 1994:1–64.

Chapter 1

1. Reeves 1976:1; Whitrow 1972:16–18.
2. Toulmin and Goodfield 1982:121–123; Whitrow 1972:24, 1989:46, 177–178.
3. Pomian 1979:567–568.
4. O'Malley 1996:12; Whitrow 1989:43, 51–54; Wilcox 1987:113.
5. Whitrow 1989:57, 65.
6. Pomian 1979:567.
7. Whitrow 1989:25.
8. E.g., Florescano 1994:69–76; Wuthnow 1980:61–63.
9. Barth 1987:48.
10. However, the idea that these people actually think spatially rather than temporally may be a distortion. It seems fairly apparent that linear patterns of thought are essential to causal reasoning, upon which our survival depends, and whether this pattern is tied to temporal signposts or spatial referents, such as campsites, does not necessarily demonstrate that the people think spatially rather than temporally.
11. Pomian 1979:566–567.
12. O'Malley 1996:12–13; Whitrow 1989:25, 31, 47, 49.
13. E.g., Skinner 1985.
14. Fortes 1958.
15. Brown 1988:20–30; Pargiter 1972:1–14, 175–179.
16. Pomian 1979:564.
17. Aveni 1989:168–177; Whitrow 1972:14; 1989:16.
18. Gell 1992:12.

19. O'Neil 1978:6–78, 34; Whitrow 1989:32–33. Aveni (1989:100–101) argues for a biological basis for a 7-day week in human biorhythms.
20. Whitrow 1989:14–17.
21. Whitrow 1989:16.
22. Aveni 1989:115–116; Crosby 1997:31; Whitrow 1989:14.
23. Ferris 1988:83–101.
24. Whitrow 1972:26–39.
25. Whitrow 1972:120–132.
26. Whitrow 1989:4.
27. The basic Aztec (and broadly, central Mexican) myths assembled from a variety of textual and codical sources are a number of different, though converging, versions, so the most general versions will be given here. To present a readable, consistent set of myths, the following are taken from Nicholson (1971:397–408) and Davies (1980), though I will also note some of the more prominent sources for the various versions. For a fuller discussion of the 5 Suns myth, see Elzey (1976).
28. E.g., Demarest and Conrad 1992.
29. Sahlins 1981, 1982, 1985, 1995.
30. Berdan 1982:144; Broda 1969:28; Brundage 1982:19; D. Carrasco 1987a:25, 1990:54; Gillespie 1989:xxiii; Gruzinski 1992:74; Ingham 1971:615; Peterson 1962:199; Thomas 1993:187; Todorov 1984:66, 74, 84. Read (1998:95, 99) argues for a spiral time in which cycles dominate within 52-year Calendar Rounds, but historical shifts occur between these, beginning at the New Fire ceremonies.
31. Berdan 1982:144; Broda 1969:28; Brundage 1982:19; D. Carrasco 1987a:25, 1990:54; Gillespie 1989:xxiii; Gruzinski 1992:74; Ingham 1971:615; Peterson 1962:199; Thomas 1993:187; Todorov 1984:66, 74, 84; Umberger 1987a:63.
32. Broda 1969:77–78; Edmonson 1988:21.
33. Davies 1987:21–31.
34. Umberger 1987a:63.
35. Durán 1967, 1:48; Sahagún 1952:49, 57, 59–61; Zorita 1963:66.
36. Berdan 1982:144–148; Bray 1968:163–171; Broda 1969:27–29; D. Carrasco 1990: 87–88; Edmonson 1992:154; Graulich 1981:48–49; Ingham 1971:623–627; Katz 1972:163; Peterson 1962:193; Michael E. Smith 1996:253–258; Soustelle 1976: 108–111.
37. Clavijero 1979, 1:293; Sahagún 1957:140.
38. Clavijero 1979, 1:290; Durán 1967, 1:293; Garibay 1973:101; Sahagún 1957:140; Torquemada 1973–83, 3:428; Veytia 1944, 1:29; Zorita 1909:302. The major exception is the Cakchiquel calendar of Ixmiche, which is based on 400 days and is non-solar (Edmonson 1988:134–135).
39. Garibay 1973:29; Sahagún 1957:138; Zorita 1909:302.
40. E.g., Códice Borbónico 1991: fols. 3–20; Tonalamatl Aubin 1981.
41. For unknown reasons, this dot-only system had, by the Postclassic period, largely supplanted a seemingly superior earlier system used by the Maya and the Zapotecs in which dots stood for ones and bars for fives, though perhaps the dot system provided greater mathematical flexibility analogous to the superiority of the Arabic decimal system over Roman numerals.
42. Motolinía 1971:56; Serna 1953:121–122; Zorita 1909:302.
43. E.g., Quiñones Keber 1995: fols. 8r–24r; Tonalamatl Aubin 1981; Codex Vaticanus 1979:11v–37r.
44. E.g., Sahagún 1957:1–125.
45. Seler 1990–96, 1:188.

46. Acosta 1954:183; Clavijero 1979, 1:293; Sahagún 1957:140; Veytia 1944, 1:29; Zorita 1909:302.
47. E.g., Codex Vaticanus 1979: 12v–37r; Códice Borbónico 1991: fols. 3–20; Quiñones Keber 1995: fols. 8r–24r; Tonalamatl Aubin 1981.
48. E.g., Códice Borbónico 1991: fols. 21–22; Tonalamatl Aubin 1981.
49. Seler 1990–96, 1:191.
50. Caso 1971:336.
51. Seler 1990–96, 1:191–193.
52. Acosta 1954:183; Alvarado Tezozomoc 1975a:319; Clavijero 1979, 1:290; Códice Borbónico 1991: fols. 21–22; Garibay 1973:29; Motolinía 1973:25; Sahagún 1957:140; 1993:fols. 283r–286r; Serna 1953:117, 118; Torquemada 1973–83, 3: 428–429; Zorita 1909:302.
53. Dibble 1971:322; Whitrow 1989:17.
54. Contrast Casas (1967, 2:185) and Cline (1973).
55. Acosta 1954:183; Clavijero 1979, 1:290; Durán 1967, 1:293; Motolinía 1973:25; Serna 1953:119; Veytia 1944, 1:29; Zorita 1909:302.
56. Motolinía 1971:48; 1973:30–31; Sahagún 1953:25.
57. Edmonson 1992:156.
58. Serna 1953:117; Torquemada 1973–83, 3:431.
59. Sahagún 1957:141; Serna 1953:117; Veytia 1944, 1:29.
60. Clavijero 1979, 1:293, 314–315; Serna 1953:117, 119–120.
61. Acosta 1954:184; Casas 1967, 2:185; Cervantes de Salazar 1985:36; Clavijero 1979, 1:289; Durán 1967, 1:221, 2:453; Garibay 1973:29, 101; López de Gómara 1965–66, 2:378; Motolinía 1971:48–49; 1973:30–31; Sahagún 1953:25; 1957: 138; Torquemada 1973–83, 3:419, 429; Veytia 1944, 1:29.
62. Bray 1968:170; Brundage 1979:22, 25–27; 1985:26–27, 36–39; D. Carrasco 1990:86; Clendinnen 1991:237–239; Couch 1985:78–87; Davies 1980:29, 94–95; Elzey 1976:131–132; Graulich 1981:47; León-Portilla 1971:50–52; Orozco y Berra 1978, 1:99–101; Paso y Troncoso 1979:102, 210–234; Pasztory 1983:61; Peterson 1962:193, 199–200; Read 1998:26; Soustelle 1976:101–102; Townsend 1992:128, 130–132, 154; Vaillant 1966:203.
63. Sahagún 1953:25–32.
64. The expected name for the hill of Huixachtecatl would be Huixachtepetl, "Hill of the Thorny Trees" (i.e., acacias), but the person form is used here, as some mountains were considered persons or gods. This hill is now called the Hill of the Star.
65. Read (1998:124) argues that it was this act that provided for the next Calendar Round.
66. Read 1998:21. In addition to the usual stylistic considerations, the depiction of a broadsword (macuahuitl) on folio 34 strongly argues for a post-Columbian date, as this weapon commonly appears in colonial codices but in no other extant pre-Conquest codex or other medium.
67. Glass and Robertson 1975:97–98. See also Dibble 1971:323.
68. Anders, Jansen, and García 1991:222; Couch 1985:83–87; Glass and Robertson 1975:97–98; Paso y Troncoso 1979:102; Robertson 1994:86–93. The ceremony is also depicted in the pre-Columbian Codex Borgia (Códice Borgia 1993:fol. 46).
69. Matos Moctezuma 1988:33. For an overview of the earlier history of Templo Mayor studies, see Boone 1987b.
70. Conquistador Anónimo 1941:34–35. The veracity of the Anonymous Conqueror's account has been questioned (Boone 1987b:10).
71. León-Portilla 1987:72–75.

72. Matos Moctezuma 1988:176.
73. Broda 1987a; Broda, Carrasco, and Matos Moctezuma 1987; D. Carrasco 1990: 55; D. Carrasco and Matos Moctezuma 1992; Florescano 1994:18–19; Heyden 1987; Klein 1987; Matos Moctezuma 1984, 1987a, 1988, 1995; Read 1998:11–12.
74. Aveni 1989:273; D. Carrasco 1987b:126–127; Matos Moctezuma 1988:123; 1989:116–120; 1992:29–34; 1995:63; Van Zantwijk 1981:73, 78–79.
75. Soustelle 1966:40.
76. This interpretation seems to conflate Coatepetl—the Hill of the Snake—as a hill needed for structural symmetry—with Coatepec, the place (i.e., town) of the Hill of the Snake.
77. León-Portilla 1987:79–81; Soustelle 1966:38.
78. Broda 1987b:72–74; D. Carrasco 1987b:134–136; Matos Moctezuma 1987b:48–57, 1988:134, 1989:195, 1992:36, 1995:66.
79. Broda 1987b:78–79; D. Carrasco 1992:126; Matos Moctezuma 1987b:57–58, 1988:136.
80. Read 1998:11.
81. Caso 1927.
82. The monument measures a maximum of 1.23 meters high, .93 meters wide, and 1 meter deep. It has a rectangular base .14 meters high, atop of which is the body of the monument, shaped like a pyramid with a set of steps up the front. This pyramidal portion is .66 meters high, with a set-back portion that is an additional .42 meters high.
83. Caso 1927:12; Códice Boturini 1964–65:lam. 1; Lehmann and Kutscher 1981: fol. 4r; Mengin 1952:pl. 18. Contra Caso, the actual recorded departure date was 1 Tecpatl, not 2 Acatl.
84. Especially Seler 1990–96, 4:104–148.
85. Seler (1990–96, 4:134–135) argues that the smoking mirror of Tezcatlipoca is also the expression for atl-tlachinolli, the hieroglyph for war. Other evidence, such as the present example, suggests that the two glyphs are distinct.
86. Caso 1927: figs. 57, 59. This glyph bears some similarity to the name glyph of Moteuczoma Xocoyotl, but Caso strongly argues against this reading, citing fundamental differences with known examples of his name glyph.
87. Caso 1927:56–57; Mengin 1952:pl. 44.
88. Caso 1971:333; Edmonson 1992:164–167.
89. Caso 1965b:943–944; 1971:334–335.
90. Caso 1971:334; Vega Sosa 1991:fols. 1–38.

Chapter 2

1. Obeyesekere 1997:8, 55–56, 177.
2. Obeyesekere 1997:56–60, 131–137.
3. Obeyesekere 1997:20.
4. Obeyesekere 1997:66–74, 179–191.
5. Caso 1971:345–346.
6. O'Neil 1978:3.
7. Whitrow 1989:15.
8. Dohrn-van Rossum 1996:114.

9. Watanabe 1983:723.
10. Whitrow 1989:19.
11. Seler 1900–1901:20, 1990–96, 1:194.
12. Sahagún 1951:21, 44, 58, 76, 98, 107, 113, 119, 130, 133, 140–141, 204; 1952:7;
    1959:63; 1970:48; 1979:56–57, 81; 1997:124.
13. Sahagún 1997:75.
14. Dohrn-van Rossum 1996:115.
15. Dohrn-van Rossum 1996:19.
16. Martir de Angleria 1964–65, 2:492.
17. Caso 1971:337.
18. Clavijero 1979, 1:289; Edmonson 1992:154; Motolinía 1971:48, 56; 1973:30–
    31; Sahagún 1953:25; Torquemada 1973–83, 3:430.
19. The main contending ideas are that the year began on a year-bearer day sign and
    that it ended on one. The latter opinion has been championed by Alfonso Caso
    (1971:345), and there is some textual evidence to support this theory. Sahagún
    (1951:21, 29) notes that great festivals were held on the last day of the month,
    at least for the fifteenth and sixteenth months, and the Tovar Calendar puts
    the festival of the first month, which it gives as Tlacaxipehualiztli, at the end
    (Kubler and Gibson 1951:22). And Casas (1967, 2:185) notes that there is a fes-
    tival on the last day of every month, though the evidence for festivals does not
    translate directly into evidence for day-naming patterns. But while Caso's theory
    has achieved a considerable following, it is based on the dates of a variety of
    monuments, Caso's own assessment of how the calendar functioned, and a cal-
    culation backward to assess the idea. He claims to have substantiated it. But the
    year-bearer-first approach has considerable logic on its side. For instance, the
    year-bearer also named the year, so a first-day position seems more logical than
    a last. Moreover, whatever the day sign, the day number must have been 1 for
    the first month of the first year of the 52-year cycle, the second year 2, and so on.
    And as that first year would also be named, say, 1 Tochtli, the second 2 Acatl,
    and so forth, the precise parallel between the name of the first day of the month
    of the year and the year name (which would thus derive from that first day of
    the year), it seems wholly consistent with Aztec calendrical thought that so too
    should the first day.
       There is, however, a neglected third option. Since the day signs are conven-
    tionally listed as beginning with cipactli, perhaps this is not merely a conven-
    tional listing, as is our week, which begins with Sunday and ends with Satur-
    day regardless of the day of the week that begins the month or year. A similar
    cipactli-initial listing marks the tonalpohualli as well.
       Perhaps this is actually the order of the day signs and, if so, that would place
    the year-bearers in the middle of each 5-day week, with the result that the
    month neither begins nor ends on a year-bearer; rather, each of the four 5-day
    weeks is supported by the middle day.
       This issue is not resolvable at present; positions can be staked out and data
    and arguments marshaled, but a definitive resolution is impossible. Achieving a
    resolution, however, is important primarily if a correlation is sought between
    Aztec and Christian calendars. But if the focus is on how the system itself func-
    tions, it does not matter a great deal which is the initial day, as the month will
    function as advertised regardless.
20. Edmonson 1988:107–109.

21. Broda 1969:88; Caso 1943:28.
22. Caso 1967:242.
23. Caso 1971:339.
24. Vivó Escoto 1964:200–203; R. C. West and Augelli 1976:40–42.
25. Castillo Farreras 1969; Hassig 1988:53–54, 65–72.
26. Clavijero 1979, 1:350; Crónica mexicana 1975:335; Durán 1967, 2:156; Saha-
    gún 1954:69; Torquemada 1973–83, 4:334; Zorita 1963:196–197. See Flores-
    cano (1965:597) and Hassig (1985:241–246) for a discussion of seasonal food
    availability in the colonial period, for which the data are much better than in the
    late pre-Conquest era.
27. Broda 1978:61.
28. Caso 1971:344.
29. Acuña 1982–87, 1:81, 100, 124, 138.
30. Relación de Michoacán 1977:186, 188–189.
31. Caso 1967:252.
32. Sahagún 1957:5.
33. Sahagún 1957:9. For other examples, see Sahagún 1957:1–133.
34. Sahagún 1957:61–64.
35. Sahagún 1957:91.
36. Caso 1971:339.
37. Whitrow 1972:58.
38. Quiñones Keber 1995:127–128.
39. Broda 1969:82.
40. Tonalamatl Aubin 1981.
41. Glass and Robertson 1975:91.
42. Broda 1969:82; Caso 1965b:945.
43. However, this evidence is not without its difficulties. The *Tonalamatl Aubin* is
    missing its first two trecena pages, though from other examples and the logic of
    the system, these can be filled in with a fair degree of confidence. In sixteen of
    the extant Aubin trecena pages, the sequence of Lords of the Night is consistent
    and unvarying, 1 through 9. But on the final two trecenas, the sequence is flawed,
    does not follow the scheme used thus far, and does not even use all of the Lords
    of the Night with the same frequency even if in an altered sequence. The Lords
    of the Night for the nineteenth trecena should be 1–9 and 1–4, with 5–9 and 1–
    8&9 for the twentieth. But the sequence actually followed for the nineteenth is
    4, 3, 2, 1, 9, 8, 6, 5, 4, 3, 2, 1, 8, and for the twentieth, it is 5, 7, 3, 8, 1, 5, 6, 7, 9,
    2, 4, 6, 8&9. Thus, the sequence differs markedly from the prevailing one: Lord
    of the Night 7 appears one fewer times than she should, and Lord of the Night 8
    appears one time more. While the last day does indeed show both Lords of the
    Night 8 and 9, the anomalous character of the last two trecenas suggests that we
    cannot have full confidence in this evidence.
        Fortunately, there is one other bit of evidence. In 1900, Charles Bowditch
    published an article on the Lords of the Night in the tonalamatl of the *Codex
    Borbonicus* that seems to have been largely overlooked in the literature on that
    manuscript (Nowotny in Codex Borbonicus 1974 is an exception). Bowditch
    notes that the two pages following the tonalamatl contain a depiction of the
    52 xihuitl years, 26 on a page, beginning with the year 1 Tochtli and ending with
    13 Calli, which is the normal sequence. But he also notes that each of these years
    has an associated Lord of the Night.

Table N–I. The 52 Xihuitl years and their associated Lords of the Night

1 Tochtli	5	1 Acatl	8	1 Tecpatl	1	1 Calli	3
2 Acatl	3	2 Tecpatl	5	2 Calli	7	2 Tochtli	1
3 Tecpatl	9	3 Calli	3	3 Tochtli	5	3 Acatl	7
4 Calli	7	4 Tochtli	9	4 Acatl	2	4 Tecpatl	4
5 Tochtli	4	5 Acatl	6	5 Tecpatl	9	5 Calli	2
6 Acatl	1	6 Tecpatl	4	6 Calli	6	6 Tochtli	8
7 Tecpatl	8	7 Calli	1	7 Tochtli	3	7 Acatl	6
8 Calli	5	8 Tochtli	8	8 Acatl	1	8 Tecpatl	3
9 Tochtli	3	9 Acatl	5	9 Tecpatl	7	9 Calli	9
10 Acatl	9	10 Tecpatl	2	10 Calli	5	10 Tochtli	7
11 Tecpatl	6	11 Calli	9	11 Tochtli	2	11 Acatl	4
12 Calli	4	12 Tochtli	6	12 Acatl	8	12 Tecpatl	2
13 Tochtli	1	13 Acatl	4	13 Tecpatl	6	13 Calli	8

Given this sequence, and assuming that the associated Lords of the Night are supposed to be those of the first day of the year, it is evident that the Lords of the Night are not offset by one each year, as would be expected if all nine Lords were counted individually in all of their cycles. That is, if there was no alteration in the 9 Lords of the Night cycle, the first day of the second xihuitl year should have gone through 365 Lords of the Night, or 40 full Lords of the Night cycles plus five additional Lords, and begin on the sixth. Since the first year, 1 Tochtli, began with the fifth Lord of the Night, an unaltered cycle would mean that the first day of the next year, 2 Acatl, should have the second Lord of the Night, but it does not; it has the third. In fact, the jump between the first year and the second is 7, the next is 6, then 7, 6, 6, 7, 6, 7, 6, 6, and so on, which Bowditch explains as the result of doubling up two of the Lords of the Night on the last day of the tonalpohualli. The reason some years jump six Lords in the sequence and others seven is that in some xihuitl years, only one tonalpohualli ends, so there is only one doubling up, while others have two, with two doublings. In the former case, a full tonalpohualli would be not 260 Lords of the Night, but 261 because two would be counted on the final day, plus the additional 105 days in the xihuitl year, for a total of 366 Lords of the Night in a 365-day. In the latter case, there would be 367 Lords of the night in a year. Bowditch's deduction makes the case that the Lords of the Night were double counted on the last day so that all three major cycles—20, 13, and the modified 9—would complete simultaneously at the end of a single 260-day tonalpohualli round.

44. Quiñones Keber 1995.
45. Read 1998:164, 173.
46. Acosta 1954:184; Casas 1967, 2:185; Clavijero 1979, 1:289; Durán 1967, 1:221, 2:453; Garibay 1973:30; Motolinía 1971:49, 1973:32; Zorita 1909:303.
47. Alvarado Tezozomoc 1975b:52; Anales de Tecamachalco 1981:6; Berdan and

Anawalt 1992, 3:11, 14, 38; Bierhorst 1992:144; Codex Azcatitlan 1995:18,21v; Códice Borbónico 1991:34; Codex Vaticanus 1979:64r, 69, 71r, 75v, 82r, 85r; Códice Boturini 1964–65:6, 10, 15, 19; Dibble 1981, 1:39; Mengin 1952:pl. 23, 31, 40, 49, 57, 46, 75; Quiñones Keber 1995:51, 58, 62, 68, 87; Sahagún 1953:25, 1997:158; Tira de Tepechpan 1978, 1:4, 7, 11, 14.

48. Hirth 1984:580.
49. Sáenz 1967:11–16; Umberger 1987a:91–92.
50. Bierhorst 1992:25; Veytia 1944, 1:39.
51. Caso 1967:168–172.
52. Caso 1967:166–186; Edmonson 1988:129; Palacios 1948:464–465; Sáenz 1961: 48, 1964:72.
53. Peñafiel 1890, 1:43; Sáenz 1967:46, 79; Seler 1888:84.
54. Lehmann and Kutscher 1981: fols. 6v, 7r.
55. Tena 1992:92.
56. Sáenz (1967:32) argues for this date, which Read (1998:27) accepts.
57. Orozco y Berra 1978, 2:43; Read 1998:92, 123.
58. Quiñones Keber 1995:229; Orozco y Berra 1978, 2:43; Read 1998:92, 123.
59. For example, contrast Durán (1967, 1:221, 2:453) and Sahagún (1957:1–13).
60. Sahagún 1953:25–32, 1957:143–144.
61. Acosta 1954:394; Casas 1967, 2:185–186; Chimalpahin 1965:229; Clavijero 1979, 1:313–315; Durán 1967, 1:221, 2:453; Motolinía 1971:49; 1973:30–31; Torquemada 1973–83, 3:419–421.
62. Sahagún 1970:68.
63. Among the recorded dates on which the Aztec xihuitl year began are February 1 (Sahagún 1997:55), February 2 (Martin de Leon, in Serna 1953:127), February 14 (Clavijero 1979, 1:290, 294), February 26 (Acosta 1954:183; Clavijero 1979, 1:290, 294), March 1 (Cervantes de Salazar 1985:36, 50; Durán 1967, 1:239), March (Kubler and Gibson 1951:22), and January, February, or March (Serna 1953:117).
64. Sahagún 1957:143.
65. Read 1998:102, 103, 124, 223. My thanks to Professor Richard Henry of the Department of Astronomy and Physics, University of Oklahoma, for providing the astronomical calculations.
66. Tena 1992:93–97.
67. Tena 1992:96. Torquemada (1973–83, 3:429) also places the New Fire ceremony in December.
68. Sahagún 1951:172.
69. Sahagún 1997:158; Umberger 1981:50.
70. Whitrow 1989:16.
71. Again, my thanks to Professor Richard Henry for suggesting this possibility.
72. Sahagún 1997:154.
73. E.g., Alvarado Tezozomoc 1975b:52, 53; Anales de Tecamachalco 1981:4, 6; Barlow 1980:40, 48, 53, 57, 61; Berdan and Anawalt 1992, 3:11, 14, 38; Chimalpahin 1965:69, 71, 73, 80–81, 100, 120, 147, 172, 180, 184, 201, 229; Códice Boturini 1964–65:6, 10, 15, 19; Codex Vaticanus 1979:66r, 69v, 71r, 72v, 82r, 85r; Dibble 1981, 1:39; Lehmann and Kutscher 1981:fols. 6v, 7r, 10r, 14v, 40v; Quiñones Keber 1995:58, 62, 68, 87; Tira de Tepechpan 1978, 1:4, 7, 11, 14.
74. Berdan and Anawalt 1992, 3:11.
75. Alva Ixtlilxóchitl 1975–77, 2:79–80; Alvarado Tezozomoc 1975b:108; Anales de Cuauhtitlan 1975:66; Barlow 1949:121; Berdan and Anawalt 1992, 3:18; Ber-

lin and Barlow 1980:16; Chimalpahin 1965:90, 93; Códice Ramírez 1975:51; Crónica mexicana 1975:249; Dibble 1981:10; Durán 1967, 2:80–81 García Icazbalceta 1886–92, 3:252; Herrera 1934–57, 6:210; Leyenda de los soles 1975:128; Mendieta 1971:150; Mengin 1952:446; Paso y Troncoso 1939–42, 10:118; Quiñones Keber 1995:65; Sahagún 1954:1; Torquemada 1975–83, 1:198.

76. Alva Ixtlilxóchitl 1975–77, 2:80, 126; Anales de Cuauhtitlan 1975:47–48, 50, 53, 66; Anales de Tula 1979:35; Barlow 1949:121–22; Berdan and Anawalt 1992, 3:18–22; Berlin and Barlow 1980:55; Chimalpahin 1965:92, 96, 101, 192–193, 198–199; Códice Ramírez 1975:60; Dibble 1981:14; Durán 1967, 2:110–111, 119–122, 125–131; García Icazbalceta 1886–92, 3:306; Herrera y Tordesilla 1934–57, 6:211; Lehmann and Kutscher 1981:36r; Leyenda de los soles 1975:128; Mendieta 1971:150; Mengin 1952:449; Paso y Troncoso 1939–42, 10:118; Sahagún 1954:1; Torquemada 1973–83, 1:200, 202–203, 207, 209, 226–227.

77. Hassig 1988:157–175.

78. Hassig 1988:125.

79. Palerm 1973:92.

80. Chimalpahin (1965:201, 229) records a New Fire ceremony on Huixachtecatl in 1455 and 1507, and appears to say that it was held there a total of four times, which would mean in 1403 and 1351 as well. However, his is a Chalca perspective and he was not in the best position to know.

81. Quiñones Keber 1995:fol. 42r; Torquemada 1973–83, 1:289.

82. Crónica mexicana 1975:318–320.

83. Orozco y Berra 1978, 3:394.

Chapter 3

1. Wolf 1999.

2. Schwaller 1985:4–9.

3. Wolf 1999:4–8.

4. Ziegler 1993:10, 210–211.

5. Ziegler 1993:15–17.

6. Kramer and Sprenger 1971:1–8, 222–230.

7. E.g., Berdan 1982:148.

8. Acosta 1954:238; Durán 1967, 2:507; Sahagún 1975:5, 9, 1989:37–38.

9. Acosta 1954:238, 283; Aguilar 1977:67; Anales de Cuauhtitlan 1975:68; Chimalpahin 1965:121, 234; Cortés 1963:19; Díaz del Castillo 1977, 1:122, 125–126; López de Gómara 1965–66, 2:52–53; Tapia 1950:40.

10. Sahagún 1961:170, 1970:69.

11. Acosta 1954:238; Durán 1967, 2:507; Florescano 1994:101; Sahagún 1975:5, 9; 1989:37–38.

12. Garibay 1973:112–116; Healan 1989b:5; Sahagún 1961:176.

13. This Cortés-as-Quetzalcoatl interpretation has been challenged by a number of historians (e.g., Lockhart 1993:20; Parry 1989:36–38). See also Pagden (in Cortés 1971:467–469, n. 42) for a discussion of this issue.

14. Acosta 1954:238; Durán 1967, 2:507; Sahagún 1975:5, 9; 1989:37–38, 41. I cannot assess the competing claims of Cook-as-god versus Cook-as-god-as-myth, but Sahlins's strong ideology-as-action stance has parallels in the conquest of Mexico, which he notes (Sahlins 1982:74, n. 1; 1985:42–43; 1995:194), and which Obeyesekere (1997:8, 16–19) identifies as a precursor to Sahlins's work,

though he questions this interpretation. I strongly oppose the Cortés-as-god interpretation in the Mexican case because it finds very little support in the earliest accounts and only appears decades after the Conquest as a way of explaining the Aztec defeat. That it has been accepted by modern scholars is, in my opinion (Hassig 1994:1–4), a deficiency of in-depth analysis.

15. Díaz 1950:15–16, 19–21; López de Gómara 1965–66, 2:16–19; Martir de Angleria 1964–65, 1:406; Oviedo y Valdés 1959, 2:135–136.
16. Acosta 1954:238; Alva Ixtlilxóchitl 1975–77, 1:450; Sahagún 1975:5–6, 1989: 34–36.
17. Florescano 1994:28; Quiñones Keber 1995: fol. 41v, 228–229; Sahagún 1953: 21–23.
18. Quiñones Keber 1995:67.
19. Quiñones Keber 1995:62.
20. Tena 1992:92.
21. Palerm 1973:18; Sanders, Parsons, and Santley 1979:222.
22. Alva Ixtlilxóchitl 1975–77, 2:111; Alvarado Tezozomoc 1975b:133; Chimalpahin 1965:97–100; Durán 1967, 1:241–242; Sahagún 1953:23, 32, 1954:2; Torquemada 1973–83, 1:300–305. I earlier argued for a good harvest in 1454 (Hassig 1981), but the pictorial evidence is against this interpretation (Quiñones Keber 1995:fol. 32), and there was clearly a crop loss in 1454.
23. Archivo General de la Nación (Mexico City), Reales Cédulas Duplicadas 3-17-9, 1587; Armillas 1971; Charlton 1970:320; Coe 1964; Mexico, Archivo General de la Nación 1940, 11:16; Moriarty 1968:469; Palerm 1973:237; Parsons 1976; Sanders 1957:304.
24. For a discussion of the various estimates, see Hassig (1985:47–53).
25. Hassig 1981, 1985:127–144.
26. Codex Vaticanus 1979:fol. 84v; Quiñones Keber 1995:fol. 41v.
27. Sahagún 1953:31, 1979:3.
28. Berdan and Anawalt 1992, 3:121–149.
29. Carrasco 1971:355; Zorita 1963:116.
30. Eliade 1974:85–90.
31. Miranda 1952:25; Zorita 1963:132.
32. G. Clark 1994:92.
33. León-Portilla 1971:51.
34. Tenayuca 1960:24–25.
35. Matos Moctezuma 1988:64–83.
36. Whitrow 1989:25, 84.
37. Nicholson 1971:398–399, 406–407.
38. E.g., Acuña 1982–87, 4:189, 203; Ruiz de Alarcón 1984:78–79.
39. E.g., Garibay 1973:102–103; Nicholson 1971:406–407; Pedro Ponce in Ruiz de Alarcón 1984:211; Sahagún 1961:169.
40. Nicholson 1971:399.
41. Garibay 1973:30–31.
42. Historia 1882:87–88.
43. Fowden 1993:34.
44. Read (1998:138–139) questions the verticality of Topan/Mictlan from a textual viewpoint, as does J. Richard Andrews (personal communication) from a linguistic perspective.
45. Nicholson 1971:406–407.
46. Durán 1967, 2:400–401.

47. This description and interpretation is based on Umberger (1981:193–208).
48. Navarrete and Heyden 1974; Pasztory 1983:170; Townsend 1979:67.
49. Umberger (1981:239) suggests that the Calendar Stone may postdate the Teo-calli, but this would not affect a 1507 or earlier date for the change from a 4-Sun to a 5-Sun world, as both monuments bear the essential depictions of this.
50. Knapp 1988:137–139; Peel 1984:112–113, 128; Townsend 1979.
51. Codex Tudela 1980:fols. 98v–103r.
52. A Teotihuacan mural of a feathered serpent above thirteen trees, bearing one cycle of 9 glyphs plus 4 repeated ones (Pasztory 1988:136–161), suggests the an-tiquity of the 9- and 13-day cycles, though their precise significance remains unclear.

Chapter 4

1. Whitrow 1989:69.
2. Whitrow 1989:16.
3. Bohannan 1953:254–255; Burman 1981:253–255; Panoff 1969:153–154.
4. Bourdieu 1988:97–109.
5. Bourdieu's complaint that writing down the calendar abstracts and falsifies it to some extent is the result not of knowing the calendar as the people using it know it, but of importing our own notions of the calendar, which are highly abstract, and trying to place the informants' notions into a formalized context, without paying due attention to the overly politicized nature of the calendar in the first place.
6. Burman 1981:252; Fabian 1983:28–31; O'Neil 1978:107; Reid 1972:468–473.
7. Rutz 1992a:4–5.
8. Rotenberg 1992.
9. Marx 1984:223–233.
10. Rutz 1992a.
11. Anales de Cuauhtitlan 1975:58; Barlow 1949a:126; Berlin and Barlow 1980:17; Códice Vaticano 1964–65:264; Durán 1967, 2:320; Paso y Troncoso 1939–42, 10:119; Torquemada 1973–83, 1:258.
12. Anales de Cuauhtitlan 1975:58; Berlin and Barlow 1980:17; Chimalpahin 1965: 115, 224; Crónica mexicana 1975:480–483; Durán 1967, 2:327, 341; Paso y Tron-coso 1939–42, 10:119; Sahagún 1954:2; Torquemada 1973–83, 1:257, 263, 267.
13. Durán 1967, 2:340.
14. Quiñones Keber 1995:225.
15. Webster 1976:814.
16. G. Clark 1994:49–50.
17. This discussion of social organization is based largely on the work of Pedro Carrasco (1971:351–356).
18. Doyle 1986:37–38. For a fuller consideration of the structure of the Aztec em-pire, see Hassig (1985, 1988).
19. Collingwood 1970:58.
20. Neill 1986:14.
21. For example, in the extant *Relaciones Geográficas* of 1579–1585, Huitzilo-pochtli is mentioned as being worshiped only in Tuztla, Tetela, Cempoala, Epa-zoyuca, Chimalhuacan Atoyac, Chicoaloapan, Tepeapulco, Teotihuacan, Te-quizistlan, Tetzcoco, Axocopan, and Hueypochtla, most of which were in or

adjacent to the Valley of Mexico, and all of which were Nahuatl speaking (Acuña 1982–87, 5:290–291, 405–407, 6:75–76, 84–86, 158–64, 171–173, 7:172–175, 233–235, 241–242, 8:54, 128–129, 143–144).

22. Sahagún 1951:168.
23. Hassig 1985:56–66, 1986.
24. Clavijero 1979, 1:355; Crónica mexicana 1975:325; Mendieta 1971:129.
25. Clavijero 1979, 1:345; Cortés 1963:76–77; Crónica mexicana 1975:634; Sahagún 1954:72.
26. Crónica mexicana 1975:412–413, 568.
27. Anales de Cuauhtitlan 1975:57; Crónica mexicana 1975:429–430; Durán 1967, 2:265, 293.
28. Dohrn-van Rossum 1996:30, 59; Landes 1983:59; Whitrow 1972:15.
29. E.g., Acuña 1982–87, 2:237, 3:87–91, 196–201, 6:216–217, 7:56–57, 227.
30. Hassig 1982.
31. E.g., W. R. Jones 1971:389.
32. Berdan 1976:138; Borah and Cook 1963:45–50.
33. Clavijero 1979, 1:293; Serna 1953:118.
34. This 13-day intercalation may be at least partly why the Aztecs expanded Topan from nine levels to thirteen. The 9-day cycle was already important and emphasized in other ways, whereas the redundant 13-day cycle was not. Thus stressing the 13 may have been a further cosmological tie-in between Topan and the sacredness of the calendrical innovation.
35. Gell 1992:307.
36. Doyle 1986:38. It has been noted, including in my own work (Hassig 1992:151), that the Aztecs did not successfully expand into areas that lacked states, despite efforts to do so. While this failure has been attributed to the lack of a suitable political structure and officeholders that would allow them to rule indirectly, another reason for this failure may well have been the absence of a sophisticated calendar, which would have hindered the adoption of an effective tribute system.
37. Anales de Cuauhtitlan 1975:64.
38. Berdan 1976:138; Berdan and Anawalt 1992, 3:47r, 4:98–99; Borah and Cook 1963:45–50; Matricula de Tributos 1980:fol. 13r. The date of this shift is confirmed by the grouping of tributaries, some of which were not conquered until Moteuczoma Xocoyotl's reign, into geographically contiguous areas.
39. Sato 1991:301.
40. Caso 1967:135.
41. Umberger 1981:122–124.
42. Quiñones Keber 1995:229.
43. Broda 1991:79–95; Townsend 1991.
44. Sahagún 1953:28, 1957:143–144.
45. Indeed, the New Fire ceremony's political role is reinforced by its one seemingly anomalous depiction. This ceremony, which is typically, though not universally, indicated by a fire drill with smoke curls, is shown at the 1487 rededication of the Great Temple (Quiñones Keber 1995:fol. 39r; Sahagún 1997:187) at a point that does not fall at the end of the Calendar Round or at any apparent division thereof. Moreover, it had no calendrical impact, such as restarting the year count. To understand this depiction requires placing it in its social and historical context. As noted earlier, this rededication occurred primarily as a venue in which wavering tributaries reaffirmed their fealty to the crown after five years of inept Aztec rule. And I would argue that this apparent New Fire ceremony

was not a ceremonial rededication of the temple, as it does not occur in similar contexts elsewhere. Rather, it was part of the political rededication that reasserted the altered calendar on which the tribute empire depended; this contention is supported by the record of the ceremony in political accounts, but not in calendrical descriptions.

46. Kubler and Gibson 1951:51–52.

47. Crónica mexicana 1975:318–320.

48. Although a flag (pantli) is used as a symbol for this month (e.g., Kubler and Gibson 1951:fig. 12; Lehmann and Kutscher 1981:42v; Veytia 1994:lams. 4, 5), flags are also used for other months (e.g., Kubler and Gibson 1951:pl. 14), and the flag here is also a symbol for Huitzilopochtli, who is celebrated this month.

49. Códice Borgia 1993:fol. 46.

50. E.g., Durán 1967, 1:239–292; Kubler and Gibson 1951:22–36; Sahagún 1997: 55–69.

51. Sahagún 1993:fols. 250r–253r.

52. It should be pointed out that the shift to Atl Cahualo as the initial month of the year began in 1455 (2 Acatl). Because this entailed shifting the start back one month, 1 Tochtli (1454) had only 17 months, not 18, which is why the *Codex Borbonicus* anomalously lists 19 months in this sequence rather than the usual 18—to clarify both the timing of the shift and its impact on the calendar system.

53. The other logical possibility for indicating year, placing a year glyph on each month of the eighteen, is impractical and does not distinguish between one year of 18 months and 18 months, each a full Calendar Round apart.

54. Because the Venus cycle is simply that, a cycle, it can be started at any point, so moving its commemoration by a year should have posed few astronomical difficulties.

55. Matos Moctezuma 1984:86.

56. Chimalpahin 1965:100, 201. See also Anales México-Azcapotzalco 1903:66.

57. Chimalpahin 1965:120, 229. The Anales México-Azcapotzalco (1903:70) mentions only Huixachtecatl for this year.

58. Sahagún 1957:143–144; Torquemada 1973–83, 3:42.

59. Chimalpahin 1965:180; Sahagún 1953:29–30; Torquemada 1973–83, 3:420–421.

60. Casas 1967, 2:185; Motolinía 1971:49.

61. Acuña 1982–87, 4:215–216.

62. Motolinía 1971:49.

63. Codex Azcatitlan 1995:18.

64. Porter 1966, 1:52–53.

65. Van Zantwijk 1981:73.

66. Aveni, Calnek, and Hartung 1988:304.

67. Matos Moctezuma 1988:70, 74.

68. Klein 1987:343.

69. Umberger 1987b:428–436.

70. Luján 1994:236–238.

71. Noguera 1961:15–27. Because the staircases vary from equality between the two sides to larger on the Huitzilopochtli side, a more detailed archaeological analysis is warranted to see whether the different pyramids varied in sync and, if not, if there is any correlation with political activities.

72. E.g., Codex Ixtlilxóchitl 1976:112v; Codex Aubin (Lehmann and Kutscher 1981: fol. 42r). The *Codex Telleriano-Remensis* (Quiñones Keber 1995:fols. 36v, 39r)

shows the left (north) side as larger, but Read (1998:14) notes that the two temples are reversed in this drawing.

73. Acuña 1982–87, 8:57–58.
74. Ignacio Bernal (1976:111–113) believed that the twin pyramid of Tenayuca was the first of its type, bringing together two temples on one pyramid, and was built by the Chichimecs during their migration into the Valley of Mexico. This early pyramid, he suggested, was dedicated to Tlaloc and Tezcatlipoca, and was copied centuries later in Tenochtitlan on a grander scale, but dedicated to Tlaloc and Huitzilopochtli. I fail to see the evidence for Tezcatlipoca at Tenayuca; indeed, Bernal's interpretation appears to be driven less by the physical remains at that site than by the assessment of Calendar Rounds between the building phases.

One difficulty with distinguishing the gods of this site from those of the other dual pyramids is that all of them share a common orientation—west— that is associated with the sun and that places the Huitzilopochtli temple on the south, as befits his name. This placement also suggests that at Tenayuca the dual occupants were Tlaloc and Huitzilopochtli, as there is no iconographic or etymological reason for orienting a Tezcatlipoca shrine toward the west or locating it on the north side. Moreover, the basic excavations of Tenayuca were carried out in the first third of the twentieth century and published in 1935. And while eight temples have been identified—an original structure and seven superpositions—the attributed dates seem too early in light of subsequent research elsewhere in the Valley of Mexico. But when Bernal wrote, these were accepted dates, and to account for them in light of the historical records of the movement of Aztecs and others into the Valley of Mexico, Tenayuca *must* have been a Chichimec site and therefore could not have commemorated Huitzilopochtli, the tutelary Aztec god. Instead, he posited the commemoration of Tezcatlipoca, the tutelary god of the Toltecs. But if the dates for Tenayuca are not accepted (and this site is ripe for reanalysis), a building sequence more in accord with Aztec construction seems likelier. With such an adjustment, the dual temples can be more plausibly seen as commemorating Tlaloc and Huitzilopochtli, as is the case with all other known dual pyramids in central Mexico.

Although the twin pyramid structure was an Aztec innovation, the emphasis on dual gods appears to have a long pedigree in central Mexico. Gods were often paired—Quetzalcoatl and perhaps Tlaloc on the Pyramid of Quetzalcoatl at Teotihuacan (Millon 1973:55; but see Sugiyama 1992:206), Quetzalcoatl and Tezcatlipoca in the numerous legends of Tollan (e.g., Garibay 1973:112–116; Sahagún 1961:170–176, 1970:69), and Tlaloc and Huitzilopochtli on the Templo Mayor in Tenochtitlan; moreover, in two, if not all three, of these cases, one god appears to have achieved ascendancy.

The ascendancy of one god does not mean the elimination of the other; after all, in a polytheistic tradition, there is little religious purpose in eliminating a god, as each has its own domain. There was no monotheistic Moses destroying the idol of the golden calf (Exodus 32). Nevertheless, there were both priestly and political purposes for a god to achieve ascendance: for the priests, an ascendant god insured more offerings going to their temple. For the political elites, an ascendant god reflected their use of a sacred idiom (Townsend 1979) to elevate themselves in the guise of a political/military deity over a more religious one.

At Teotihuacan, god ascendancy is uncertain, as there are no written records, precious little sculpture that was not removed for re-use elsewhere, and only a small selection of murals (most of which are sixth century and later) and ceramic figures. Nevertheless, Tlaloc and Quetzalcoatl are co-represented on the Pyramid of Quetzalcoatl, though this structure was destroyed and covered over in an expansion in A.D. 150 (Sugiyama 1989:90–98). Whether that represented a change in the relative importance of the two gods is unknown, but the history of Teotihuacan clearly indicates a major shift in organization with the razing of the early residences and relocation in apartment compounds, and the rise of a militaristic emphasis after A.D. 600, as evident in ceramic figures and murals (Barbour 1975:140; Millon 1976:239–240; 1981:242, n. 26; Pasztory 1978a:14).

At Tollan, both legends and archaeology attest to a struggle between Tezcatlipoca and Quetzalcoatl, with the former ascendant. No dual structures were found, but sections of the city apparently associated with Quetzalcoatl were abandoned and remained largely vacant (Diehl 1981:280, 1983:45; Healan, Cobean, and Diehl 1989:244), reflecting the loss of status of that god in relation to Tezcatlipoca, and a corresponding rise of emergent secular rulers over more traditional, sacred ones.

75. Townsend 1979:15, 41–63.
76. Townsend 1979:49.
77. Townsend 1979:53.
78. Townsend 1979:54.
79. Townsend 1979:71.
80. Umberger 1981:172–193, 1984:63.
81. Boone 1989:15; Umberger 1984:72–78.
82. Umberger 1981:190.
83. Despite my doubt regarding the identity of the first figure as Xiuhteuctli, it would be convenient for my interpretation of the intercalary days, as well as Serna's statements, because it would further evidence the monument's commemorative nature reflecting the calendrical change.
84. See Hassig 1992:238–241, n. 105.
85. The Huixachtecatl temple dedicated to Huitzilopochtli has only one stairway, but apparently lacks any reference to Tlaloc.
86. Sáenz 1967:24–26.
87. Hassig 1988:128–130.
88. Seler 1990–96, 4:104.
89. Seler 1990–96, 4:115–116.
90. Seler 1990–96, 4:119–121.
91. Seler 1990–96, 4:121–124.
92. J. Richard Andrews, personal communication.
93. Códice de Huamantla 1984:lams. 17, 42–46, 49–50.
94. Chimalpahin 1965:99. See also Hassig 1988:171.
95. Crónica mexicana 1975:541; Durán 1967, 2:360; Hassig 1988:215.

Chapter 5

1. Sahagún 1959:1–2.
2. Burgoa 1934, 1:332–333; De Landa 1973:105; Read 1998:12. See the pictures of Spanish priests burning native temples and ritual paraphernalia, which doubtlessly included books, in Muñoz Camargo (Acuña 1982–87, 4:pl. 9, 10, 12).
3. E.g., Anales de Tula 1979; Berdan and Anawalt 1992, 3; Codex Azcatitlan 1995; Codex Vaticanus 1979; Dibble 1981:4–5; Lehmann and Kutscher 1981; Lock-

hart 1992:377; Mengin 1952; Quiñones Keber 1995; Wilcox 1987:190. See also Florescano 1994:36.

4. E.g., Berdan and Anawalt 1992, 3:12, 14, 16, 22, 27, 31, 33, 38; Codex Azcatitlan 1995:13v, 14v, 15v, 16v, 17v, 18v, 20v; Codex Vaticanus 1979:73v, 74r–v, 77v, 78r, 80v, 84r; Lehmann and Kutscher 1981:27v, 29v, 31v, 32r, 33v, 37r, 37v, 38r; Mengin 1952:pl. 53, 56, 71, 74; Quiñones Keber 1995:62, 64, 65, 66, 72, 75, 80, 81, 85.

5. E.g., Berdan and Anawalt 1992, 3:16, 19, 22, 27; Codex Azcatitlan 1995:14, 15, 16, 17, 19; Codex Vaticanus 1979:73v, 74r–v, 77v, 78r, 80v, 84r, 85v, 86v; Códice de Xicotepec 1995:secs. 1–2, 8; Lehmann and Kutscher 1981:29r, 31v, 32r, 33v; Mengin 1952:pl. 51, 56, 48, 71, 74; Quiñones Keber 1995:61, 62, 64, 65, 66, 72, 75, 80, 81, 82, 85.

6. E.g., Berdan and Anawalt 1992, 3:11, 12, 14, 15, 18, 19, 22, 23, 27, 28, 31, 33, 34, 38, 39, 40; Codex Azcatitlan 1995:8, 9v, 10, 11; Codex Vaticanus 1979:74r, 76v, 77r, 79r–v, 83r, 85r–v, 86r; Códice de Xicotepec 1995:sec. 10; Lehmann and Kutscher 1981:36v, 37r, 37v, 40v, 41r; Mengin 1952:pl. 57, 60, 69, 70, 71; Quiñones Keber 1995:61, 65, 71, 76, 88, 89.

7. E.g., Codex Azcatitlan 1995:14; Codex Vaticanus 1979:81v; Códice de Xicotepec 1995:sec. 8; Lehmann and Kutscher 1981:38r, 38v; Mengin 1952:pl. 71; Quiñones Keber 1995:81.

8. E.g., Codex Vaticanus 1979:85v; Quiñones Keber 1995:77, 82, 87, 88, 91.

9. E.g., Codex Vaticanus 1979:76r–v, 77v, 80r, 85v; Lehmann and Kutscher 1981:38v; Mengin 1952:pl. 69, 72; Quiñones Keber 1995:69, 70, 72, 79, 84, 87, 88.

10. E.g., Quiñones Keber 1995:67, 89, 91.

11. E.g., Codex Vaticanus 1979:75r; Lehmann and Kutscher 1981:30r, 34v, 39r; Quiñones Keber 1995:68.

12. E.g., Codex Vaticanus 1979:84v; Códice Aubin 1980:60, 68, 77; Quiñones Keber 1995:86.

13. Florescano 1994:49–50.

14. D. Carrasco 1990:54.

15. MacNeish, Nalken-Terner, and Johnson 1967:55, 150–152.

16. Toulmin and Goodfield 1982:23, 29.

17. Códice Boturini 1964–65:lam. 1.

18. Florescano 1994:50.

19. Codex Vaticanus 1979:66v.

20. Códice Boturini 1964–65:lam. 1.

21. Códice Boturini 1964–65:lams. 5–6.

22. Berdan and Anawalt 1992, 3:11–12.

23. Florescano 1994:52; Hassig 1988:125–235.

24. Of the surviving pre-Columbian codices, there are five in the Borgia group (Borgia, Cospi, Féjéváry-Mayer, Laud, and Vaticanus B), six from western Oaxaca (Aubin Ms. no. 20, Becker no. 1, Bodley, Colombino, Nuttall, and Vienna), and four from the Maya area (Dresden, Grolier, Madrid, and Paris) (Glass 1975:11; Lee 1985).

25. Durán 1967.

26. Chimalpahin 1965.

27. Brown 1988:7–9, 304.

28. Códice Boturini 1964–65:13.

29. E.g., Codex Vaticanus 1979:66r, 69, 71r.

30. Quiñones Keber 1995:58.

31. Quiñones Keber 1995:41r, 42v, 229, 274.
32. Pasztory 1983:60. See also Códice Boturini 1964–65:passim.
33. Caso 1971:335.
34. Broda 1969:29.
35. Umberger 1987a:92.
36. Durán 1967, 1:223.
37. But Durán (1967, 1:223) claims it was, which may suggest a need for closer reexamination.
38. Sharer 1994:568.
39. Berdan 1982:144; Broda 1969:28; Brundage 1979:22, 1982:146; Léon-Portilla 1971:50–51; Todorov 1984:85.
40. Sahagún 1953:25.
41. Payne and Closs 1988:223–224.
42. E.g., Pasztory 1983:165.
43. Caso 1967:135, 138; Pasztory 1983:165; Umberger 1981:122–124.
44. Quiñones Keber 1995.
45. Acuña 1982–87, 4:215–216.
46. Edmonson 1988:21, 27; Furst 1978:231.
47. Furst 1978:232.
48. Caso 1967:135.
49. Note that the departure from Aztlan is not on, nor does it begin, a Calendar Round count, which suggests that there is a pre-Aztec period during which the Calendar Round of that time began, which may have been used to cover the prehistorical events of the Aztec mythical past.
50. Breisach 1983:25–26, 30.
51. Breisach 1983:36; G. Clark 1994:98; Toulmin and Goodfield 1982:281; Whitrow 1989:67; Wilcox 1987:83–93.
52. Berdan and Anawalt 1992, 3:12, 14, 16, 19, 22, 27, 31, 33, 38; Codex Vaticanus 1979:73v, 74r–v, 77v, 78r, 80v, 84r, 85v, 86v; Lehmann and Kutscher 1981:27v, 29r, 29v, 31v, 32r, 33v, 37r, 37v, 38r; Quiñones Keber 1995:61, 62, 64, 65, 66, 72, 75, 80, 81, 82, 85.
53. E.g., Anales de Tecamachalco 1981:6; Anales de Tula 1979:lam. 2; Códice de Huichapan 1992:lams. 14, 38, 60.
54. New Catholic Encyclopedia 1967, 3:653, 10:250; Whitrow 1989:70.
55. New Catholic Encyclopedia 1967, 3:653, 10:250.
56. Africa 1991:374–375; Potter 1987:192.
57. New Catholic Encyclopedia 1967, 10:250.
58. Whitrow 1972:19, 1989:70; Wilcox 1987:142–144, 203–208.
59. Sato 1991:279.
60. Códice Boturini 1964–65:lam. 1; Umberger 1981:209–213.
61. Read 1998:11; Umberger 1981:213.
62. Wilcox 1987:9.
63. Aveni 1989:127–135.
64. Sahagún 1951:75.
65. Cook and Borah 1971:9–10; Sanders 1976:150.
66. See Christian (1981) for an interesting account of Catholicism as actually practiced in Spain in the late sixteenth century.
67. E.g., Sobel 1995.
68. E.g., Malmström 1997:100.
69. Broda 1969:77–78; Edmonson 1988:98–101.

70. Broda 1969:84–85; Caso 1967:143–162; Edmonson 1988:101–102.
71. Broda 1969:80–81; Caso 1965a; Cline and Cline 1975; Franch 1966; Seler 1904.
72. Broda 1969:84–85; Caso 1967:166–168; Edmonson 1988:129; Palacios 1948: 464–465; Peñafiel 1890, 1:43; Sáenz 1967:11–16, 46; Seler 1888:84.
73. Caso 1967.
74. Edmonson 1988, 1992:164–167.
75. Caso 1971:333.
76. Aveni 1989:116–117; Crosby 1997:87; O'Neil 1978:11; Moyer 1982; Whitrow 1989:116–118.
77. Aveni 1989:117–118; Whitrow 1989:119. This 10-day shift, plus the 20-day shift from the Tlacaxipehualiztli to Atl Cahualo year beginning accounts for most of the disparate dates the Spaniards recorded for the beginning of the Aztec year.
78. Broda 1969:78.
79. This division parallels that between the Olmec and Maya syllabary writing systems, on one hand, where the zero-date calendar prevailed, and the Mexican pictographic and ideographic glyph systems, on the other, where the non-zero-date calendar was used, and which may indicate an origin among the Zapotecs, who left the earliest Mexican calendrical glyphs (Broda 1969:77, 80–81).
80. Landes 1983:26.
81. Sato 1991:220.
82. There is only fragmentary evidence for the calendar of Teotihuacan (A.D. 1–750), capital of the first major empire in Mexico. It appears to have had the tonalpohualli (Broda 1969:84; Caso 1967:143–153), and thus presumably the 13 day numbers and 20 day symbols as well, which are sufficient to operate a complete Calendar Round system (the xihuitl months, if they existed at this time, as presumably they did, are not usually recorded even in the Aztec system, so their absence at Teotihuacan is not unexpected). The Teotihuacanos, however, used the bar-dot numbering system (each bar equals 5 and each dot equals 1) rather than the Aztec dot-only system, a 2–14 day-number count rather than 1–13 (Edmonson 1988:5, 11; 1992:160), and different day symbol glyphs, though some may have had the same meaning as Aztec day symbols (Broda 1969:84; Caso 1967:155). There are also possible year dates (Caso 1967:154) and apparently a glyph for year (Edmonson 1988:33). A set of four similar murals from Teotihuacan that are identified as the Maguey Priest murals (Miller 1973:170) or the Maguey Bloodletting Ritual (Millon 1988) show a priestly figure flanked by two sets of maguey leaves before what has been identified as a rectangular or terraced field. The rectangular fields may also be year bundles and depict a Binding of the Years ceremony at Teotihuacan (Millon 1988:199–200), a commemoration that would be expected given the pieces of their calendar that are known. During Teotihuacan times, relative calendrical uniformity dominated, but with that empire's demise, at least seven different calendars came into use (Edmonson 1988:101–102).

Xochicalco (A.D. 650–900) emerged not as an imperial capital but as a regional center during the interregnum between Teotihuacan and Tollan. The calendar system borrowed glyphic elements from Teotihuacan and Monte Albán, as well as employing some that are unique and that apparently originated there. It had the tonalpohualli and a 1–13 day-number count employing those numbers, and some of the day symbols were changed, although only eight can be clearly identified (Broda 1969:84–85). A new set of year bearers came into use, along with a new year symbol and a new way of distinguishing a year date from a day date, and there was use of both the bar-dot and dot-only numerical systems. Moreover, the Xochicalcans apparently initiated, or restarted and recalibrated, the New Fire ceremony, recording the (or "a") first New Fire ceremony in the year 1 Tochtli (Sáenz 1967). Since such ceremonies are unnecessary for internal purposes, these political events are aimed at subordinate centers; this, together with the recalibrated calendar, suggests the emergence of a tributary empire, though of uncertain extent. The calendar is incompletely known for Tollan, with only some of the day symbols being identified (Edmonson 1988:252–254, 1992:159), but the Toltecs employed the same calendar system (Alva Ixtlilxó-chitl 1975–77, 1:283), although their year started with 1 Tochtli (Bierhorst 1992: 25), and it was from this calendar that the Aztecs derived theirs (Edmonson 1992:166).

How far Tollan's influence extended can be seen in Oaxaca. In the eleventh century, the Mixtec king 8 Deer (1011–1063) conquered 75 to 100 towns and unified the Mixteca Alta and the coastal Mixtecs in a polity centered at Ti-lantongo (Caso 1966:145; Marcus and Flannery 1983:218; Paddock 1966b:202; Mary E. Smith 1963:227, 288; 1966:151). But this small empire does not appear to have been entirely independent. It did not perform a New Fire ceremony and, in fact, the Mixtecs had shifted to the Toltec calendar (Caso 1965a:955; Flannery and Marcus 1983a:185), indicating at least some degree of political subordination beyond the symbolic that is suggested by 8 Deer's investiture at Tollan (Caso 1966:128–129; J. Clark 1912:20–21; Flannery and Marcus 1983a:185).

83. Charlot 1931, 1:311, 2:pl. 59; Justeson et al. 1985:70; Lincoln 1986:154.
84. G. Clark 1994:99; O'Neil 1978:9–10, 79; Whitrow 1989:26, 66–67.
85. Doyle 1986:19.
86. Bricker 1981:6; Love 1994:73; Satterthwaite 1965:613–617.
87. Chase and Chase 1996, 1998; Culbert 1988.
88. New Catholic Encyclopedia 1967, 2:1065.
89. Chichen Itza was taken over by a Mexicanized group now known as the Putun (Thompson 1970:3–47), whose identity is debated. Mayanists generally resist the idea that they were Toltecs, while Mexicanists generally accept it. And the intrusion of Mexican architecture, sculpture, glyphs, and Nahuatl (spoken by the Toltecs) at this time strongly argue in favor of the Toltec invasion thesis (Andrews 1965:314–315, 317; Andrews and Sabloff 1986:434, 445–449; Fowler 1989:41–42; Justeson et al., 1985:70; Morley, Brainerd, and Sharer 1983:160–164; Pollock 1965:433; Proskouriakoff 1965:491, 496; Willey 1986:32–33), as do the lack of Maya equivalents in central Mexico.
90. Ball 1985:236, 243; 1986:383; Chase 1986:101–110; Chase and Chase 1985:9–13, 17.
91. Whitrow 1989:120.
92. Aveni 1989:144–145; Landes 1983:286. The nationalistic French similarly insisted that the zero meridian should be calculated from Paris, rather than Greenwich, where it was first established as voted in 1884 by the International Meridian Conference.
93. Gossen 1974:27.
94. Pedro Carrasco, personal communication.
95. De Landa 1973:60–65.
96. Hassig 1988:53–54.

Chapter 6

1. Cartas de Indias 1970, 1:56; Mendieta 1971:213–215; Motolinía 1971:258–262; Torquemada 1973–83, 5:198–199.
2. Gibson 1964:155, 161.
3. Madsen 1960:118.
4. Ricard 1974:217–235.
5. Gibson 1964:382; Ricard 1974:217–235.
6. Breisach 1983:140–142; Burkhart 1989:74–81. Crosby (1997:30) notes that medieval Europeans saw the world in stages that changed abruptly, rather than gradually. This is also true of the Aztecs and their five Suns, in which the present Sun could end at any point, but within a Sun was an eternal present. See also Phelan (1970:41) for Mendieta's view of the world in terms of ages.
7. Burkhart 1989:79–82; Florescano 1994:81–90; Phelan 1970:passim. Sahagún, however, did not share this apocalyptic perspective (Phelan 1970:27).
8. Gibson 1964:166.
9. Durán 1967, 1:3–6, 236–237.
10. See Foster (1960:167–226) for a discussion of ritual days in Christian Latin America.
11. E.g., Chimalpahin 1965; Lehmann and Kutscher 1981.
12. Wilcox 1987:190.
13. Breisach 1983:154.
14. Breisach 1983:159. See Díaz del Castillo's reliance on Paolo Giovio and Gonzalo de Illescas in his *Historia verdadera* (Díaz del Castillo 1977, 1:71, 79).
15. E.g., Martínez 1948.
16. Lockhart 1992:216; Zorita 1963:132.
17. Durán 1967, 2:453.
18. E.g., Cline and Cline 1975; Franch 1966:123.
19. Weitlaner 1963:198–201.
20. Ruiz de Alarcón 1984:141–155.
21. Sahagún 1957:144.
22. Landes 1983:26, 29.
23. Sahagún 1997:124.
24. Aveni 1989:92; Landes 1983:25, 59, 92; Le Goff 1980:49; O'Malley 1996:10.
25. Aveni 1989:91; Dohrn-van Rossum 1996:19, 113–117; Landes 1983:77; O'Neil 1978:4; Rotenberg 1992:28; Whitrow 1972:58, 1989:28–29.
26. Dohrn-van Rossum 1996:57–59; Landes 1983:57.
27. Dohrn-van Rossum 1996:21–24; Landes 1983:24; Pacey 1992:34–36; Whitrow 1972:10, 1989:27–28. But see Cipolla (1978:103). See also Berdini (1962) for a fuller treatment of the water clock, and the use of mercury instead of water.
28. Dohrn-van Rossum 1996:18–21, 57; Landes 1983:24, 68.
29. Whitrow 1972:67.
30. Landes 1983:229.
31. Balmer 1978:615; Dohrn-van Rossum 1996:117–118, 252, 273.
32. G. Clark 1994:104; Crosby 1997:77–78; Landes 1983:60–66; Whitrow 1989:83, 101–102.
33. Cipolla 1978:103–104; Le Goff 1980:34–39.
34. Crosby 1997:77–78; Dohrn-van Rossum 1996:33–39, 47, 64.
35. Crosby 1997:76; Landes 1983:122, 128; O'Malley 1996:56; O'Neil 1978:12, 33; Whitrow 1989:108.

36. O'Malley 1996:63.
37. Aveni 1989:96–97; Dohrn-van Rossum 1996:348; O'Malley 1996:61; Whitrow 1989:159.
38. Landes 1983:285; Stephens 1989:3–4, 16–21.
39. O'Malley 1996:64–67, 74–79, 90–94.
40. O'Malley 1996:80–82; Stephens 1989:7–11.
41. Bartky 1989; O'Malley 1996:100–101.
42. Whitrow 1972:69.
43. Piña Garza 1994:64–66.
44. Other non-clock visual timekeepers found elsewhere, such as time balls that drop at designated points, usually noon, remain as historical oddities, like the one at the Royal Observatory in Greenwich, England. This timekeeper, which was not used in Mexico, survives as the ball that marks the New Year in Times Square, New York (Aveni 1989:96; O'Malley 1996:87).
45. Dohrn-van Rossum 1996:232–236; Landes 1983:26, 59, 72; O'Malley 1996: 23–24.
46. Dohrn-van Rossum 1996:39.
47. Dohrn-van Rossum 1996:197–213, 294–300.
48. Landes 1983:229–230.
49. Azcapotzalco was a center of metalworking generally and produced bronze church bells (Kubler 1972, 1:176), which were commonly found in church towers throughout central Mexico (Kubler 1972, 2:passim). See Toussaint (1967: 267–269) on bell manufacturing in colonial Mexico.
50. Dohrn-van Rossum 1996:125–128, 138–140; Whitrow 1972:62.
51. Piña Garza 1994:94.
52. Bejarano 1889–1916, 5:226–227.
53. Piña Garza 1994:95.
54. Altman 1991:430–431.
55. Bejarano 1889–1916, 12:135. In contrast to Mexico, in England, clock makers—or ironworkers, who also made clocks—were found as early as the thirteenth century and had become sufficiently numerous to become one of the fourteen formal branches of ironworkers in London by 1422 (Geddes 1991:17–82).
56. Altman 1991:416–417. There was enough of an impact on the Indians that clocks were occasionally mentioned in indigenous records, as in the *Anales de Tecamachalco* for 1561 (Anales de Tecamachalco 1981:29).
57. For the postcolonial continuation of such time practices in Guatemala, see Hawkins (1984:167–168).
58. Landes 1983:94.
59. Fernandez and Fernandez 1996:221.
60. Landes 1983:37–40.
61. Wasserstrom 1983:240–251.
62. Chance and Taylor 1985.
63. Gibson 1964:356–357; Hassig 1982, 1985:231–237.
64. Dohrn-van Rossum 1996:245–251.
65. Hassig 1985:231–237.
66. Gell 1992:12.
67. Hassig 1988:232–237.
68. Archivo General de la Nación (Mexico City), General de Parte 1-355-81, 1575; 2-957-226, 1580.
69. Gibson 1964:100; Mendieta 1971:226–230.

70. Schwaller 1985:5–9.
71. Ruiz de Alarcón 1984:passim.
72. Bejarano 1889–1916, 1:12.
73. Anales de Tecamachalco 1981:9; Chimalpahin 1965:258; Quiñones Keber 1995: fol. 45r.
74. Gibson 1964:166–185.
75. Haskett 1991:194–195.
76. Robertson 1975:253–265.
77. E.g., Códice de San Antonio 1993; Códice García Granados 1992; Códice de Huixquilucan 1993.
78. Bricker 1981:8–9.

Chapter 7

1. E.g., Boone 1989; Brundage 1979, 1985; D. Carrasco 1990; Carrasco and Matos Moctezuma 1992; Clendinnen 1991; Conrad and Demarest 1984.
2. E.g., Boone 1989; Burkhart 1989.
3. E.g., Berdan 1982; Hassig 1985, 1988; Katz 1972; Peterson 1962; Vaillant 1966.
4. Ferris 1988:96–101.
5. There are, of course, fervently held religious beliefs that are strikingly at odds with the world as we know it; however, those who adhere to such beliefs must necessarily withdraw from the world—into cloistered orders as religious hermits—or risk dissolution.
6. Southwold 1979.
7. Knapp 1988:138.
8. Feuchtwang 1993:35–36, 48.
9. Skinner and Winckler 1969.
10. Bartlett 1993:72, 82–83, 300–306.
11. E.g., see Fowden's (1993) discussion of the breakdown of archaic empires that are also integrated by a shared religion.
12. Durán 1967, 1:3; Mendieta 1971:9; Motolinía 1973:1; Sahagún 1982:45–46.
13. Córdoba 1970:105–115; Durán 1967, 1:5–6; Ruiz de Alarcón 1984:45; Sahagún 1951:39–41; 1969:114–115, 201–202, 213; 1970:24–27, 33, 107.
14. E.g., Ruiz de Alarcón 1984:45–47.
15. E.g., Ciruelo 1977:83, 91, 103, 108–109; Ruiz de Alarcón 1984:47–48, 53, 62, and passim.
16. Córdoba 1970.
17. Sahagún 1969:201–202.
18. Sahagún 1969:213.
19. Sahagún 1969:29–34, 1970:24–27.
20. Sahagún 1952:5–6, 1970:33.
21. Sahagún 1952:39.
22. Sahagún 1951:193–201, 1969:209–218.
23. Gibson 1964:100–101; Ricard 1974:33; Sahagún 1951:39–41, 1969:114–115.
24. E.g., Ruiz de Alarcón 1984:63.
25. See also Ruiz de Alarcón 1984:45.
26. New Catholic Encyclopedia 1967, 2:1064–1065, 5:865–868, 9:317–318.
27. Aveni 1989:128; Bloomfield 1975:44–51; Breisach 1983:141–142; Crosby 1997:

28–29; Toulmin and Goodfield 1982:56, 71–72; Whitrow 1989:74–75, 80–82; Wilcox 1987:126–127.

28. E.g., Anales de Tecamachalco 1981; Chimalpahin 1965; Lehmann and Kutscher 1981.

29. Berdan 1982:144; Broda 1969:27; Brundage 1979:25; 1982:63, 137; 1985:26–27, 70–71; C. A. Burland 1967:129; D. Carrasco 1990:54; Clendinnen 1991:35; Edmonson 1988:1; Gruzinski 1992:74; León-Portilla 1992; Thomas 1993:187; Todorov 1984:66, 69, 84.

30. Berdan 1982; Brundage 1979, 1982, 1985; Burland 1967; Burland and Forman 1980; D. Carrasco 1990; Clendinnen 1991; Davies 1980; León-Portilla 1971, 1992; Peterson 1962; Townsend 1992.

31. Graham 1988:123; Houston 1988:126.

32. Aveni 1989:193, 249; Whitrow 1972:12–13, 1989:93, 95.

33. Compare Eliade's (1974) position with that of Read (1998).

34. Culbert 1988:135–136.

35. E.g., Carmack 1983:235–237; Scholes and Thompson 1977:65.

36. E.g., Bricker 1981:8.

37. E.g., Ruiz de Alarcón 1984:89.

38. E.g., Hunt 1977:179–180, 184–203; Read 1998:15–16.

39. E.g., Gossen 1974:24–29; Tedlock 1992:89–104.

Bibliography

Acosta, José de. 1954. *Obras*. Madrid: Ediciones Atlas.

Acuña, René. 1982–87. *Relaciones geográficas del siglo XVI*. 9 vols. Mexico City: Universidad Nacional Autónoma de México.

Africa, Thomas W. 1991. *The Immense Majesty: A History of Rome and the Roman Empire*. Arlington Heights, Ill.: Harlan Davidson, Inc.

Aguilar, Francisco de. 1977. *Relación breve de la conquista de la Nueva España*. Mexico City: Universidad Nacional Autónoma de México.

Altman, Ida. 1991. "Spanish Society in Mexico City after the Conquest." *Hispanic American Historical Review* 71:413–445.

Alva Ixtlilxóchitl, Fernando de. 1975–77. *Obras completas*. 2 vols. Mexico City: Universidad Nacional Autónoma de México.

Alvarado Tezozomoc, Hernando. 1975a. *Crónica mexicana y Códice Ramírez*. Mexico City: Editorial Porrúa.

———. 1975b. *Crónica Mexicáyotl*. Mexico City: Universidad Nacional Autónoma de México.

Anales de Cuauhtitlan. 1975. "Anales de Cuauhtitlan." In *Códice Chimalpopoca* 1975:3–118.

Anales de Tecamachalco. 1981. *Anales de Tecamachalco: Crónica local y colonial en idioma náhuatl: 1398 y 1590*. Mexico City: Editorial Innovación.

Anales de Tula. 1979. *Anales de Tula*. Graz, Austria: Akademische Druck-u.

Anales México-Azcapotzalco. 1903. "Anales México-Azcapotzalco." *Anales del Museo Nacional de México* 7:49–74.

Anders, Ferdinand, Maarten Jansen, and Luis Reyes García. 1991. *El Libro del Ciuacoatl: Homenaje para el año del Fuego Nuevo*. Mexico City: Fondo de Cultura Económica.

Andrews, E. Wyllys V. 1965. "Archaeology and Prehistory in the Northern Maya Lowlands: An Introduction." *Handbook of Middle American Indians*, 2, *Archaeology of Southern Mesoamerica*, part 1: 288–330.

Andrews, E. Wyllys V, and Jeremy A. Sabloff. 1986. "Classic to Postclassic: A Summary Discussion." In Sabloff and Andrews 1986: 433–456.

Antigüedades de México. 1964–65. *Antigüedades de México*. 4 vols. Mexico City: Secretaría de Hacienda y Crédito Público.

Armillas, Pedro. 1971. "Gardens on Swamps." *Science* 174:653–661.

Aveni, Anthony F. 1989. *Empires of Time: Calendars, Clocks, and Cultures*. New York: Basic Books.

Aveni, Anthony F., and Gordon Brotherston. 1989. *World Archaeology.* Cambridge: Cambridge University Press.

Aveni, Anthony F., E. E. Calnek, and H. Hartung. 1988. "Myth, Environment, and the Orientation of the Templo Mayor of Tenochtitlan." *American Antiquity* 53:287–309.

Ball, Joseph. 1985. "The Postclassic Archaeology of the Western Gulf Coast: Some Initial Observations." In Chase and Rice 1985:235–253.

———. 1986. "Campeche, the Itza, and the Postclassic: A Study in Ethnohistorical Archaeology." In Sabloff and Andrews 1986:379–408.

Balmer, R. T. 1978. "The Operation of Sand Clocks and Their Mechanical Development." *Technology and Culture* 19:615–632.

Barbour, Warren. 1975. "The Figurines and Figurine Chronology of Ancient Teotihuacán, Mexico." Ph.D. diss., University of Rochester. Ann Arbor, Mich.: University Microfilms.

Barlow, Roberto H. 1949. "El Códice Azcatitlán." *Journal de la Société des Américanistes* 38:101–135.

———. 1980. *Anales de Tlatelolco y Códice de Tlatelolco.* Mexico City: Ediciones Rafael Porrúa.

Barth, Fredrik. 1987. *Cosmologies in the Making: A Generative Approach to Cultural Variation in Inner New Guinea.* Cambridge: Cambridge University Press.

Bartky, Ian R. 1989. "The Adoption of Standard Time." *Technology and Culture* 30:25–56.

Bartlett, Robert. 1993. *The Making of Europe: Conquest, Colonization and Cultural Change, 950–1350.* Princeton: Princeton University Press.

Bejarano, Ignacio. 1889–1916. *Actas de Cabildo de la Ciudad de México.* 54 vols. Mexico City.

Benson, Elizabeth P. 1981. *Mesoamerican Sites and World-Views.* Washington, D.C.: Dumbarton Oaks.

Berdan, Frances F. 1976. "A Comparative Analysis of Aztec Tribute Documents." *Actas del XLI Congreso International de Americanistas* 2:131–142.

———. 1982. *The Aztecs of Central Mexico: An Imperial Society.* New York: Holt, Rinehart, and Winston.

Berdan, Frances F., and Patricia Rieff Anawalt. 1992. *The Codex Mendoza.* 4 vols. Berkeley and Los Angeles: University of California Press.

Berdini, Silvio A. 1962. "The Compacted Cylindrical Clepsydra." *Technology and Culture* 3:115–141.

Bergesen, Albert. 1980. *Studies of the Modern World System.* New York: Academic Press.

Berlin, Heinrich, and Robert H. Barlow. 1980. *Anales de Tlatelolco.* Mexico City: Ediciones Rafael Porrúa.

Berlo, Janet Catherine. 1992. *Art, Ideology, and the City of Teotihuacan.* Washington, D.C.: Dumbarton Oaks.

Bernal, Ignacio. 1976. *Tenochtitlan en una isla.* Mexico City: Utopía.

Berrin, Kathleen. 1988. *Feathered Serpents and Flowering Trees: Reconstructing the Murals of Teotihuacan.* San Francisco: Fine Arts Museums of San Francisco.

Bierhorst, John, trans. 1992. *History and Mythology of the Aztecs: The Codex Chimalpopoca.* Tucson: University of Arizona Press.

Blair, John, and Nigel Ramsay. 1991. *English Medieval Industries: Craftsmen, Techniques, Products.* London: Hambledon Press.

Bloomfield, M. 1975. "Joachim of Flora: A Critical Survey of His Canon, Teachings, Sources, Biography, and Influence." In D. C. West 1975:29–91.

Bohannan, Paul. 1953. "Concepts of Time among the Tiv of Nigeria." *Southwestern Journal of Anthropology* 9:251–262.

Boone, Elizabeth Hill. 1987a. *The Aztec Templo Mayor.* Washington, D.C.: Dumbarton Oaks.

———. 1987b. "Templo Mayor Research, 1521–1978." In Boone 1987a:5–69.

———. 1989. *Incarnations of the Aztec Supernatural: The Image of Huitzilopochtli in Mexico and Europe.* Transactions of the American Philosophical Society. Vol. 79, part 2.

Borah, Woodrow, and Sherburne F. Cook. 1963. *The Aboriginal Population of Central Mexico on the Eve of the Spanish Conquest.* Ibero-Americana 45.

Bourdieu, Pierre. 1988. *Outline of a Theory of Practice.* Cambridge: Cambridge University Press.

Bowditch, Charles P. 1900. "The Lords of the Night and the Tonalamatl of the Codex Borbonicus." *American Anthropologist* 2:145–154.

———. 1901. "Memoranda on the Maya Calendars Used in the Books of Chilan Balam." *American Anthropologist* 3:129–138.

Bray, Warwick. 1968. *Everyday Life of the Aztecs.* New York: G. P. Putnam's Sons.

Breisach, Ernst. 1983. *Historiography: Ancient, Medieval, and Modern.* Chicago: University of Chicago Press.

Bricker, Victoria R. 1981. *The Indian Christ, the Indian King: The Historical Substrate of Maya Myth and Ritual.* Austin: University of Texas Press.

Broda, Johanna. 1969. *The Mexican Calendar as Compared to Other Mesoamerican Systems.* Vienna: Acta Ethnologica et Linguistica, no. 15.

———. 1978. "El tributo en trajes guerreros y la estructura del sistema tributario mexica." In P. Carrasco and Broda 1978:113–174.

———. 1987a. "The Provenience of the Offerings: Tribute and *Cosmovision.*" In Boone 1987b:211–256.

———. 1987b. "Templo Mayor as Ritual Space." In Broda, Carrasco, and Matos Moctezuma 1987:61–123.

———. 1991. "The Sacred Landscape of Aztec Calendar Festivals: Myth, Nature, and Society." In Carrasco 1991:74–120.

Broda, Johanna, Davíd Carrasco, and Eduardo Matos Moctezuma. 1987. *The Great Temple of Tenochtitlan: Center and Periphery in the Aztec World.* Berkeley and Los Angeles: University of California Press.

Brown, Donald E. 1988. *Hierarchy, History, and Human Nature: The Social Origins of Historical Consciousness.* Tucson: University of Arizona Press.

Brundage, Burr Cartwright. 1979. *The Fifth Sun: Aztec Gods, Aztec World.* Austin: University of Texas Press.

———. 1982. *The Phoenix of the Western World: Quetzalcoatl and the Sky Religion.* Norman: University of Oklahoma Press.

———. 1985. *The Jade Steps: A Ritual Life of the Aztecs.* Salt Lake City: University of Utah Press.

Burgoa, Francisco de. 1934. *Geográfica descripción.* 2 vols. Mexico City: Archivo General de la Nación.

Burkhart, Louise M. 1989. *The Slippery Earth: Nahua-Christian Moral Dialogue in Sixteenth-Century Mexico.* Tucson: University of Arizona Press.

Burland, C. A. 1967. *The Gods of Mexico.* New York: G. P. Putnam's Sons.

Burland, Cottie, and Werner Forman. 1980. *The Aztecs: Gods and Fate in Ancient Mexico.* New York: Galahad Books.

Burman, Rickie. 1981. "Time and Socioeconomic Change in Simbu." *Man* 16:251–267.

Carmack, Robert M. 1983. "Spanish-Indian Relations in Highland Guatemala, 1800–1944." In MacLeod and Wasserstrom 1983:215–252.

Carrasco, Davíd. 1987a. "Aztec Religion." In Eliade 1987, 2:23–29.

———. 1987b. "Myth, Cosmic Terror, and the Templo Mayor." In Broda, Carrasco, and Matos Moctezuma 1987:124–162.

———. 1990. *Religions of Mesoamerica*. San Francisco: Harper and Row.

———. 1991. *To Change Place: Aztec Ceremonial Landscapes*. Niwot: University Press of Colorado.

———. 1992. "Toward the Splendid City: Knowing the Worlds of Moctezuma." In D. Carrasco and Matos Moctezuma 1992:99–148.

Carrasco, Davíd, and Eduardo Matos Moctezuma. 1992. *Moctezuma's Mexico: Visions of the Aztec World*. Niwot: University Press of Colorado.

Carrasco, Pedro. 1971. "Social Organization of Ancient Mexico." *Handbook of Middle American Indians* 10:349–375.

Carrasco, Pedro, and Johanna Broda. 1978. *Economía política e ideología en el México prehispánico*. Mexico City: Editorial Nueva Imagen.

Cartas de Indias. 1970. *Cartas de Indias*. 2 vols. Guadalajara: Edmundo Aviña Levy.

Casas, Bartolomé de las. 1967. *Apologética historia sumaria*. 2 vols. Mexico City: Universidad Nacional Autónoma de México.

Caso, Alfonso. 1927. *El Teocalli de la Guerra Sagrada*. Mexico City: Publicaciones de la Secretaría de Educación Pública.

———. 1943. "The Calendar of the Tarascans." *American Antiquity* 9:11–28.

———. 1958. "El calendario mexicano." *Memorias de la Academia Mexicana de Historia* 17:41–96.

———. 1965a. "Mixtec Writing and Calendar." *Handbook of Middle American Indians* 3:948–961.

———. 1965b. "Zapotec Writing and Calendar." *Handbook of Middle American Indians* 3:931–947.

———. 1966. *Interpretation of the Codex Colombino*. Mexico City: Sociedad Mexicana de Antropología.

———. 1967. *Los calendarios prehispánicos*. Mexico City: Universidad Nacional Autónoma de México.

———. 1971. "Calendrical Systems of Central Mexico." *Handbook of Middle American Indians* 10:333–348.

———. 1974. *El Pueblo del Sol*. Mexico City: Fondo de Cultura Económica.

Castillo, Cristóbal del. 1991. *Historia de la venida de los mexicanos y otros pueblos e historia de la conquista*. Mexico City: Instituto Nacional de Antropología e Historia.

Castillo Farreras, Victor M. 1969. "Caminos del mundo náhuatl." *Estudios de Cultura Náhuatl* 8:175–187.

Cervantes de Salazar, Francisco. 1985. *Crónica de la Nueva España*. Mexico City: Editorial Porrúa.

Chance, John K., and William B. Taylor. 1985. "Cofradías and Cargos: An Historical Perspective on the Mesoamerican Civil-Religious Hierarchy." *American Ethnologist* 12:1–26.

Charlot, Jean. 1931. "Bas-Reliefs from Temple of the Warriors Cluster." In Morris, Charlot, and Morris 1931, 2:133–136.

Charlton, Thomas. 1970. "Contemporary Agriculture of the Valley." In Sanders, Kovar, Charlton, and Diehl 1970:253–383.

Chase, Arlen F. 1986. "Time Depth or Vacuum: The 11.3.0.0.0 Correlation and the Lowland Maya Postclassic." In Sabloff and Andrews 1986:99–140.

Chase, Arlen F., and Diane Z. Chase. 1985. "Postclassic Temporal and Spatial Frames for the Lowland Maya: A Background." In Chase and Rice 1985:9–22.

———. 1996. "More than Kin and King: Centralized Political Organization among the Late Classic Maya." *Current Anthropology* 37:803–830.

———. 1998. *Late Classic Maya Political Structure, Polity Size, and Warfare Arenas.* In Ciudad Ruiz, Fernández Marquínes, García Campillo, Ponce de León, García-Gallo, and Sanz Castro 1998:11–29.

Chase, Arlen F., and Prudence M. Rice. 1985. *The Lowland Maya Postclassic.* Austin: University of Texas Press.

Chimalpahin Cuauhtlehuanitzin, Francisco de San Antón Muñón. 1965. *Relaciones originales de Chalco Amaquemecan.* Mexico City: Fondo de Cultura Económica.

Christian, William A. Jr. 1981. *Local Religion in Sixteenth-Century Spain.* Princeton: Princeton University Press.

Cipolla, Carlo M. 1978. *Clocks and Culture, 1300–1700.* New York: Norton.

Ciruelo, Pedro. 1977. *A Treatise Reproving All Superstitions and Forms of Witchcraft.* Cranbury, N.J.: Associated University Presses.

Ciudad Ruiz, Andrés, Yolanda Fernández Marquínes, José Miguel García Campillo, Maria Josefa Iglesias Ponce de León, Alfonso Lacadena García-Gallo, and Luís T. Sanz Castro. 1998. *Anatomía de una civilización: Aproximaciones interdisciplinarias a la cultura maya.* Madrid: Sociedad Española de Estudios Mayas.

Clark, J. Cooper. 1912. *The Story of "Eight Deer" in Codex Colombino.* London: Taylor and Francis.

Clark, Grahame. 1994. *Space, Time and Man: A Prehistorian's View.* Cambridge: Cambridge University Press.

Clavijero, Francisco Javier. 1979 [1787]. *The History of Mexico.* 2 vols. New York: Garland.

Cleland, Charles. 1976. *Cultural Change and Continuity: Essays in Honor of James Bennett Griffin.* New York: Academic Press.

Clendinnen, Inga. 1991. *The Aztecs: An Interpretation.* Cambridge: Cambridge University Press.

Cline, Howard F. 1973. "The Chronology of the Conquest: Synchronologies in Codex Telleriano-Rememsis and Sahagún." *Journal de la Société des Américanistes* 62:9–34.

Cline, Howard F., and Mary W. Cline. 1975. "Ancient and Colonial Zapotec and Mixtec Calendars." *The Americas* 31:272–288.

Closs, Michael P. 1988. *Native American Mathematics.* Austin: University of Texas Press.

Codex Azcatitlan. 1995. *Codex Azcatitlan.* Paris: Bibliothèque Nationale de France/Société des Américanistes.

Codex Borbonicus. 1974. *Codex Borbonicus.* Graz, Austria: Akademische Drück-u.

Codex Ixtlilxóchitl. 1976. *Codex Ixtlilxóchitl.* Graz, Austria: Akademische Druck-u.

Codex Tudela. 1980. *Codex Tudela.* Madrid: Ediciones Cultura Hispánica.

Codex Vaticanus. 1979. *Codex Vaticanus 3738.* Graz, Austria: Akademische Druck-u.

Códice Aubin. 1980. *Códice Aubin.* Mexico City: Editorial Innovación.

Códice Borgia. 1993. *Códice Borgia.* Mexico City: Fondo de Cultura Económica.

Códice Borbónico. 1991. *Códice Borbónico.* Mexico City: Fondo de Cultura Económica.

Códice Boturini. 1964–65. *Códice Boturini.* In *Antigüedades de México* 1964–65, 2:7–29.

Códice Chimalpopoca. 1975. *Códice Chimalpopoca: Anales de Cuauhtitlan y Leyenda de los Soles.* Mexico City: Universidad Nacional Autónoma de México.

Códice de Huamantla. 1984. *Códice de Huamantla.* Mexico City.

Códice de Huichapan. 1992. *El Códice de Huichapan.* Mexico City: Telecomunicaciones de México.

Códice de Huixquilucan. 1993. *Códice Techialoyan de Huixquilucan (Estado de México).* Toluca: El Colegio Mexiquense.

Códice de San Antonio. 1993. *Códice de San Antonio Techialoyan.* Toluca: Instituto Mexiquense de Cultura.

Códice de Xicotepec. 1995. *El Códice de Xicotepec.* Mexico City: Gobierno del Estado de Puebla/Centro Francés de Estudios Mexicanos y Centroamericanos/ Fondo de Cultura Económica.

Códice García Granados. 1992. *Códice Techialoyan García Granados.* Toluca: El Colegio Mexiquense.

Códice Ramírez. 1975. "Códice Ramírez." In Alvarado Tezozomoc 1975a:9–161.

Códice Vaticanus. 1964–65. "Codice Vaticano Latino 3738." In *Antigüedades de México* 1964–65, 3:7–313.

Coe, Michael D. 1964. "The Chinampas of Mexico." *Scientific American* 211:90–98.

Collingwood, R. G. 1970. *Roman Britain.* Oxford: Oxford University Press.

Conquistador Anónimo. 1941. *Relación de algunas cosas de la Nueva España y de la gran ciudad de Temestitan Mexico.* Mexico City: Editorial América.

Conrad, Geoffrey W., and Arthur A. Demarest. 1984. *Religion and Empire: The Dynamics of Aztec and Inca Expansionism.* Cambridge: Cambridge University Press.

Cook, Sherburne F., and Woodrow Borah. 1971. *Essays in Population History.* Vol. 1. Berkeley and Los Angeles: University of California Press.

Córdoba, Pedro. 1970. *Christian Doctrine: For the Instruction and Information of the Indians.* Coral Gables: University of Miami Press.

Cortés, Hernan. 1963. *Cartas y documentos.* Mexico City: Editorial Porrúa.

———. 1971. *Letters from Mexico.* A. R. Pagden, trans. and ed. New York: Orion.

Couch, N. C. Christopher. 1985. *The Festival Cycle of the Aztec Codex Borbonicus.* Oxford: BAR International Series 270.

Crónica mexicana. 1975. "Crónica mexicana." In Alvarado Tezozomoc 1975a:162–701.

Crosby, Alfred W. 1997. *The Measure of Reality: Quantification and Western Society, 1250–1600.* Cambridge: Cambridge University Press.

Culbert, T. Patrick. 1988. "Political History and the Decipherment of Maya Glyphs." *Antiquity* 62:135–152.

Davies, Nigel. 1980. *The Aztecs: A History.* Norman: University of Oklahoma Press.

———. 1987. *The Aztec Empire: The Toltec Resurgence.* Norman: University of Oklahoma Press.

De Landa, Diego. 1973. *Relación de las cosas de Yucatan.* Mexico City: Editorial Porrúa.

Demarest, Arthur A., and Geoffrey W. Conrad. 1992. *Ideology and Pre-Columbian Civilizations.* Santa Fe: School of American Research Press.

Denevan, William M. 1976. *The Native Population of the Americas in 1492.* Madison: University of Wisconsin Press.

Díaz, Juan. 1950. "Itinerario de Juan de Grijalva." In Yáñez 1950:3–26.

Díaz del Castillo, Bernal. 1977. *Historia verdadera de la conquista de la Nueva España.* 2 vols. Mexico City: Editorial Porrúa.

Dibble, Charles E. 1971. "Writing in Central Mexico." *Handbook of Middle American Indians* 10:322–332.

———. 1981. *Codex en Cruz*. 2 vols. Salt Lake City: University of Utah Press.

Diehl, Richard A. 1981. "Tula." *Handbook of Middle American Indians*, Supplement 1, *Archaeology*:277–295.

———. 1983. *Tula: The Toltec Capital of Ancient Mexico*. New York: Thames and Hudson.

Dohrn-van Rossum, Gerhard. 1996. *History of the Hour: Clocks and Modern Temporal Orders*. Chicago: University of Chicago Press.

Doyle, Michael W. 1986. *Empires*. Ithaca: Cornell University Press.

Durán, Diego. 1964. *The Aztecs: The History of the Indies of New Spain*. New York: Orion.

———. 1967. *Historia de las Indias de Nueva España e islas de la tierra firme*. 2 vols. Mexico City: Editorial Porrúa.

———. 1971. *Book of the Gods and Rites and the Ancient Calendar*. Norman: University of Oklahoma Press.

Edmonson, Munro S. 1988. *The Book of the Year: Middle American Calendrical Systems*. Salt Lake City: University of Utah Press.

———. 1992. "The Middle American Calendar Round." *Handbook of Middle American Indians*, Supplement 5, *Epigraphy:* 154–167.

Eliade, Mircea. 1974 [1954]. *The Myth of the Eternal Return, or, Cosmos and History*. Princeton: Princeton University Press.

———. 1987. *The Encyclopedia of Religion*. 16 vols. New York: Macmillan.

Elzey, Wayne. 1976. "The Nahua Myth of the Suns: History and Cosmology in Pre-Hispanic Mexican Religions." *Numen* 23:114–135.

Etzioni, Amatai. 1969. *A Sociological Reader on Complex Organizations*. 2d ed. New York: Holt, Rinehart, and Winston.

Fabian, Johannes. 1983. *Time and the Other: How Anthropology Makes Its Object*. New York: Columbia University Press.

Fernandez, M. P., and P. C. Fernandez. 1996. "Precision Timekeepers of Tokugawa Japan and the Evolution of the Japanese Domestic Clock." *Technology and Culture* 37:221–248.

Ferris, Timothy. 1988. *Coming of Age in the Milky Way*. New York: William Morrow.

Feuchtwang, Stephan. 1993. "Historical Metaphor: A Study of Religious Representation and the Recognition of Authority." *Man* 28:35–49.

Flannery, Kent V., and Joyce Marcus. 1983a. "The Changing Politics of A.D. 600–900." In Flannery and Marcus 1983b:186.

———. 1983b. *The Cloud People: Divergent Evolution of the Zapotec and Mixtec Civilizations*. New York: Academic Press.

Florescano, Enrique. 1965. "El abasto y la legislación de granos en el siglo XVI." *Historia Mexicana* 14:567–630.

———. 1994. *Memory, Myth, and Time in Mexico: From the Aztecs to Independence*. Austin: University of Texas Press.

Fortes, Meyer. 1958. "Introduction." In Goody 1958:1–14.

Foster, George. 1960. *Culture and Conquest: America's Spanish Heritage*. Chicago: Quadrangle Books.

Fowden, Garth. 1993. *Empire to Commonwealth: Consequences of Monotheism in Late Antiquity*. Princeton: Princeton University Press.

Fowler, William R. Jr. 1989. *The Cultural Evolution of Ancient Nahua Civilizations: The Pipil-Nicarao of Central America.* Norman: University of Oklahoma Press.

Franch, José Alcina. 1966. "Calendarios Zapotecos prehispánicos según documentos de los siglos XVI y XVII." *Estudios de Cultura Náhuatl* 6:119–133.

Furst, Jill Leslie. 1978. *Codex Vindobonensis Mexicanus I: A Commentary.* Albany: Institute for Mesoamerican Studies, no. 4.

García Icazbalceta, Joaquín. 1886–92. *Nueva colección de documentos para la historia de México.* 5 vols. Mexico City: Francisco Díaz de León.

Garibay, Angel Maria, ed. 1973. *Teogonía e historia de los mexicanos: Tres opúsculos del siglo XVI.* Mexico City: Editorial Porrúa.

Geddes, Jane. 1991. "Iron." In Blair and Ramsay 1991:167–188.

Gell, Alfred. 1992. *The Anthropology of Time: Cultural Constructions of Temporal Maps and Images.* Oxford: Berg.

Gibson, Charles. 1964. *The Aztecs under Spanish Rule: A History of the Indians of the Valley of Mexico, 1519–1810.* Stanford: Stanford University Press.

Gillespie, Susan D. 1989. *The Aztec Kings: The Construction of Rulership in Mexica History.* Tucson: University of Arizona Press.

Glass, John B. 1975. "A Survey of Native Middle American Pictorial Manuscripts." *Handbook of Middle American Indians* 14:3–80.

Glass, John B., and Donald Robertson. 1975. "A Census of Native Middle American Pictorial Manuscripts." *Handbook of Middle American Indians* 14:81–252.

Goody, Jack. 1958. *The Developmental Cycle in Domestic Groups.* Cambridge: Cambridge University Press.

Gossen, Gary H. 1974. *Chamulas in the World of the Sun: Time and Space in a Maya Oral Tradition.* Cambridge: Harvard University Press.

Graham, Ian. 1988. "Homeless Hieroglyphs." *Antiquity* 62:122–126.

Graulich, Michel. 1981. "The Metaphor of the Day in Ancient Mexican Myth and Ritual." *Current Anthropology* 22:45–60.

Gruzinski, Serge. 1992. *The Aztecs: Rise and Fall of an Empire.* New York: Thames and Hudson.

Haskett, Robert. 1991. *Indigenous Rulers: An Ethnohistory of Town Government in Colonial Cuernavaca.* Albuquerque: University of New Mexico Press.

Hassig, Ross. 1981. "The Famine of One Rabbit: Ecological Causes and Social Consequences of a Pre-Columbian Calamity." *Journal of Anthropological Research* 37:171–181.

———. 1982. "Periodic Markets in Pre-Columbian Mexico." *American Antiquity* 47:346–355.

———. 1985. *Trade, Tribute, and Transportation: The Sixteenth-Century Political Economy of the Valley of Mexico.* Norman: University of Oklahoma Press.

———. 1986. "One Hundred Years of Servitude: Tlamemes in Early New Spain." *Handbook of Middle American Indians,* Supplement 4, *Ethnohistory:* 134–152.

———. 1988. *Aztec Warfare: Imperial Expansion and Political Control.* Norman: University of Oklahoma Press.

———. 1992. *War and Society in Ancient Mesoamerica.* Berkeley and Los Angeles: University of California Press.

———. 1994. *Mexico and the Spanish Conquest.* London: Longman.

Hawkins, John. 1984. *Inverse Images: The Meaning of Culture, Ethnicity, and Family in Postcolonial Guatemala.* Albuquerque: University of New Mexico Press.

Healan, Dan M. 1989a. *Tula of the Toltecs: Excavations and Survey.* Iowa City: University of Iowa Press.

————. 1989b. "Tula, Tollan, and the Toltecs in Mesoamerican Prehistory." In Healan 1989a:3–6.

Healan, Dan M., Robert H. Cobean, and Richard A. Diehl. 1989. "Synthesis and Conclusions." In Healan 1989a:239–251.

Herrera y Tordesilla, Antonio de. 1934–57. *Historia general de los hechos de los castellanos en las islas y tierra firme del mar oceano.* 17 vols. Madrid.

Heyden, Doris. 1987. "Symbolism of Ceramics from the Templo Mayor." In Boone 1987a:109–130.

Hirth, Kenneth. 1984. "Xochicalco: Urban Growth and State Formation in Central Mexico." *Science* 225:579–586.

Historia. 1882. *Historia de los Mexicanos por sus pinturas.* Anales del Museo Nacional de México 2:85–106.

Histoyre du Mechique. 1905. "Histoyre du Mechique." *Journal de la Société des Américanistes de Paris* 2:1–41.

Houston, Stephen D. 1988. "The Phonetic Decipherment of Mayan Glyphs." *Antiquity* 62:126–135.

Hunt, Eva. 1977. *The Transformation of the Hummingbird: Cultural Roots of a Zinacantan Mythical Poem.* Ithaca: Cornell University Press.

Ingham, John M. 1971. "Time and Space in Ancient Mexico: The Symbolic Dimensions of Clanship." *Man* 6:615–629.

Izard, Michael, and Pierre Smith. 1982. *Between Belief and Transgression: Structuralist Essays in Religion, History, and Myth.* Chicago: University of Chicago Press.

Jones, Grant D. 1977. *Anthropology and History in Yucatan.* Austin: University of Texas Press.

Jones, W. R. 1971. "The Image of the Barbarian in Medieval Europe." *Comparative Studies in Society and History* 13:376–407.

Justeson, John S., William M. Norman, Lyle Campbell, and Terrence Kaufman. 1985. *The Foreign Impact on Lowland Mayan Language and Script.* New Orleans: Middle American Research Institute, Publication 53.

Katz, Friedrich. 1972. *The Ancient American Civilizations.* New York: Praeger.

Klein, Cecilia F. 1987. "The Ideology of Autosacrifice at the Templo Mayor." In Boone 1987a:293–370.

Knapp, A. Bernard. 1988. "Ideology, Archaeology, and Polity." *Man* 23:133–163.

Kramer, Heinrich, and James Sprenger. 1971. *The Malleus Maleficarum of Heinrich Kramer and James Sprenger.* New York: Dover.

Kubler, George. 1972. *Mexican Architecture of the Sixteenth Century.* 2 vols. Westport, Conn.: Greenwood Press.

Kubler, George, and Charles Gibson. 1951. "The Tovar Calendar: An Illustrated Mexican Manuscript of ca. 1585." *Memoirs of the Connecticut Academy of Arts and Sciences* 11.

Kuhn, Thomas S. 1962. *The Structure of Scientific Revolutions.* Chicago: University of Chicago Press.

Landes, David S. 1983. *Revolution in Time: Clocks and the Making of the Modern World.* Cambridge: Harvard University Press.

Lee, Thomas A. Jr. 1985. *Los Códices Mayas.* Tuxtla Gutiérrez: Universidad Autónoma de Chiapas.

Le Goff, Jacques. 1980. *Time, Work, and Culture in the Middle Ages.* Chicago: University of Chicago Press.

Lehmann, Walter, and Gerdt Kutscher. 1981. *Geschichte Der Azteken: Der Codex*

Aubin verwandte Dokumente Quellenwerke zur Alten Geschichte Amerikas. Berlin: Gebr. Mann Verlag.

León-Portilla, Miguel. 1971. *Aztec Thought and Culture.* Norman: University of Oklahoma Press.

———. 1987. "The Ethnohistorical Record for the Huey Teocalli of Tenochtitlan." In Boone 1987a:71–95.

———. 1992. *The Aztec Image of Self and Society: An Introduction to Nahua Culture.* Salt Lake City: University of Utah Press.

Leyenda de los soles. 1975. "Leyenda de los soles." In Códice Chimalpopoca 1975: 119–142.

Lincoln, Charles E. 1986. "The Chronology of Chichen Itza: A Review of the Literature." In Sabloff and Andrews 1986:141–196.

Lockhart, James. 1992. *The Nahuas after the Conquest: A Social and Cultural History of the Indians of Central Mexico, Sixteenth through the Eighteenth Centuries.* Stanford: Stanford University Press.

———. 1993. *We People Here: Nahuatl Accounts of the Conquest of Mexico.* Berkeley and Los Angeles: University of California Press.

López de Gómara, Francisco. 1965–66. *Historia general de las Indias.* 2 vols. Barcelona: Obras Maestras.

Love, Bruce. 1994. *The Paris Codex: Handbook for a Maya Priest.* Austin: University of Texas Press.

Luján, Leonardo López. 1994. *The Offerings of the Templo Mayor of Tenochtitlan.* Niwot: University Press of Colorado.

MacLeod, Murdo J., and Robert Wasserstrom. 1983. *Spaniards and Indians in Southeastern Mesoamerica: Essays on the History of Ethnic Relations.* Lincoln: University of Nebraska Press.

MacNeish, Richard S., Antoinette Nelken-Terner, and Irmgard W. Johnson. 1967. *The Prehistory of the Tehuacan Valley.* Vol. 2. *Nonceramic Artifacts.* Austin: University of Texas Press.

Madsen, William. 1960. "Christo-Paganism: A Study of Mexican Religious Syncretism." *Middle American Research Institute Bulletin* 19:105–179.

Malmström, Vincent H. 1997. *Cycles of the Sun, Mysteries of the Moon: The Calendar in Mesoamerican Civilization.* Austin: University of Texas Press.

Marcus, Joyce, and Kent V. Flannery. 1983. "The Postclassic Balkanization of Oaxaca." In Flannery and Marcus 1983b:217–226.

Martínez, Henrico. 1948. *Repositorio de los tiempos: Historia Natural de Nueva España.* Mexico City: Secretaría de Educación Pública.

Martir de Angleria, Pedro. 1964–65. *Decadas del Nuevo Mundo.* 2 vols. Mexico City: Editorial Porrúa.

Marx, Karl. 1984. *Capital.* Vol. 1, *A Critical Analysis of Capitalist Production.* New York: International Publishers.

Matos Moctezuma, Eduardo. 1984. "The Great Temple of Tenochtitlan." *Scientific American* 251:2:80–89.

———. 1987a. "Symbolism of the Templo Mayor." In Boone 1987a:185–209.

———. 1987b. "The Templo Mayor of Tenochtitlan: History and Interpretation." In Broda, Carrasco, and Matos Moctezuma 1987:15–60.

———. 1988. *The Great Temple of the Aztecs: Treasures of Tenochtitlan.* New York: Thames and Hudson.

———. 1989. *The Aztecs.* New York: Rizzoli.

————. 1992. "Aztec History and Cosmovision." In D. Carrasco and Matos Moctezuma 1992:3–98.

————. 1995. *Life and Death in the Templo Mayor.* Niwot: University Press of Colorado.

Matricula de Tributos. 1980. *Matricula de Tributos (Códice de Moctezuma).* Graz, Austria: Akademische Druck-u.

Mendieta, Gerónimo de. 1971. *Historia eclesiástica indiana.* Mexico City: Editorial Porrúa.

Mengin, Ernest. 1952. "Commentaire du Codex Mexicanus Nos 23–24." *Journal de la Société des Américanistes* 41:387–498.

Mexico, Archivo General de la Nación. 1940. *Boletín.* Mexico City: Archivo General de la Nación.

Miller, Arthur G. 1973. *The Mural Painting of Teotihuacán.* Washington, D.C.: Dumbarton Oaks.

Millon, René. 1973. *The Teotihuacán Map.* Part 1, *Text.* Austin: University of Texas Press.

————. 1976. "Social Relations in Ancient Teotihuacán." In Wolf 1976:205–248.

————. 1981. "Teotihuacan: City, State, and Civilization." *Handbook of Middle American Indians,* Supplement 1, *Archaeology:*198–243.

————. 1988. "Where Do They All Come from? The Provenance of the Wagner Murals from Teotihuacan." In Berrin 1988:78–113.

Miranda, José. 1952. *El tributo indígena en el Nueva España durante el siglo XVI.* Mexico City: El Colégio de México.

Moriarty, J. R. 1968. "Floating Gardens (Chinampas) Agriculture in the Old Lakes of Mexico." *American Indígena* 28:461–484.

Morley, Sylvanus G., George Brainerd, and Robert J. Sharer. 1983. *The Ancient Maya.* Stanford: Stanford University Press.

Morris, Earl H., Jean Charlot, and Ann Axtell Morris. 1931. *The Temple of the Warriors at Chichen Itzá.* 2 vols. Washington, D.C.: Carnegie Institution of Washington, Publication 406.

Motolinía [Toribio de Benavente]. 1971. *Memoriales o libro de las cosas de la Nueva España y de los naturales de ella.* Mexico City: Universidad Nacional Autónoma de México.

————. 1973. *Historia de los Indios de la Nueva España.* Mexico City: Editorial Porrúa.

Moyer, Gordon. 1982. "The Gregorian Calendar." *Scientific American* 246, no. 5: 144–152.

Navarrete, Carlos, and Doris Heyden. 1974. "La cara central de la piedra del sol: Una hipótesis." *Estudios de Cultura Náhuatl* 11:355–376.

Neill, Stephen. 1986. *A History of Christian Missions.* London: Penguin.

New Catholic Encyclopedia. 1967. *New Catholic Encyclopedia.* 15 vols. New York: McGraw-Hill.

Nicholson, Henry B. 1971. "Religion in Pre-Hispanic Central Mexico." *Handbook of Middle American Indians* 10:395–446.

Noguera, Eduardo. 1961. *Archaeological Sites of the State of Morelos.* Mexico City.

Obeyesekere, Gananath. 1997. *The Apotheosis of Captain Cook: European Mythmaking in the Pacific.* Princeton: Princeton University Press.

O'Malley, Michael. 1996. *Keeping Watch: A History of American Time.* Washington, D.C.: Smithsonian Institution Press.

O'Neil, W. M. 1978. *Time and the Calendars*. Sydney: Sydney University Press.

Orozco y Berra, Manuel. 1978. *Historia antigua y de la conquista de México*. 4 vols. Mexico City: Editorial Porrúa.

Oviedo y Valdés, Gonzalo Fernández de. 1959. *Historia general y natural de las Indias*. 5 vols. Madrid: Ediciones Atlas.

Pacey, Arnold. 1992. *Technology in World Civilization: A Thousand-Year History*. Cambridge: MIT Press.

Paddock, John. 1966a. *Ancient Oaxaca: Discoveries in Mexican Archaeology and History*. Stanford: Stanford University Press.

———. 1966b. "Oaxaca in Ancient Mesoamerica." In Paddock 1966a:83–240.

Palacios, Enrique Juan. 1948. "La estimación del año natural en Xochicalco, acorde con la ciencia." *Actes du XXVIIIe Congres International des Américanistes* 461–466.

Palerm, Angel. 1973. *Obras hidráulicas prehispánicas en el sistema lacustre del valle de México*. Mexico City: Instituto Nacional de Antropología e Historia.

Palerm, Angel, and Eric Wolf. 1972. *Agricultura y civilización en Mesoamérica*. Mexico City: SepSetentas.

Panoff, Michel. 1969. "The Notion of Time among the Maenge People of New Britain." *Ethnology* 8:153–166.

Pargiter, F. E. 1972. *Ancient Indian Historical Tradition*. Delhi: Motilal Banarsidass.

Parry, J. H. 1989. *Spain and Its World, 1500–1700*. New Haven: Yale University Press.

Parsons, Jeffrey R. 1976. "The Role of Chinampa Agriculture in the Food Supply of Aztec Tenochtitlan." In Cleland 1976:233–257.

Paso y Troncoso, Francisco del. 1939–42. *Epistolario de Nueva España*. 16 vols. Mexico City: Editorial Porrúa.

———. 1979 [1898]. *Descripción, historia y exposición del Códice Borbónico*. Mexico City: Siglo Veintiuno.

Pasztory, Esther. 1978a. "Historical Synthesis of the Middle Classic Period." In Pasztory 1978b:3–22.

———. 1978b. *Middle Classic Mesoamerica: A.D. 400–700*. New York: Columbia University Press.

———. 1983. *Aztec Art*. New York: Harry N. Abrams.

———. 1988. "Feathered Serpents and Flowering Trees with Glyphs." In Berrin 1988:136–161.

Payne, Stanley E., and Michael Closs. 1988. "A Survey of Aztec Numbers and Their Uses." In Closs 1988:213–235.

Peel, J. D. Y. 1984. "Making History: The Past in the Ijesha Present." *Man* 19:111–132.

Peñafiel, Antonio. 1890. *Monumentos del arte mexicano antiguo*. 3 vols. Berlin: A. Ascher and Co.

Peterson, Frederick. 1962. *Ancient Mexico: An Introduction to the Pre-Hispanic Cultures*. New York: Capricorn Books.

Phelan, John Leddy. 1970. *The Millennial Kingdom of the Franciscans in the New World*. Berkeley and Los Angeles: University of California Press.

Piña Garza, Eduardo. 1994. *Los Relojes de México*. Mexico City: Universidad Autónoma Metropolitana.

Pollack, Harry E. D. 1965. "Architecture of the Maya Lowlands." *Handbook of Middle American Indians*, 2, *Archaeology of Southern Mesoamericans*, part 1:378–440.

Pomian, Krzysztof. 1979. "The Secular Evolution of the Concept of Cycles." *Review* 2:563–646.

Porter, Arthur Kingsley. 1966. *Medieval Architecture: Its Origins and Development.* 2 vols. New York: Hacker Art Books.

Potter, Timothy W. 1987. *Roman Italy.* Berkeley and Los Angeles: University of California Press.

Proskouriakoff, Tatiana. 1965. "Sculpture and Major Arts of the Maya Lowlands." *Handbook of Middle American Indians,* 2, *Archaeology of Southern Mesoamerica,* part 1:469–497.

Quiñones Keber, Eloise. 1995. *Codex Telleriano-Remensis: Ritual, Divination, and History in a Pictorial Aztec Manuscript.* Austin: University of Texas Press.

Read, Kay Almere. 1998. *Time and Sacrifice in the Aztec Cosmos.* Bloomington: Indiana University Press.

Reeves, Marjorie. 1976. *Joachim of Fiore and the Prophetic Future.* London: SPCK.

Reid, Herbert. 1972. "The Politics of Time: Conflicting Philosophical Perspectives and Trends." *The Human Context* 4:456–483.

Relación de Michoacán. 1977. *Relación de las ceremonias y ritos y población y gobierno de los indios de la provincia de Michoacán.* Morelia, Michoacán, México: Balsal Editores, S.A.

Ricard, Robert. 1974. *The Spiritual Conquest of Mexico: An Essay on the Apostolate and the Evangelizing Methods of the Mendicant Orders in New Spain: 1523–1572.* Berkeley and Los Angeles: University of California Press.

Robertson, Donald. 1975. "Techialoyan Manuscripts and Paintings, with a Catalog." *Handbook of Middle American Indians, Guide to Ethnohistorical Sources,* Part Three 14:253–280.

———. 1994. *Mexican Manuscript Painting of the Early Colonial Period: The Metropolitan Schools.* Norman: University of Oklahoma Press.

Rotenberg, Robert. 1992. "The Power to Time and the Time to Power." In Rutz 1992b:18–36.

Ruiz de Alarcón, Hernando. 1984. *Treatise on the Heathen Superstitions and Customs That Today Live among the Indians Native to This New Spain, 1629.* Norman: University of Oklahoma Press

Rutz, Henry J. 1992a. "Introduction: The Idea of a Politics of Time." In Rutz 1992b: 1–17.

———. 1992b. *The Politics of Time.* Washington, D.C.: American Ethnological Society Monograph Series, no. 4.

Sabloff, Jeremy A., and E. Wyllys Andrews V. 1986. *Late Lowland Maya Civilization: Classic to Postclassic.* Albuquerque: University of New Mexico Press.

Sáenz, César A. 1961. "Tres estelas en Xochicalco." *Revista Mexicana de Estudios Antropológicos* 17:39–65.

———. 1964. "Las Estelas de Xochicalco." *XXXV Congreso International de Americanistas, 1962* 2:69–82.

———. 1967. *El Fuego Nuevo.* Mexico City: Instituto Nacional de Antropología e Historia.

Sahagún, Bernardino de. 1951. *General History of the Things of New Spain: Florentine Codex.* Book 2, *The Ceremonies.* Arthur J. O. Anderson and Charles E. Dibble, trans. Salt Lake City: University of Utah Press.

———. 1952. *General History of the Things of New Spain: Florentine Codex.* Book 3, *The Origin of the Gods.* Arthur J. O. Anderson and Charles E. Dibble, trans. Salt Lake City: University of Utah Press.

————. 1953. *General History of the Things of New Spain: Florentine Codex*. Book 7, *The Sun, Moon, and Stars, and the Binding of the Years*. Arthur J. O. Anderson and Charles E. Dibble, trans. Salt Lake City: University of Utah Press.

————. 1954. *General History of the Things of New Spain: Florentine Codex*. Book 8, *Kings and Lords*. Arthur J. O. Anderson and Charles E. Dibble, trans. Salt Lake City: University of Utah Press.

————. 1957. *General History of the Things of New Spain: Florentine Codex*. Book 4, *The Soothsayers*, and Book 5, *The Omens*. Arthur J. O. Anderson and Charles E. Dibble, trans. Salt Lake City: University of Utah Press.

————. 1959. *General History of the Things of New Spain: Florentine Codex*. Book 9, *The Merchants*. Arthur J. O. Anderson and Charles E. Dibble, trans. Salt Lake City: University of Utah Press.

————. 1961. *General History of the Things of New Spain: Florentine Codex*. Book 10, *The People*. Arthur J. O. Anderson and Charles E. Dibble, trans. Salt Lake City: University of Utah Press.

————. 1969. *General History of the Things of New Spain: Florentine Codex*. Book 6, *Rhetoric and Moral Philosophy*. Arthur J. O. Anderson and Charles E. Dibble, trans. Salt Lake City: University of Utah Press.

————. 1970. *General History of the Things of New Spain: Florentine Codex*. Book 1, *The Gods*. Arthur J. O. Anderson and Charles E. Dibble, trans. Salt Lake City: University of Utah Press.

————. 1975. *General History of the Things of New Spain: Florentine Codex*. Book 12, *The Conquest of Mexico*. Arthur J. O. Anderson and Charles E. Dibble, trans. Salt Lake City: University of Utah Press.

————. 1979. *Códice Florentino*. 3 vols. Mexico City: Archivo General de la Nación.

————. 1982. *General History of the Things of New Spain: Florentine Codex: Introductions and Indices*. Arthur J. O. Anderson and Charles E. Dibble, trans. Salt Lake City: University of Utah Press.

————. 1989. *Conquest of New Spain: 1585 Revision*. Salt Lake City: University of Utah Press.

————. 1993. *Primeros Memoriales*. Facsimile Edition. Norman: University of Oklahoma Press.

————. 1997. *Primeros Memoriales*. Norman: University of Oklahoma Press.

Sahlins, Marshall. 1981. *Historical Metaphors and Mythical Realities: Structure in the Early History of the Sandwich Islands Kingdom*. Ann Arbor: University of Michigan Press.

————. 1982. "The Apotheosis of Captain Cook." In Izard and Smith 1982:73–102.

————. 1985. *Islands of History*. Chicago: University of Chicago Press.

————. 1995. *How Natives Think: About Captain Cook, for Example*. Chicago: University of Chicago Press.

Sanders, William T. 1957. "Tierra y Agua (Soil and Water)." Ph.D. diss., Harvard University.

————. 1976. "The Population of the Central Mexican Symbiotic Region, the Basin of Mexico, and the Teotihuacán Valley in the Sixteenth Century." In Denevan 1976:85–150.

Sanders, William T., Anton Kovar, Thomas Charlton, and Richard Diehl. 1970. *The Natural Environment, Contemporary Occupation, and Sixteenth Century Population of the Valley—The Teotihuacan Valley Project: Final Report*. Vol. 1. Pennsylvania State University, Occasional Papers in Anthropology, no. 3.

Sanders, William T., Jeffrey R. Parsons, and Robert S. Santley. 1979. *The Basin of*

Mexico: Ecological Processes in the Evolution of a Civilization. New York: Academic Press.

Sato, Masayuki. 1991. "Comparative Ideas of Chronology." *History and Theory* 30: 275–301.

Satterthwaite, Linton. 1965. "Calendrics of the Maya Lowlands." *Handbook of Middle American Indians* 3:603–631.

Scholes, France V., and Eric Thompson. 1977. "The Maya and the Colonizing of Belize in the Nineteenth Century." In G. D. Jones 1977:43–68.

Schwaller, John Frederick. 1985. *Origins of Church Wealth in Mexico: Ecclesiastical Revenues and Church Finances, 1523–1600.* Albuquerque: University of New Mexico Press.

Séjourné, Laurette. 1981. *El Pensamiento Náhuatl cifrado por los calendarios.* Mexico City: Siglo Veintiuno.

———. 1987. "Mesoamerican Calendars." In Eliade 1987, 3:11–16.

Seler, Eduard. 1888. "Die Ruinen von Xochicalco." *Zeitschrift für Ethnologie* 20:94–111. (English translation in *Collected Works,* Vol. 2, pt. 2, no. 2, pp. 80–97)

———. 1900–1901. *The Tonalamatl of the Aubin Collection: An Old Mexican Picture Manuscript in the Paris National Library.* Mexican Manuscript nos. 18–19. Berlin and London.

———. 1904. "The Mexican Chronology, with Special Reference to the Zapotec Calendar." *Bureau of American Ethnology, Bulletin* 28:11–56.

———. 1990–96. *Collected Works in Mesoamerican Linguistics and Archaeology.* 5 vols. Culver City, Calif.: Labyrinthos.

Serna, Jacinto de la. 1953. *Tratado de las idolatrías, supersticiones, dioses, ritos, hechicerías, y otras costumbres gentílicas de las razas aborigenes de México.* Mexico: Ediciones Fuente Cultural.

Sharer, Robert J. 1994. *The Ancient Maya.* Stanford: Stanford University Press.

Skinner, G. William. 1985. "Presidential Address: The Structure of Chinese History." *Journal of Asian Studies* 44:271–292.

Skinner, G. William, and Edwin A. Winckler. 1969. "Compliance Succession in Rural Communist China: A Cyclical Theory." In Etzioni 1969:410–438.

Smith, Mary Elizabeth. 1963. "The Codex Colombino: A Document of the South Coast of Oaxaca." *Tlalocan* 4:276–288.

———. 1966. *The Glosses of Codex Colombino.* Mexico City: Sociedad Mexicana de Antropología.

Smith, Michael E. 1996. *The Aztecs.* Cambridge: Blackwell.

Sobel, Dava. 1995. *Longitude: The True Story of a Lone Genius Who Solved the Greatest Scientific Problem of His Time.* New York: Walker.

Soustelle, Jacques. 1966. "Terrestrial and Celestial Gods in Mexican Antiquity." *Diogenes* 56:20–50.

———. 1976. *Daily Life of the Aztecs on the Eve of the Spanish Conquest.* Stanford: Stanford University Press.

Southwold, Martin. 1979. "Religious Belief." *Man* 14:628–644.

Stephens, Carlene. 1989. "'The Most Reliable Time': William Bond, the New England Railroads, and Time Awareness in Nineteenth-Century America." *Technology and Culture* 30:1–24.

Sugiyama, Saburo. 1989. "Burials Dedicated to the Old Temple of Quetzalcoatl at Teotihuacan, Mexico." *American Antiquity* 54:85–106.

———. 1992. "Rulership, Warfare, and Human Sacrifice at the Ciudadela: An Iconographic Study of Feathered Serpent Representations." In Berlo 1992:205–230.

Tapia, Andrés de. 1950. "Relación de Andrés de Tapia." In Yáñez 1950:27–78.
Tax, Sol. 1951. *The Civilization of Ancient America.* Chicago.
Tedlock, Barbara. 1992. *Time and the Highland Maya.* Albuquerque: University of New Mexico Press.
Tena, Rafael. 1992. *El calendario mexica y la cronografía.* Mexico City: Instituto Nacional de Historia e Antropología.
Tenayuca. 1935. *Tenayuca: Estudio arqueológico de la piramide de este lugar, hecho por el Departamento de Monumentos de la Secretaría de Educación Pública.* Mexico City: Museo Nacional de Arqueología, Historia, y Etnografía.
———. 1960. *Tenayuca: Official Guide of the Instituto Nacional de Antropología e Historia.* Mexico City: Instituto Nacional de Antropología e Historia.
Thomas, Hugh. 1993. *Conquest: Montezuma, Cortés, and the Fall of Old Mexico.* New York: Simon and Schuster.
Thompson, J. Eric S. 1970. *Maya History and Religion.* Norman: University of Oklahoma Press.
Tira de Tepechpan. 1978. *Tira de Tepechpan: Códice colonial procedente del Valle de México.* 2 vols. Mexico City: Biblioteca Enciclopédica del Estado de México.
Todorov, Tzvetan. 1984. *The Conquest of America: The Question of the Other.* New York: Harper and Row.
Tonalamatl Aubin. 1981. *El Tonalamatl de la Colección de Aubin,* Mexico City.
Torquemada, Juan de. 1973–83. *Monarquía indiana.* 7 vols. Mexico City: Universidad Nacional Autónoma de México.
Toulmin, Stephen, and June Goodfield. 1982. *The Discovery of Time.* Chicago: University of Chicago Press.
Toussaint, Manuel. 1967. *Colonial Art in Mexico.* Austin: University of Texas Press.
Townsend, Richard Fraser. 1979. *State and Cosmos in the Art of Tenochtitlan.* Washington, D.C.: Dumbarton Oaks.
———. 1991. "The Mt. Tlaloc Project." In D. Carrasco 1991:26–30.
———. 1992. *The Aztecs.* New York: Thames and Hudson.
Umberger, Emily. 1981. "Aztec Sculptures, Hieroglyphs, and History." Ph.D. diss., Columbia University.
———. 1984. "El Trono de Moctezuma." *Estudios de Cultura Náhuatl* 17:63–87.
———. 1987a. "Antiques, Revivals, and References to the Past in Aztec Art." *Res* 13:62–105.
———. 1987b. "Events Commemorated by Date Plaques at the Templo Mayor: Further Thoughts on the Solar Metaphor." In Boone 1987a:411–449.
Vaillant, George C. 1966. *Aztecs of Mexico: Origin, Rise, and Fall of the Aztec Nation.* Baltimore: Pelican Books.
Van Zantwijk, Rudolf. 1981. "The Great Temple of Tenochtitlan: Model of Aztec Cosmovision." In Benson 1981:71–86.
Vega Sosa, Constanza. 1991. *Códice Azoyú 1: El Reino de Tlachinollan.* Mexico City: Fondo de Cultura Económica.
Veytia, Mariano. 1944. *Historia Antigua de México.* 2 vols. Mexico City: Editorial Leyenda, S. A.
———. 1994. *Los Calendarios mexicanos.* Mexico City: Editorial Porrúa.
Vivó Escoto, Jorge A. 1964. "Weather and Climate of Mexico and Central America." *Handbook of Middle American Indians* 1:187–215.
Wasserstrom, Robert. 1983. *Class and Society in Central Chiapas.* Berkeley and Los Angeles: University of California Press.

Watanabe, John. 1983. "In the World of the Sun: A Cognitive Model of Mayan Cosmology." *Man* 18:710–728.

Webster, David. 1976. "On Theocracies." *American Anthropologist* 78:812–828.

Weitlaner, Robert J., and Irmengard Weitlaner Johnson. 1963. "Nuevas versiones sobre calendarios mixes." *Revista Mexicana de Estudios Antropológicos* 16:183–209.

West, Delno C. 1975. *Joachim of Fiore in Christian Thought: Essays on the Influence of the Calabrian Prophet.* New York: Burt Franklin.

West, Robert C., and John P. Augelli. 1976. *Middle America: Its Lands and Peoples.* Englewood Cliffs, N.J.: Prentice-Hall.

Whitrow, G. J. 1972. *The Nature of Time.* Baltimore: Penguin.

———. 1989. *Time in History: Views of Time from Prehistory to the Present Day.* Oxford: Oxford University Press.

Wilcox, Donald J. 1987. *The Measure of Times Past: Pre-Newtonian Chronologies and the Rhetoric of Relative Time.* Chicago: University of Chicago Press.

Willey, Gordon R. 1986. "The Postclassic of the Maya Lowlands: A Preliminary Overview." In Sabloff and Andrews 1986:433–456.

Wolf, Eric R. 1976. *The Valley of Mexico.* Albuquerque: University of New Mexico Press.

———. 1999. *Envisioning Power: Ideologies of Dominance and Crisis.* Berkeley and Los Angeles: University of California Press.

Wuthnow, Robert. 1980. "World Order and Religious Movements." In Bergesen 1980:57–75.

Yáñez, Agustín. 1950. *Crónicas de la conquista de México.* Mexico City: Ediciones de la Universidad Nacional Autónoma.

Ziegler, Philip. 1993. *The Black Death.* Bath, England: Alan Sutton.

Zorita, Alonso de. 1909. *Historia de la Nueva España.* Vol. 1. Madrid: Librería General de Victoriano Suárez.

———. 1963. *Breve y sumaria relación de los señores de la Nueva España.* Mexico City: Universidad Nacional Autónoma de México.

Index